THE SECOND
BRITISH EMPIRE

Recent Titles in
Contributions in Comparative Colonial Studies
Series Editor, Robin W. Winks

Social Engineering in the Philippines: The Aims, Execution, and Impact
of American Colonial Policy, 1900-1913
Glenn Anthony May

The Politics of Dependency: Urban Reform in Istanbul
Stephen T. Rosenthal

Rhodes, the Tswana, and the British: Colonialism, Collaboration, and
Conflict in the Bechuanaland Protectorate, 1885-1889
Paul Maylam

Between Black and White: Race, Politics, and the Free Coloreds
in Jamaica, 1792-1865
Gad J. Heuman

British Rule in Malaya: The Malayan Civil Service and Its
Predecessors, 1867-1942
Robert Heussler

Economic Control and Colonial Development:
Crown Colony Financial Management in the Age of Joseph Chamberlain
Richard M. Kesner

Constraint of Empire: The United States and Caribbean Interventions
Whitney T. Perkins

Toward a Programme of Imperial Life: The British Empire at the Turn
of the Century
John H. Field

European Colonial Rule, 1880-1940: The Impact of the West on India,
Southeast Asia, and Africa
Rudolf von Albertini, with Albert Wirz
Translated by John G. Williamson

An Empire for the Masses: The French Popular Image of Africa,
1870-1900
William H. Schneider

Western Women in Colonial Africa
Caroline Oliver

The Emergence of Modern South Africa: State, Capital, and the
Incorporation of Organized Labor on the South African Gold Fields,
1902-1939
David Yudelman

THE SECOND BRITISH EMPIRE

Trade, Philanthropy, and Good Government, 1820–1890

JOHN P. HALSTEAD

CONTRIBUTIONS IN COMPARATIVE
COLONIAL STUDIES, NUMBER 14

GREENWOOD PRESS
WESTPORT, CONNECTICUT • LONDON, ENGLAND

Library of Congress Cataloging in Publication Data

Halstead, John P.
    The second British Empire.

    (Contributions in comparative colonial studies,
ISSN 0163-3813 ; no. 14)
    Bibliography: p.
    Includes index.
    1. Great Britain—Colonies—Administration—History—
19th century.   2. Great Britain—Colonies—Commerce—
History—19th century.   3. Great Britain—Foreign
relations—19th century.   I. Title.   II. Series.
JV1060.H34   1983   325'.341'09   82-20965
ISBN 0-313-23519-8 (lib. bdg.)

Library of Congress Catalog Card Number: 82-20965
ISBN: 0-313-23519-8
ISSN: 0163-3813

First published in 1983

Greenwood Press
A division of Congressional Information Service, Inc.
88 Post Road West
Westport, Connecticut 06881

Printed in the United States of America

10 9 8 7 6 5 4 3 2 1

To Susan

CONTENTS

LIST OF MAPS

PREFACE

This book says a great deal at the outset about British foreign policy and the pursuit of Britain's aims abroad, but only incidentally as a device for seeing the British Empire in a broader context. It is primarily concerned with the motives behind imperial expansion in the nineteenth century. It is not an attempt to challenge the many competing interpretations of imperialism in general but to suggest a way of looking at one particular imperialism that I think has been neglected and deserves fuller consideration. I do not presume to settle a controversy, but if I can inject a new dimension, which can be legitimately defended and which serves to complement or even embellish other interpretations, I will have accomplished my purpose.

A work of this scope is almost necessarily incomplete. In the course of two research trips to England supported by the State University of New York's Joint Awards Council and its Research Foundation, I have searched widely but selectively in the papers of the Foreign, Colonial, and India offices and in as many collections of private papers as possible, but many sources that undoubtedly would shed light or provide differing perspectives on the subject have escaped my view. This I can only regret and hope that other scholars will do me the honor of rectifying my omissions.

In the course of ten years, one accumulates a great many obligations, and it is now my happy task to acknowledge them. Many generous people, including the following, helped me to refine some of the basic ideas in the book at various stages of my research: Alison and Roger Des Forges, Sir Percival Griffiths, Anthony Hopkins, Sidney Kanya-Forstner, Frederick Madden, Nicholas Mansergh, Philip Mason, Christopher Platt, Agatha Ramm, Ronald Robinson, Bernard Semmel, Alison Smith, Claude Welch, and Ivor Wilkes. To the seminars conducted by Jack Gallagher at Oxford, Gerald Graham at King's College (London), and Roland

Oliver and G. A. Sanderson at the University of London's School of Oriental and African Studies I owe a great debt for broadening and deepening my perspectives. Eight very busy men took the time to screen portions of the manuscript for errors of fact and judgment. They are not responsible for my conclusions, but they are responsible for many of the improvements made in the final manuscript: Dewitt Ellinwood, David Fieldhouse, John Flint, John S. Galbraith, Peter Holt, Sir Cyril Philips, John Tosh, and Malcolm Yapp. Robin Winks was kind enough to help me sort out an early version of part I. Two former graduate assistants, Serafino Porcari and George Thomas, who have gone on to library work and teaching, respectively, aided me at an early stage in expanding my bibliography. Elizabeth Rodenbeck drew the maps.

I am indebted to the Broadlands Archives Trust for permission to consult and quote from the Palmerston papers and to J. M. Fewster and the staff of the Department of Paleography and Diplomatic at the University of Durham for their help in using the papers of the third Earl Grey. I am especially grateful to Robert Blake (now Lord Blake) for his hospitality when provost of Queen's College, Oxford, and for the use of the papers of the fourteenth Earl of Derby then in his keeping. For access to the papers of the third Marquess of Salisbury, I wish to thank both the Marquess of Salisbury and Robin Harcourt Williams at Hatfield House and P. G. J. Pulzer and the library staff at Christ Church, Oxford.

Felicity Ranger and the staff of the National Register of Archives were most helpful in guiding me to numerous collections of private papers, as were S. C. Sutton, Joan Lancaster, and the staff of the India Office Library for their guidance, patient assistance, and microfilming services. Quotations of Crown copyright records from the Foreign Office and Colonial Office Records in the Public Record Office appear by permission of the Controller of H. M. Stationery Office. Extracts from C. D. Cowan, *Nineteenth Century Malaya: The Origins of British Political Control*, and from C. H. Philips, *The Correspondence of Lord William Bentinck: Governor-General of India, 1828-1835*, are used by permission of Oxford University Press. Production of the bibliographic essay was assisted by a grant from the Research and Conference Grant Program of the American University in Cairo.

There is a special kind of appreciation for Katharine Becker, Dorothy Ward, Ruth Fassbaugh, Mary Wagner, and Gregoire Tcherasson whose skill and patience with endless revisions ultimately produced the finished manuscript. And finally, no expression of gratitude can fully acknowledge the forbearance of my wife and children during various stages of writing.

John P. Halstead
The American University in Cairo

THE SECOND
BRITISH EMPIRE

INTRODUCTION

Our understanding of modern imperialism has suffered from tunnel vision. It has been treated as a discrete phenomenon, historically comparable to the Renaissance, or the Industrial Revolution, or the rise of European nationalism. We have assumed that it possessed its own inner drives, achieved a certain momentum, was ultimately discredited by higher ideals, and retreated when faced by colonial nationalism. The discrete view of imperialism has been reinforced by its very study. Those fascinated by it have glued their eyes to it; they have sought to identify its causes and motives, traced its origins to conditions in the mother countries or in the future colonies themselves, and studied its course through stages of conquest, rule, reform, and decolonization, leaving the impression that these constituted the principal international thrust of modern Europe.

The proliferation of area studies has served to foster this view. The Africanist and Asianist tend to see imperialism as the dominant external factor affecting the non-Western world during the past century or two, and it may have been. But it does not follow that imperialism equally dominated the affairs of the great powers. While a temporary reverse in Tonkin may have unseated Jules Ferry, then premier of France, it did nothing to alter the main lines of French foreign policy. And even at the height of what was perhaps the greatest colonial crisis of the late nineteenth century—Fashoda—neither the House of Commons nor the Chamber of Deputies lost its head sufficiently to sack Lord Salisbury or Théophile Delcassé who had seemingly led their countries to the brink of war. In the larger orbit of British and French national affairs, most African and Oriental countries were very small moons indeed.

As a result, imperialism has been made to seem more important to the Western world than it actually was. It was, in fact, auxiliary to the main concerns of the European powers who engaged in it but was not comparable historically to the Renaissance, the Industrial Revolution, or the rise of national states, each of which was central to Western historical evolution. Perhaps if we cut imperialism down to size it will become less puzzling to understand.

Attempts have been made to do this. Marxist historians have usually seen imperialism in a broader context, either as an expansion of capitalism or as one aspect of global capitalist exploitation. Non-Marxist historians, less encumbered by doctrine, have discovered a somewhat greater variety of motivations. Both Nicholas Mansergh and William Langer saw imperialism as a function of diplomacy. In their view, the colonies were mainly pawns in a larger game whose objectives and concerns were situated in Europe rather than in Africa or Asia.[1] C. J. Lowe sees it as a function of European power politics, more particularly as one British response to declining influence in continental affairs and to the vulnerability of India's land frontier.[2] Archibald Thornton has also advanced a power theory to the effect that the British governing classes of the late nineteenth century felt they had been endowed with a vocation for exercising power responsibly at home and abroad, and British imperialism was simply the Asian and African expression of their felt duty.[3] The most fruitful interpretations have been the studies of John Gallagher, Ronald Robinson, David K. Fieldhouse, and D. C. M. Platt.

In their 1953 article, Gallagher and Robinson saw British imperialism as one facet of Britain's effort to maximize free trade around the world.[4] They felt this created a continuity in British expansion throughout the century and that the "Scramble" for African territory which concluded the century was only the final chapter of a story that began with informal controls and ended with formal annexations. The continuity theory was one of the more original and controversial of their contributions to the historiography of modern imperialism. It accounts for a great deal of early and mid-nineteenth-century imperialist activity that cannot otherwise be explained. In their later study, *Africa and the Victorians*, Robinson and Gallagher tentatively advanced another concept: the importance of local conditions to imperial expansion.[5] More fully developed by Robinson in a 1972 essay and by Fieldhouse in *Economics and Empire*, this view attempts to revise the older Eurocentric theories by recognizing the importance of native collaboration or of local problems as stimuli to imperialism without losing sight of the role played by the official mind.[6] This is a sensible and fruitful corrective, which I have used in this book.

The most perceptive of all recent theories, in my view, has been that of Christopher Platt.[7] Elaborating on Gallagher and Robinson's 1953 suggestion that imperialism occurred in inverse proportion to the political and economic security of the places where Britain sought to trade, Platt relegates imperialism to the status of an auxiliary of foreign policy and shows that in pursuit of Britain's worldwide financial and commercial aims, imperialism was the method used against "barbarous" countries to achieve aims which in more "civilized" countries would be achieved by the usual diplomatic methods. Although one might object to the terms used, this conception seems to me valid and fertile and might profitably be developed. Platt's book, the 1953 article by Gallagher and Robinson, Robinson's 1972 essay, and Fieldhouse's book are probably the most significant recent attempts to rise above the discrete view of imperialism and to place it in the larger perspective of international relations. My debt to them and to the other authors mentioned above are apparent.

Each of these explanations, however, as well as the more widely known Hobson-Lenin thesis, presents some distinct difficulties, and none offers a completely satisfactory explanation of nineteenth-century British expansion. Platt has demonstrated that before 1870 the British were not seeking large-scale investment abroad. Investors were preoccupied by the domestic market, and such capital as found its way overseas went either to the United States or to already existing dependencies.[8] Langer has also shown that there was little or no coincidence, geographically or chronologically, between British overseas expansion and investment.[9] It does not seem necessary to comment further on the Hobson-Lenin thesis. This whole book is essentially in disagreement with it.

With regard to Gallagher and Robinson's early article, trade was the sole factor considered; noneconomic motives were ignored. And through no fault of their own the continuity theme became lost in a debate over the essentially sterile issue of "formal" versus "informal" empire in which the definition of imperialism hangs on the technicalities of the imperial apparatus, a debate which in my view can best be resolved by using the conception of "paramountcy" which defines imperialism in terms of effective control, however formal or informal, as explained in chapter 4. Their later work, *Africa and the Victorians*, went off on the tangent of imperialism as a function of security, thereby stressing the late nineteenth century, losing the continuity theme, and underrating the economic motives.

The superbly balanced and large-scale work of David Fieldhouse ostensibly begins in 1830 but actually gives insufficient attention to the critical phases of expansion in the early nineteenth century. Robinson's recent theory of collaboration cannot be applied to Burma, Sind, Natal, the Sudan, or Northern Nigeria where collaboration was conspicuously absent in the expansionist stage. Finally, as perceptive as Platt's insight into Britain's relations with less-advanced peoples might be, he sees no continuity from the early to the late nineteenth century, limits his study to financial and commercial matters, and apart from Egypt and a cursory treatment of Africa, focuses on regions that do not coincide with the areas of greatest British expansion.

This work is an amalgamation of the most valid conceptions of the preceding authors with certain perceptions of my own portraying nineteenth-century British imperialism as the by-product, or auxiliary, of the global pursuit of British interests, for as Lord Palmerston put it in a letter to Lord Clarendon: "When people ask me . . . for what is called a [foreign] policy, the only answer is that we mean to do what may seem to be best, upon each occasion as it arises, making the Interests of Our Country one's guiding principle."[10] As we shall see, the Victorians had some very concrete interests clearly in mind as they sought to persuade the rest of the world to cooperate with Britain in their pursuit. Those interests transcended economics and mere "getting," often rising to the level of giving, although enlightened self-interest might be said to have been the norm.

Not only were Britain's interests concrete, they were fairly rational as well. To contend as Schumpeter did that the rational (capitalist) elements in British society were consistently anti-imperialist and that the Empire was the work of the remnants of the feudal aristocracy exercising its ingrained lust for power seems erroneous to me and somewhat beside the point. Everyone likes to wield power. It is not very enlightening to cite this fact as the principal cause of a particular social or political development when most of our social, political, and economic ills can be traced, in part at least, to this trait of human nature. We need no study such as Schumpeter's to prove that human behavior is irrational. But to attribute to the lust for power a complex phenomenon such as imperialism is to reduce history to psychoanalysis. National pride and pride of empire, vague yearnings for romance and adventure, the compulsion to kick the gong around or to lord it over peoples considered inferior undoubtedly tinged the atmosphere in which decisions to expand, or not to expand, were made. It can be maintained, as I do in this book, that these factors colored British expansion less than others. To deal with these emotive factors in an evidential manner is largely beyond the scope and the capability of historians and lies in the bailiwick of social psychologists. Historians must never forget them, but for the most part they must deal with a more superficial level of conduct where people try to rationalize their behavior. Here is where most evidence is to be found—in the form of comparatively rational trade statistics, committee reports, departmental memoranda, and official and private correspondence, all justifying lines of conduct. Occasionally a correspondent makes a Freudian slip, but even here readers must beware, for it may not be a true augury of conduct. The statesman who felt racial prejudice or for whom national prestige and wielding power were important often made decisions for reasons that transcended these emotions.

The British Empire, more than any other, was founded by this kind of decision making. Those who would brush off imperialism as a monolithic perversion of nationalism should read the documents of the British Foreign and Colonial offices and the private papers of those who staffed those offices. One might ask: What would Britain's imperialism have been like if, during its unchallenged industrial and naval preponderance from 1815 to the 1870s, it had been ruled by the Hohenzollerns or Romanovs? As it was, the Empire was ruled—or guided—by an enlightened, reforming, and sometimes benevolent aristocracy whose practice, however, often failed to measure up to the purity of intent. But it was intent that often motivated expansion, and the extent to which it did so will be explored in this book.

What, then, were these concrete, rational, and relatively high-minded interests? One would assume that national security would be a primary concern of all British governments at all times, but as a factor shaping British foreign policy, national security was somewhat in abeyance in the seven decades after 1820. From 1815 until the construction of the German High Seas Fleet, which was almost the entire period when Britain's modern empire was acquired, Britain did not feel its national security seriously threatened.[11] A reading of the foreign policy documents for this period leaves one with a sense of British equanimity throughout. None of the so-called crises seems to have threatened the fundamental security of the country, an impression corroborated by Lord Salisbury who was probably in a better position than any other foreign secretary of the nineteenth century to evaluate Britain's standing in Europe. Responding in 1901 to Count Hatzfeldt's warning that Britain's isolation was a dangerous indulgence, Salisbury asked: *"Have we ever felt that danger practically? . . .* Except during his [Napoleon's] reign we have never even been in danger."[12] From Waterloo until the German naval bills of 1897, British policy was to maintain a European balance of power as the best guarantor of peace, a policy so successful that Britain's European frontiers were more secure than they had been for centuries. In these benign circumstances, British statesmen could afford the luxury of directing their attention, as they never could before, to the pursuit of Britain's other interests abroad. Those interests which can be subsumed under three headings—trade, philanthropy, and good government—reflected accurately the character and needs of nineteenth-century British society and constituted the major aims of British foreign policy.

NOTES

1. Nicholas Mansergh, *The Coming of the First World War: A Study in the European Balance, 1878-1914* (London, 1949); William L. Langer, *European Alliances and Alignments, 1871-1890* (New York, 1931) and *The Diplomacy of Imperialism, 1890-1902*, 2d ed. (New York, 1935).

2. C. J. Lowe, *The Reluctant Imperialists*, vol. 1: *British Foreign Policy 1878-1902* (London, 1967).

3. Archibald P. Thornton, *The Imperial Idea and Its Enemies: A Study in British Power* (London, 1959) and *Doctrines of Imperialism* (New York, 1965).

4. John Gallagher and R. Robinson "The Imperialism of Free Trade," *Economic History Review*, 2d ser., 6, no. 1 (1953): 1-15.

5. Ronald Robinson and J. Gallagher, *Africa and the Victorians: The Official Mind of Imperialism* (London, 1961).

6. Ronald Robinson, "Non-European Foundations of European Imperialism: Sketch for a Theory of Collaboration," in Roger Owen and Bob Sutcliffe, *Studies in the Theory of Imperialism* (London, 1972); David K. Fieldhouse, *Economics and Empire, 1830-1914* (Ithaca, N.Y., 1973).

7. D.C.M. Platt, *Finance, Trade and Politics in British Foreign Policy, 1815-1914* (Oxford, 1968).

8. D.C.M. Platt, "British Portfolio Investment Overseas before 1870: Some Doubts," *Economic History Review*, (February 1980): 1-2.

9. William L. Langer, "A Critique of Imperialism," *Foreign Affairs* 14 (1935).

10. Palmerston to Clarendon, July 20, 1856, quoted in H. W. V. Temperley and L. M. Penson, eds., *Foundations of British Foreign Policy from Pitt to Salisbury, 1792-1902* (Cambridge, 1938), 88.

11. Ronald Hyam's comments about British sea power tend to confirm this. See *Britain's Imperial Century, 1815-1914* (New York, 1976), 21-25.

12. Salisbury memorandum, May 29, 1901, quoted in G. P. Gooch and H. W. V. Temperley, eds., *British Documents on the Origins of the War, 1898-1914* (London, 1927-1938), 2:68.

PART I

THE SUBSTANCE OF BRITISH IMPERIALISM

1

BRITISH INTERESTS AND FOREIGN POLICY

TRADE

Britain's insularity does not of itself account for the startling nineteenth-century expansion of its foreign trade. The English did not go to sea simply because they were surrounded by it. If they are willing to live at a subsistence level, islanders have no need of foreign trade, and until the sixteenth century the English were less noteworthy as seafarers than many other Europeans. It was England's industrialization, which began in the Tudor era with the population movement into the iron-producing regions of the north-west, that transformed it into a trading nation. The acceleration of that process in the late eighteenth and early nineteenth centuries—an acceleration so rapid it has been termed a revolution—made England the world's trading nation.

In the eighteenth century, however, foreign trade was of little importance to most English. From 1760 to 1790 its volume was virtually static and in the early 1790s hovered around the £35 million mark. Thereafter it experienced a slow and uneven growth until the mid-nineteenth century. By 1818 it had risen to £84 million, and Britain had become sufficiently dependent on the trade to cause deep concern over the recurrent trade crises that plagued the post-Napoleonic era.[1] The celebrated response of British statesmen was not further government controls but the liberation of trade from the remaining shackles of mercantilism. The old emphasis on maritime power (the focus of mercantilist doctrine) was to be displaced by a new emphasis on trade as such. To buy in the cheapest market and sell in the dearest became more important than subsidizing a supply of skilled seamen or safeguarding the vested interests of the declining West Indian planters and East Indian nabobs. To the Select Committee on Foreign Trade, reporting in 1820, all of the evidence pointed to the folly of maintaining the old restrictive system under the new circumstances. William Pitt, the Younger, who foresaw so much, had foreseen the need for this as well. His Commutation Act of 1784, which reduced tea duties from 100 percent to 12.5 percent and transformed Britain into a nation of tea drinkers, had shown what could be accomplished in the case of a particular trade item. After the committee report of 1820 the reforms accelerated. The Timber Act of 1821 equalized the duties on American and European lumber, to the benefit of both the British government and the British consumer. In 1822 the navigation laws pertaining to the West Indies and British North America were eased. William Huskisson's Reciprocity of Duties Act of 1823 inaugurated an era of nearly a hundred years in which the basic instrument of British trade policy was to be the commercial treaty. It differed from the older mercantilist treaties in aiming not at the exclusion of other powers but at opening the doors to all alike and ensuring that Britain received equal treatment. Its essence was the most-favored-nation clause.[2] In 1825 Huskisson opened the colonies to trade with all countries and reduced the duties on selected imports. The East India Company's one remaining monopoly, that of the China trade, was abolished by the Charter Act of 1833. And then came Robert Peel's sweeping dismantlement of the 1840s.

The results were astonishing and seemed to prove that a "fair field and no favor" was all that British merchants and manufacturers required. While the restrictions were being dismantled, British foreign trade rose gradually to £125 million in 1840, after which it shot upward. Between 1800 and 1893 it expanded tenfold, most of the rise taking place between 1840 and 1870. By 1850 nearly 25 percent of Britain's grain was imported. By 1867 it was 40 percent; by 1878 over 50 percent. As of 1850 approximately 60 percent of the world's merchant fleet was British, and the British merchant fleet was five times as large as the French. By 1900 it was nine times as large. Within ten years after the inauguration of the Suez Canal, British shipping accounted for 75 percent of total. Ten years more it was nearly 80 percent.[3]

For most of the nineteenth century, cotton was the backbone of British trade, and it was entirely supported by foreign raw materials. Reckoned by value, raw cotton imports constituted one-fourth to one-third of the total imports of raw materials, and cotton exports accounted for an equal or larger fraction of total exports. The cotton textile industry depended on the export market for its survival. As early as 1820 two-thirds of the cotton yarn produced in England was exported, either directly or in the form of cloth. By 1880 the proportion had risen to over 80 percent.[4]

That these statistics profoundly affected the thinking of British statesmen can hardly be denied. Very early in the nineteenth century it had become clear that trade was vital to Britain's existence. Confident that British manufactures could compete anywhere in the world if left free to do so, British statesmen were not equally confident that the freedom to do so would be willingly granted, and they were prepared to heed Adam Smith's other admonition that laissez-faire did not absolve them from the responsibility of protecting Britain's trade abroad as a "necessary part of the duty of the executive power."[5] Pitt's comment that "British policy is British trade" reflected Smith's concern and accurately foreshadowed the thinking of his nineteenth-century disciples.[6]

George Canning's interest in Latin America, the Iberian peninsula, and Greece seems beyond question to have been motivated by his concern for British trade. His first treaties with the revolted Spanish colonies, such as those of 1824 with Argentina, Colombia, and Mexico, were commercial treaties. It was only in 1825 that Canning got around to recognizing their political independence. His concern over the French intervention in Spain in 1823 was aroused largely because he feared French interference with the trade of Spain's ex-colonies. His Polignac memorandum of October 1823 (and there is no reason to believe it does not reflect his true concerns) clearly demonstrates that Canning was seeking nothing more than "Amity and Commercial Intercourse." He specifically rejected commercial preference and asked for most-favored-nation status. It also appears that Canning's position on the Greek revolt —his leaning ever so slightly to the Greek side—followed upon his belief that Greek autonomy would favor British trade. Trade was the main end. Naval preponderance over a threatened resurgence of Muslim sea power in the eastern Mediterranean was simply the means to that end.[7]

Lord Palmerston, who guided British foreign policy longer than anyone else in the nineteenth century, wrote in 1836, on the occasion of a spat with Portugal, that the Political Relations of the Two Countries are inseparably connected with Commercial Intercourse. . . . Political Connections between Governments are neither useful nor lasting, unless they are rooted in the Sentiments and Sympathies of Nations; and it is only by extensive Commercial Intercourse that a Community of Interests can be permanently established between the People of different Countries.[8]

Five years later, in the middle of the Afghan crisis, he had occasion to remind Lord Auckland, then Governor-General of India, that "it is the business of Government to open and to secure the roads for the merchant."[9]

Lord Granville's celebrated memorandum on foreign policy of 1852, produced on the Queen's command for the edification of his successor, Lord John Russell, shows the same awareness. Granville pointed out that "one of the first duties of a British Government must always be to obtain for our Foreign Trade that security which is essential for its success." The context of this paragraph of the memorandum is that foreign commerce is a powerful civilizing force, but the sense of economic necessity is clearly conveyed in the admonition that Britain should achieve this worthy end by "pushing our manufactures by any means into every possible corner of the globe."[10] That this memorandum was derided (by that diligent diarist, Charles Greville) as "a series of commonplaces" confirms that it reflected the goals and principles upon which British foreign policy was commonly founded.

Benjamin Disraeli understood the primacy of trade early on. In 1842 he pointed out to his colleagues in the House of Commons that "in a country where commerce was one of the principal sources of public wealth . . . a commercial interest was a public interest of the highest class."[11] Lord Clarendon, Foreign Secretary at three times from 1853 to 1870, agreed with Pitt that commercial policy was all-important to a Foreign Secretary.[12] And Professor Dike, in his noted monograph on British trade in West Africa, concludes that for the period he treats (1830-1885) commerce was "the chief end of British enterprise overseas."[13]

The rising competition and depressions of the late nineteenth century did not fundamentally alter the attitude of British statesmen. Surveys conducted in the 1880s and 1890s by the Board of Trade and others showed that foreign trade rivalry was neither cutting significantly into British markets nor growing rapidly in relation to British trade and that British shipping was effectively maintaining itself against competition. After the 1886 report of the Royal Commission on the Depression of Trade and Industry, however, British officials became more concerned about the unfair, protectionist policies of foreign governments, a concern reflected in the tariffs imposed in the name of fair trade. But even modest retaliation of this sort was grudging. The underlying optimism reflected in the reports of the Board of Trade carried free trade through to the more prosperous years of the early twentieth century, and British trade policy did not fundamentally change until the Great Depression of the 1930s. Whatever new departure there was in government aid to commerce amounted to no more than a greater effort to provide more accurate commercial intelligence.[14]

Thus British laissez-faire emerged basically intact out of the protectionist threat of the fin de siècle. But the scare had served to remind British statesmen—if they needed reminding—of the function of trade in Britain's life and of their duty to uphold and protect it. Sir Philip Currie, Permanent Under Secretary for Foreign Affairs, said in 1889 that "an ambassador's or minister's duty is to look after British interest, and our commercial interests are naturally the most important."[15] Somewhat later, Joseph Chamberlain asserted that "commerce was the greatest of all political interests" and that the Foreign Office, Colonial Office, War Office, and Admiralty, despite their frequent differences, were together "chiefly engaged in finding new markets and defending old ones."[16] The judicious support of trade by the British government was personified by Sir Robert Giffen, head of the Board of Trade from 1876 to 1897, when he testified before the Select Committee on Steamship Subsidies in 1902. Giffen was optimistic that British commerce could compete in a free market, but he was worried that foreign governments, by subsidies and protection, were erecting unfair hurdles for British trade. Under these circumstances, Giffen felt that the government "owed something to individuals whose living is threatened by the action of powerful [foreign] governments."[17]

Policy makers were no less conscious of the preeminence of trade in Britain's foreign relations before the 1870s than they were after the later depressions and foreign competition set in. All nineteenth-century British statesmen were sensitive to Britain's dependence on trade, and although they rarely stooped to bailing out a particular entrepreneur who got into trouble overseas, all of them pursued policies conducive to British foreign trade in general. Thus there was a continuity throughout the nineteenth century in the official view of the government's role in the protection and fostering of trade.

PHILANTHROPY

The pursuit of philanthropic goals, as a matter of private concern and public policy alike, has been peculiarly characteristic of the English-speaking people in modern times. The philanthropic impulse of private citizens from the age of Elizabeth I onward was uncommonly reinforced in England by the philosophies of the Enlightenment and by the rise of evangelicalism in the eighteenth century. By the nineteenth century this impulse had thoroughly permeated the public sector, and nearly every institution of British society was guided to some extent by a real concern for the underdog. One reflection of this was the long series of legislation, spanning the whole century, that concerned itself with the working poor: the repeal of the Combination Acts in the 1820s, the gradual abolition of the Corn Laws from the 1820s to the 1840s, the response to the ten-hour movement in the 1830s and 1840s, the series of factory acts scattered across several decades, housing for the poor such as the Artisans' Dwelling Act of 1875, the series of late Victorian education acts designed to eradicate illiteracy, the legislation designed to cope with rising problems of public health and sanitation, acts removing religious disabilities, and the reform of the criminal code, which by 1830 had removed more than a hundred felonies from the list of capital crimes. All of this was the result of bipartisan effort and rose from an impulse far deeper than party tactics.

Abroad the impulse found its expression in a genuine, if paternalistic, compulsion to carry civilization to the heathen, a compulsion most pronounced in the missionary societies. More closely related to the purposes of this book were the activities of the various aborigines protection societies formed to publicize and put a stop to the mistreatment of Khoikhoi and Griqua in South

Africa, Maori in New Zealand, and blacks everywhere in the Empire. The impulse was expressed most dramatically in the century-long battle to put an end to the slave trade. It may be true that slavery was in process of becoming uneconomic, but the slave-owners did not think so, and the antislavery movement triumphed over a vigorous and powerful vested interest when it did only because it won the steadfast support of the most eminent and influential men and women in British public life.

Testimonials abound. In Lord Castlereagh's time "there was nothing that the Country had more at heart than the abolition of the slave trade."[18] Canning was an ardent champion of slave trade abolition and fought for it vigorously in Parliament from 1798 onward. Over the course of years he wrote more than a thousand dispatches in his attempts to persuade other countries to adopt and enforce abolition.[19] For Palmerston the abolition of the slave trade was a personal passion, part of the "world bettering" to which he devoted much of his long public life. When he was at the Foreign Office, the suppression of the slave trade occupied more office time than any other single activity,[20] and no one can read his numerous memoranda on the subject in the Foreign Office papers or in his private correspondence and retain a shred of doubt that he was in earnest. In July 1844 he made a speech against the slave trade that was so eloquent that it was later published as a tract by the Anti-Slavery Society.[21] He later recalled that "during the many years that I was at the Foreign Office, there was no subject that more constantly or more intensely occupied my thoughts, or constituted the aim of my labours [than] the extirpation of that abominable crime."[22] Clarendon corroborated this in 1853 when he sought Palmerston's advice at the time the French were proposing to ship bonded labor to their West Indian colonies, remarking that "no one has done so much as you for putting down the S[lave] Trade."[23] Finally, we have Lady Gwendolyn Cecil's remark about her father, that practitioner of realpolitik, to the effect that his antislavery attitude was Salisbury's "only crusading impulse."[24]

The dogged persistence of British antislavery activity that resulted from this commitment is further testimony to its preeminence in the British mind. As early as 1789 Britain had declared illegal the slave trade from East Africa to India. The blanket declaration of 1807 (several months before President Thomas Jefferson's comparable declaration) revealed that William Wilberforce's obsession, thanks to the labors of the Clapham Sect and the Anti-Slavery Society, had permeated the seats of power to some extent. Evidence shows that in 1814 the British emissaries at Vienna were more interested in pressing for the abolition of the slave trade than they were in settling the outstanding problems of Europe.[25] Prior to 1822 scattered protocols were negotiated to effect cooperation with the Preventive Squadrons, Castlereagh concluding antislavery treaties with Spain, the Netherlands, and Madagascar in this period. But it was in Canning's time that the movement gained the momentum that carried it through the rest of the century.

Between 1820 and 1890 upward of 170 treaties dealing with the abolition of the slave trade or of its related evils, bonded emigrant labor and apprenticeship, were negotiated by Britain with nearly every other nation of the world and with over fifty African chiefs. Most of the treaties fall within the early years, 1820-1852, coinciding with the peak of antislavery pressure on British politicians. There was a lull in treaty making for the next two decades as Britain sought, successfully, to enforce the treaties then in existence. The Preventive Squadrons were so busy in these years that a separate Slave Trade Department was formed within the Foreign Office. The revival of treaty making in the 1870s and 1880s was a result of the intensification of slaving on the east coast of Africa after the Atlantic trade had largely been eliminated. Depending on whether one takes as authoritative the Foreign Office List of Protocols or the lists of treaties found in the General Indexes of the Parliamentary Papers, antislavery and aborigines protection treaties accounted for either 13 percent or 28 percent of all treaties concluded by Britain from 1820 to 1890. Whichever figure is correct, it represents a significant part of Foreign Office effort, especially considering that Britain realized no profit, indeed sustained great expense, inconvenience, and opprobrium, for its efforts.

A. P. Newton, for long the Rhodes Professor of Imperial History at the University of London, points out that Britain's persistent efforts to abolish the trade touched every maritime nation and "demanded for many years a large share of the attention of every succeeding Foreign Secretary."[26] Britain was the only major power so completely committed to the abolition of the slave trade. It was partly because they understood this, and that the trade would continue were it not for their perseverance, that British Foreign Secretaries kept this aspect of philanthropy in the forefront of their concerns throughout the century.

GOOD GOVERNMENT

If trade and slavery abolition were Britain's principal foreign interests, a derivative interest of comparable importance was good government. The belief that good government and the salutary conditions that stemmed from it provided the best possible climate for the conduct of foreign trade and that peaceful commercial relations conducted in an atmosphere of freedom and justice offered the best prospects for human happiness the world over seemed axiomatic to nineteenth-century Englishmen. That the final suppression of the slave trade depended ultimately on the justice and integrity of governments everywhere, in Africa and Asia as well as in the West, seemed equally axiomatic. Wars and revolutions, which undermined these conditions, were therefore to be avoided and could be avoided, and British Foreign Secretaries before and after Palmerston concurred with his belief that the surest preventative of war and revolution was enlightened government, by which he meant constitutional government. Palmerston could not "recollect any Country in which a Constitutional system of Government has been established that has not on the whole been better off in consequence of that system than it had been before."[27]

Castlereagh and Canning had pointed the way. Each had contributed to the substance and theory of good government. Castlereagh's "just equilibrium" established the policy of preserving the peace by maintaining a balance of power in Europe, while Canning stressed constitutional government and the sanctity of treaties. Henceforth, until the end of the century, while all other European powers at one time or another pursued aggressive policies, Britain alone stood forth consistently as the peacemaker, the arbiter. Different Foreign Secretaries pursued this goal in different ways. Castlereagh's was nonintervention. Canning and Palmerston interpreted nonintervention quite differently. Nearly all of them were prepared to use force if necessary, but the overall goal was peace, and altogether they were so successful that their handiwork is referred to as the pax Britannica.

The evangelicals and humanitarians added another dimension to the conception of good government with their civilizing mission. The Committee on Aborigines chaired by Thomas Fowell Buxton, Wilberforce's successor as leader of the antislavery group in the Commons, reported in 1837:

> The British Empire has been singularly blessed by Providence, and her eminence, her strength, her wealth, her prosperity, her intellectual, her moral and her religious advantages, are so many reasons for peculiar obedience to the laws of Him who guides the destiny of nations. These were given for some higher purpose than commercial prosperity or military renown [though many Englishmen would have valued these higher than Buxton]. ...Can we suppose otherwise than that it is our office to carry civilization and humanity, peace and good government, and, above all, the knowledge of the true God, to the uttermost end of the earth?[28]

While Buxton's rhetoric may not have carried away Palmerston, it nevertheless reflected the sentiments of a large number of Englishmen, and even Palmerston meant "to keep England on the side of liberal opinions."[29] Granville, however, could rise to Buxton's heights: "Having possessions scattered over the whole globe, and priding itself on its advanced state of civilization... [it was] the duty and the interest [of Britain] to encourage moral, intellectual and physical progress among all other nations."[30]

One is tempted to attribute all this to hypocrisy, but if good government for other people was the goal, Britain was no less demanding of itself. Not only did its rulers impose good government upon themselves from the time of Pitt and Burke onward, in terms of East India regulating acts and the parliamentary reform and social legislation that preoccupied nineteenth-century Parliaments, they sought as well to make Britain the exemplar of international behavior. For all his "Palmerstonian blows," Pam did "keep England on the side of liberal opinions," as evidenced by the undying hatred he inspired in the hearts of corrupt despots throughout the world. Gladstone is perhaps the most shining example where he succeeded, if the most pathetic where he failed. For him good government in all its aspects—justice, economy, international cooperation, equality of nations, freedom, and order—was the basic principle and objective of British foreign policy.[31] Britain's acquiescence in the arbitration of the Alabama claims is a good example of his commitment to put the British government on the line, even at its own expense. He told the House of Commons: "It is not particularly agreeable to have to pay money to a foreign Power . . . [but] . . . the good sense of the country has . . . [acknowledged] . . . the large interests of humanity and civilization involved in this mode of dealing with international disputes."[32]

At century's end, a distinguished public servant, Sir Eyre Crowe, characterized the main historical thrust of British foreign policy. He was commenting on the danger inherent in the universal jealousy and fear that Britain's sea power inspired in other nations, nations that in concert could overwhelm a small island kingdom whose people were not trained to arms.

This danger can in practice only be averted—and history shows that it has been so averted—on condition that the national policy . . . is so directed as to harmonize with the general desires and ideals common to all mankind, and more particularly that it is closely identified with the primary and vital interests of a majority, or as many as possible, of the other nations.[33]

For any number of reasons, then, the British thought it was in their interests to promote good government throughout the world. Guided by the practical imperatives of trade, the moral imperatives of philanthropy, the certainty that wars and revolutions were best avoided by enlightened rule, a conviction of righteousness and the superiority of English institutions, the dictates of Palmerstonian and Gladstonian liberalism, and the limitations of British power, British statesmen made the pursuit of good government the third component of their foreign policy.

Britain's nineteenth-century emphasis on trade (especially free trade), its philanthropic bent, and its obsession with good government had grown from seeds planted in the eighteenth century, respectively, by Adam Smith, by Granville Sharp and John Wesley, and by William Pitt and Edmund Burke. None except Pitt and Burke had much affected British policy making until the end of the Napoleonic crisis allowed Britain to attend to other matters, but in the comparatively halcyon, security-free years after 1815 they matured and formed the main trunk of British foreign policy. Throughout the nineteenth century British officials and private citizens alike were to be found, more than any other people, scattered around the world. An unusual concatenation of circumstances had infused British society with vigor, confidence, and expansiveness, which, owing to Britain's maritime supremacy, were channeled quite naturally into overseas activities. Convinced that the world was their oyster in which they would cultivate the pearls of free trade, free people, and free institutions, the British roamed the world with comparative impunity, striking Palmerstonian blows at protectionism, slavery, and tyranny.

Can we generalize about how the British went about pursuing these aims? It was quite apparent that what worked with France availed little with Turkey. What sufficed with Turkey was inappropriate when dealing with the Zulu. About the most that can be said is that the measures adopted were pragmatic. If they worked, they were used; if not, they were discarded. Perhaps it will be more helpful if we now shift our thinking away from the interests pursued to the means used to pursue them in order to demonstrate the contention made at the outset that the imperialism of Britain is best understood when viewed as an auxiliary of foreign policy.

NOTES

1. Leone Levi, *History of British Commerce and of the Economic Progress of the British Nation, 1763-1870* (London, 1872), 26; Arthur L. Bowley, *A Short Account of England's Foreign Trade in the 19th Century: Its Economic and Social Results* (New York, 1905), frontispiece chart and pp. 5-6.

2. D. C. M. Platt, *Finance, Trade and Politics in British Foreign Policy, 1815-1914* (Oxford, 1968), 85-86, 92-95.

3. Bowley, *Short Account*, frontispiece chart; Sir John H. Clapham, *An Economic History of Modern Britain* (Cambridge, 1926-1938), 2:211, 215, 218-19, and *The Economic Development of France and Germany* (Cambridge, 1921), 356.

4. David S. Landes, *The Unbound Prometheus: Technological Change and Industrial Development in Western Europe from 1750 to the Present* (Cambridge, Mass., 1969), 238-39.

5. Platt, *Finance, Trade*, xxxiii, citing Adam Smith, *Wealth of Nations*, chap. 1.

6. Ibid., xiii.

7. See H. W. V. Temperley and L. M. Penson, eds., *Foundations of British Foreign Policy from Pitt to Salisbury, 1792-1902* (Cambridge, 1938), 68-76, and Robert W. Seton-Watson, *Britain in Europe, 1789-1914: A Survey of Foreign Policy* (Cambridge, 1937), 98-118.

8. Quoted in Jasper Ridley, *Lord Palmerston* (London, 1970), 185-86.

9. Quoted in D. C. M. Platt, "The Imperialism of Free Trade: Some Reservations," *Economic History Review*, 2d ser., 21, no. 2 (August 1968): 297.

10. Temperley and Penson, *Foundations*, 184.

11. Platt, *Finance, Trade*, xxi, quoting *Parliamentary Debates*, March 8, 1842.

12. Ibid., xiv-xv.

13. Kenneth O. Dike, *Trade and Politics in the Niger Delta, 1830-1885: An Introduction to the Economic and Political History of Nigeria* (Oxford, 1956), 167.

14. Platt, *Finance, Trade*, 107, 141-42.

15. Ibid., 363.

16. Ibid., xvi, quoting speech to Birmingham Chamber of Commerce, November 1896.

17. Ibid., 103.

18. Algernon Cecil, *British Foreign Secretaries, 1807-1916: Studies in Personality and Policy* (London, 1927), 39.

19. Wendy Hinde, *George Canning* (London, 1973), 342.

20. Donald Southgate, *"The Most English Minister"... The Policies and Politics of Palmerston* (New York, 1966), 147, 151.

21. Ridley, *Lord Palmerston*, 297.

22. Palmerston to Sir John Crampton, Feb. 17, 1864, in Temperley and Penson, *Foundations*, 304.

23. Clarendon to Palmerston, Broadlands Mss., GC/CL/553.

24. Richard Faber, *The Vision and the Need: Late Victorian Imperialist Aims* (London, 1966), 61.

25. Reginald Coupland, *The British Anti-Slavery Movement*, 2d ed. (New York, 1964), 154.

26. *Cambridge History of British Foreign Policy* (New York, 1923), 2:235.

27. Palmerston to Granville, March 19, 1841, in Temperley and Penson, *Foundations*, 111-12.

28. Report of Committee on Aborigines, *Parliamentary Papers*, 1837, vii (425) 76, quoted in Philip Curtin, *The Image of Africa: British Ideas and Action, 1780-1850* (Madison, Wis., 1964), 458.

29. Temperley and Penson, *Foundations*, 100-101.

30. Ibid., 183.

31. Ibid., 391-94.

32. Ibid., 329.

33. Crowe's memorandum of Jan. 1, 1907, quoted in G. P. Gooch and H. W. V. Temperley, eds., *British Documents on the Origins of the War, 1898-1914* (London, 1927-1938), 3:402.

2

IMPERIALISM AS A
FUNCTION OF
FOREIGN POLICY

RATIONALIZED AND UNRATIONALIZED SOCIETIES

Of all the nations of Europe, the Britain of the early nineteenth century had been most deeply affected by the four great revolutions that transformed medieval European society: the Renaissance, the Reformation, the Enlightenment, and the Industrial Revolution. Britain had become the most rationalized society in the world, in the sense of the word that means modern, efficient, and enlightened methods of operation. Three centuries of trial and error had hammered out the best functioning, most liberal government in Europe. Britain's response to the possibilities of industrialization had led to a material productivity such as the world had never seen and could not think to rival for another half-century. Enlightenment ideas had permeated social behavior as in no other country in the world, notably in the form of the evangelical humanitarianism, which reached into every walk of English social life. The established religion was not so much a national creed as a device for banking the fires of religious controversy that had deeply divided and embittered the rest of Europe. English society was pleased, though hardly satisfied, with itself. Change and reform were in the air and in the works, inevitably affecting Britain's outlook on the rest of the world and shaping the way the nation pursued her national interests overseas. When she encountered less rationalized societies, she found that their interests did not coincide with Britain's; the less rationalized the less likely were their interests to coincide.

When Britain came in contact with powerful, rationalized states, such as the leading European and North American powers, the usual diplomatic devices functioned to gain whatever ends were in view. These states formed a club whose members adhered more or less to international law because experience had shown that in the long run it was expedient to do so. Since members of the club understood the importance of honoring agreements, the customary instrument was the bilateral treaty. In cases where a club member balked, Britain had little recourse other than reliance on a concert of powers, a still gentlemanly way of putting on the squeeze to make bilateralism work. The ultimate weapon, warfare, was employed by Britain against a major power only once during the period under examination. For the most part, arbitrary unilateral action in these relationships was unthinkable because of the clear and present danger of effective retaliation. Although Britain coerced dozens of minor states into anti-slave-trade treaties in the first half of the nineteenth century, it was unsuccessful in reaching effective agreements with France or the United States until after mid-century. In matters of trade, Britain had deprived itself of the only effective commercial weapon by its commitment to free trade. Unwilling to retaliate in kind against protectionism, it was forced to rely on diplomatic or political weapons to achieve commercial ends. Nor would coercion work in trying to enforce minimum standards of good government. Here Britain had to, and normally could, rely on the usual diplomatic instruments such as postal agreements, copyright conventions, and disarmament conferences or alternatively on the moral effect of setting a Gladstonian example of upright international conduct. When dealing with equals, then, Britain displayed the utmost circumspection, partly because it was forced to, but partly because this was the way modern, enlightened nations behaved.

Britain was somewhat less restrained in its treatment of smaller and weaker states such as Greece, Portugal, or the Latin American republics. Although partly rationalized, these states were less stable and seemed less able to abide by their international agreements. Even so Britain often showed restraint in dealing with them, as in 1837 when Argentina decided to raise its protective tariffs. On that occasion Palmerston directed the British Minister at Buenos Aires to remonstrate unofficially (to do so officially would have been improper) and to urge upon Argentina the merits of free trade and the dangers of high tariffs, and nothing more.[1] Britain repeatedly engaged countries of this category in antislavery protocols, hoping that they would have some effect. Every independent state of Latin America was so engaged at least once, often twice, between 1825 and 1850. Portugal signed four such protocols with Britain between 1825 and 1842; Greece ten between 1828 and 1850. Nonetheless a measure of coercion often crept into Britain's relations with these countries. The Aberdeen Act of 1845 is a good example of the high-handed approach Britain could take in such cases. Essentially this was a unilateral British effort to put a stop to the Brazilian slave trade. When Brazil asked Britain to repeal the act and substitute a bilateral treaty, Palmerston pointed out that such treaties with Portugal had had little effect and that repeal of the act would simply inundate Brazil once again with African slaves.[2] Another example was the Anglo-Venezuelan Commercial Treaty of 1825, which preserved Britain's most-favored-nation rights indefinitely despite repeated Venezuelan appeals to fix a time limit.[3] With these states the bilateral treaty was the ostensible instrument, but it was often attended by a degree of coercion inconsistent with true bilateralism.

In the case of Asiatic governments such as Turkey, Persia, Afghanistan, or China, antiquated and deteriorating or in turmoil but still recognized as sovereign states, Britain normally avoided outright domination because it led to unfortunate incidents and involvement with the other powers.[4] Such states, however, were extremely vulnerable to coercion, and the treaties negotiated with them had a decidedly unilateral flavor. Duress was all the more permissible in these cases because they were non-Christian peoples who, it was thought, could lapse into atrocious barbarism, and only by stern policing or international pressure could they be made to reform their corrupt governments and to cooperate in maintaining a climate favorable to free trade and the protection of minorities or submerged classes. In these cases duress could run the gamut from intimidation to outright occupation, as happened in Afghanistan and China. But where occupation took place, the troops were eventually withdrawn, and the victim's independence and sovereignty were qualified mainly by the threat of a recurrent occupation or by the establishment of European spheres of influence.[5]

In dealing with these first three categories of nations, the British government customarily felt that its role was fulfilled once it had concluded the standard commercial or anti-slave-trade treaty. Thereafter traders, investors, and missionaries could fend for themselves, and it was left to the Preventive Squadrons[6] to strengthen the weak resolve of other nations to abide by their antislavery agreements unless conditions once again grew so bad that a "Palmerstonian blow" was called for to bring errant despots back on course.

Among less rationalized societies, sophisticated modes of international conduct did not prevail. Whether Britain was dealing with traditional Oriental governments such as were found in the Indian and Malay states, Burma, or Zanzibar, or with the tribal states of tropical Africa, it invariably found that they were unable or unwilling to cooperate effectively as sovereign states in the achievement of Britain's three major interests. They were either too conservative to desire free trade and slavery abolition, or too weak and disorganized to work for them if they had wanted to. Nor did they display any enthusiasm to eliminate the pervading corruption (as understood by the British) in their governments or to maintain peace, order, and justice for the benefit of either their own peoples or the Europeans who appeared increasingly on their shores. The slaving kings of West Africa were all too satisfied with the profitable trade in which the British had first encouraged them. Why should they give up their livelihood because the British had experienced a change of heart? As for the imperatives of legitimate trade —the maintenance of order, the sanctity of contracts, guaranteed delivery, the improvement of transport, the commercialization of agriculture—most Africans and Asians neither understood nor cared, at least not by British standards.

Among such peoples, the framework of international law that guided the affairs of more rationalized societies was either unknown or unrecognized. However we may feel today about the right of self-determination, the right of any country to determine for itself what levels of corruption and inefficiency are supportable, the nineteenth century was not much impressed with that right, and the British felt justified in using varying degrees of force to reach the same objectives reached elsewhere by less rigorous methods. Starting with the high tone, Britain progressed to the threat of force and then the use of force. Out of extraterritoriality grew advice, protection, and ultimately dominion. Repugnant as the British government found the trouble and expense of ruling such peoples, it seemed clear that in the interest of trade, aborigines protection, and good government, the British had the capacity to do the job and therefore should.

Viewed in this context, imperialism is revealed not as an end in itself or as an objective of foreign policy but rather as a means, or a method, or an instrument of foreign policy. Unlike many Frenchmen who regarded their empire as the hallmark of France's great-power status, the British sensed that the dependent empire was not central to Britain's wealth and power. Its power lay in the navy and the free dominions, its wealth in industry and trade. Thus imperial expansion was simply one method of several employed by Britain in pursuit of overseas interests in the nineteenth and early twentieth centuries. It was a method adopted by a technologically, organizationally, and humanistically advanced society—a rationalized society—in its dealings with peoples whose technology, organization, and humanism were comparatively undeveloped.

THE NINETEENTH-CENTURY VIEW OF IMPERIALISM

Most Victorians viewed imperialism as an acceptable and effective means of dealing with uncooperative, non-European peoples. One reason was that the exercise of power, the coercion of weak states by strong, was not yet regarded as immoral. Indeed power was the name of the game, in the theory as well as in the practice of nineteenth-century international politics. For the British aristocracy in particular, paternalistic, public minded, and bigoted as it was, it seemed beyond question that the world's best chance for peace, justice, and prosperity lay in opening itself to the refreshing current of free trade. Where less rationalized societies were concerned, this might well mean acquiescing in British control. It was not only that Britain had the capacity to dominate such peoples; it had the will to do so, and, accordingly, it was felt, the right to do so. If any British statesman questioned the application of force to less-developed nations, it was not to question that right but only to ascertain that the effort would have a practical effect, that it be applied justly, and that it not be too costly. In the aristocratic tradition, the use of power was always justified by benevolence, and the methods customarily employed by Britain were benevolent by nineteenth-century standards. Few political philosophers have denied the principle of the just use of force.

A second reason for the acceptability of imperialism to the Victorians was the conviction of superiority. By all the criteria that mattered to the Victorian English—political, social, technological, moral, spiritual—English society was manifestly superior to the rest of the world. The British were proud of their society: their free institutions, their industrial might, their navy, their part in Napoleon's defeat. Convinced that commerce and Christianity were the royal roads to civilization, they were proud of British leadership in both. The Victorians were economic determinists in the sense that their good society was to be based on prosperity. They were certain that a rising standard of living would be attended by moral and intellectual improvement; and was not Britain showing the way? Most profound of all was their pride in the English character: in diligence, thrift, ingenuity, moral fiber, self-reliance, cheerfulness, and aplomb.

Whether the Englishman thought of his superiority over Africans and Asians as temporary or permanent, as racial or cultural, are sterile and overworked debates. It existed, was taken for granted, and, it was assumed, was taken for granted by others as well. It was therefore expected, prior to mid-century at least, that British norms and techniques would be accepted by Africans and Asians more or less voluntarily, if not enthusiastically. When that view proved to be naive, when Africans and Asians turned their backs on the arts of civilization or proved clumsy in their acquisition, some coercion was called for. Britain reasoned that it had the right and duty to impose where example and exhortation had failed. Carried to extremes this attitude was labeled jingoism, but essentially it did not have to be jingoistic. For many Victorians who subscribed to it, it epitomized not the expansion of power but the transfer of superior modes of life to societies that were inferior because, in British eyes, they were deficient in the fundamentals of rationalized existence: free commerce, humanity, and good governance.

Today's indignation over this attitude hardly existed in the nineteenth century, even among the anti-imperialists. Except for a few people, domination over Africans and Asians was not thought to be immoral. Indeed Africans and Asians were "lucky to be exposed to civilization."[7] If anyone questioned the practice, it was mainly because it was troublesome and expensive, not because it was unethical to deprive Oriental tyrants of their much abused sovereignties or their benighted subjects of freedoms, which scarcely existed. Gladstone did not believe empire to be immoral. He thought Disraeli immoral because of his jingoistic foreign policy, but Gladstone could separate jingoism from empire. While Colonial Secretary and after, he testified many times to his belief in the civilizing mission of an enlightened and superior Britain.

Why is imperialism no longer acceptable today? Among other things, Europeans have lost their will to power, their self-confidence, and their easy optimism about the potential for cultural change in Africa and Asia. There exists today a greater differential in economic and military power between Europe and all of its former colonies put together, both absolutely and relatively, than existed in the nineteenth century. The great European empires of the nineteenth century are gone, and for the same reason that the Roman Empire collapsed—the loss of will.[8] The tough-minded imperialists have been retired because their way of handling relations between Western and non-Western peoples is frowned upon by the world's leaders. The experts on international affairs in the West who prevail today are the tender-minded. Today the former imperial powers are ordinarily restrained by a higher morality concerning the rights of weaker states, and the paternalistic sense of duty, characteristic of nineteenth-century British government, is derided and out of fashion.

With the will to power has disappeared the old certainty of European racial or cultural superiority. No longer are there "superior" peoples. African and Asian "backwardness" is now seen as an accident of history, just as European backwardness was an accident of history at the time of the Muslim preponderance in the Mediterranean. Once the European sense of righteousness and superiority had been undermined, imperialism went on the defensive and could no longer be maintained in the face of the growing confidence of non-Western peoples. Finally, for the Western powers, imperialism has the additional disadvantage that it is no longer worthwhile, either economically or politically.

In examining an historical phenomenon chronologically as close to us and emotionally as evocative as modern imperialism, we must make an extra effort to gain a balanced perspective. Archibald Thornton has pointed out that there has been far too much romanticizing about the uses and abuses of power and that historians of modern imperialism must come to terms with their subject, as most historians of ancient imperialisms have succeeded in doing.[9] Mid-twentieth-century strictures on imperialism are beside the point and not very enlightening. They are somewhat like condemning feudalism because it was medieval. To impose twentieth-century mores on an era when they did not prevail is to misunderstand what happened and why. For example, to condemn as unjust the lopsided treaties then imposed on African chiefs is to ignore the realities of power as seen by the nineteenth century. The fact is that Africans and Asians deprived of sovereignty, conscripted for labor, and obligated to pay strange taxes also received in return benefits, if only in terms of an end to the internecine warfare, which, with endemic sickness, was the most debilitating defect of tribal society. We can avoid a good deal of confusion in our perception of modern imperialism by rejecting the moralistic approach, acknowledging the mores of the nineteenth century, and seeing Western imperialism for what it was: a passing phase in international relations. (Imperialism has not passed out of fashion in the Soviet Union, but Russia is not a wholly Western state. And of course, many believe that the West is still engaged in neocolonialism.)

It is not the purpose of this book to praise or blame British imperialism or to enter into the increasingly convoluted economic debate about European expansion. What I have tried to do is to reconstruct the motives and sentiments of the times as dispassionately as possible in order to show how British people felt and thought and how this led to the expansion of their empire. If some of their motives or sentiments were humane and some vicious, some benevolent and some acquisitive, we might perceive them more clearly if we refrain from passing judgment on them and accept them for what they are: a reflection of human nature. The ethical assumptions and moral standards of the nineteenth century were different from ours.

NOTES

1. D. C. M. Platt, *Finance, Trade and Politics in British Foreign Policy, 1815-1914* (Oxford, 1968), 143.

2. Palmerston to Russell, July 31, 1862, in H. W. V. Temperley and L. M. Penson, eds., *Foundations of British Foreign Policy from Pitt to Salisbury, 1792-1902* (Cambridge, 1938), 303-4.

3. Platt, *Finance, Trade*, 90-92.

4. Egypt might also be placed in this category, but the British could not

avoid outright domination there owing to the special circumstances of the Suez Canal.

5. China is a borderline case, which can fit into this or the next category because its government remained sovereign while small pieces of its territory were occupied or periodically violated.

6. British naval patrols assigned to the African coasts and Atlantic slave trade routes to enforce the antislavery treaties.

7. Richard Faber, *The Vision and the Need: Late Victorian Imperialist Aims* (London, 1966), 42.

8. Archibald P. Thornton, *Doctrines of Imperialism* (New York, 1965), 124.

9. Ibid., chap. 1.

3

BRITISH INTERESTS
AND IMPERIALISM

The pursuit of its three fundamental global interests led Britain to imperial expansion. Not surprisingly the relative importance of each interest shifted from time to time and from place to place.

TRADE

The absolute volume of trade with Asia and Africa was rising significantly throughout the nineteenth century. British exports to Africa rose from £1 million in 1840 to £13 million in 1870; to Asia from £7 million to £37 million.[1] These figures embraced all African and Asian countries, whether British dependencies or not. It was to be expected that British dependencies would account for the larger portion of the total since British India and South Africa were the most highly developed trading countries in their respective continents. In this period British exports to South Africa (the Cape and Natal) rose from £400,000 to £2 million.[2]

India was by far Britain's foremost non-Western trading partner in the nineteenth century, although it took a while after the Napoleonic period for this to become apparent. In 1814, besides the East India Company, there were six private firms in Calcutta handling trade with Britain; by 1833 there were about twenty, partly resulting from the abolition of the Company's monopoly and partly from the general expansion of trade. Thereafter British exports to India, chiefly cotton goods, began to rise rapidly, trebling in the decade 1839-1849 while they only doubled to other world markets. In 1840 Britain's exports to India totaled £5 million; by 1850 they were £7 million, by 1860 £17 million, by 1870 £19 million, and by 1880 India had surpassed the United States as a market for British goods (£27 million to £24 million). British import figures have not been used because they do not show as dramatic a rise (from Asia and Africa) as do export figures, although here too India was the exception. Before 1870 India was second only to the United States as a supplier to Great Britain. Thereafter India conceded second place to France.[3]

If the proportion of African and Asian trade to the whole is considered, the figures are even more compelling. British exports to Africa as a proportion of total exports rose from 0.6 percent in 1815 to 2.9 percent in 1840, to 6.8 percent in 1870, and to 14.5 percent in 1903. Asia's share rose from 5.6 percent in 1815, to 14.5 percent in 1840, to 18.9 percent in 1870, and to 20.9 percent in 1903. From 1840 to 1870 alone British exports to Africa rose 1,200 percent (from £1 million to £13 million) and to Asia, about 430 percent (from £7 million to £37 million), while total British exports rose only 300 percent (£51 million to £200 million). The import figures are less striking; if anything they show a proportionate decline. Africa continued to supply Britain with minerals and raw materials at about the same rate throughout the century, but Asia supplied a declining percentage of British imports after mid-century, with the exception of cotton, for obvious reasons, during the U.S. Civil War years.[4]

These indicators of the rising importance of African and Asian trade were not lost on Victorian statesmen. Whatever can be said about the limited absolute volume of that trade, it was apparent that Asians and Africans were fast becoming better customers of Britain, and the trend showed no signs of abating. Even if Africa and Asia seemed relatively less important as sources of raw materials, their rising importance as markets for British goods seemed to be established beyond question. British statesmen were persuaded that exports to tropical countries were headed for a long-term rise, which nothing should be permitted to disturb.[5] To encourage this trend was doubly important because the rising industrial states of the West—while still Britain's best customers—were taking a shrinking proportion of Britain's exports.

Where did British dependencies fit into this picture? It was clear that British India, in terms of absolute volume, accounted for the bulk of the rise in exports to Asia, taking £5 million out of a total of £7 million in 1840, £19 million out of £37 million in 1870. But a calculation of percentage increases of absolute volumes is more interesting. During the period when British exports to all of Asia were rising 430 percent (1840-1870), British exports to India rose only 230 percent (£5 million to £9 million). And while British exports to all of Africa were rising 1,200 percent in the same period, British exports to South Africa rose only 450 percent (£400,000 to £2 million). In other words, exports were rising at a faster rate to countries other than the two oldest dependencies. Apparently a country's status as a British dependency did not automatically guarantee trade advantages to Britain. As has been pointed out by Robinson and Gallagher and many others, British statesmen were not convinced that empire was a prerequisite for trade. As a rule it appeared more important that the trade be free, and hopefully British rule, which was expensive and troublesome, would not be necessary to achieve that end. Even as late as 1877 Sir Robert Morier, Ambassador to Portugal, could write to Lord Derby that it would be best not to encourage Portugal to sell any of its African possessions, for other European powers would inevitably enter the bidding and would be less desirable neighbors than the Portuguese. He pointed out that it was fortunate that only Portugal, Britain, Egypt, and Zanzibar were important African landowners, that "Egypt and Zanzibar do pretty well what we tell them to do," and that Portugal could probably be persuaded to see that it was in its best interests not to sell but to open its territories to free trade.[6]

Nevertheless where free trade was interrupted, British statesmen, however hesitant, hardly ever failed to intervene forcefully. Some were less hesitant than others. Palmerston wrote in 1860 that Britain's West African trade was "an object which ought to be actively and perseveringly pursued" and protected if necessary by a "physical effort."[7] Prior to the Scramble the chief danger to the free and peaceful flow of trade came from local wars or hostility to European incursions. British statesmen counteracted such disruptions "by . . . influence if they could; but by imperial rule if they must."[8] In thus stating the case for the "informal empire of trade," Robinson and Gallagher were trying to show that prior to about 1882, influence was sufficient and very little formal imperialism took place. Compared to the vast annexations and grandiose protectorates of the Scramble period, this is true. But the fact remains that a good deal of British imperialism was resorted to even before the Scramble for purposes of fostering trade. As the case studies later in the book show, more authentic imperialist expansion than can be passed off as mere influence took place before 1870 in Burma, in Sind and the Punjab, in Malaya, along the South African coast, and on the Gold and Niger coasts, to name only those regions dealt with in this book. In all cases, trade was either a significant or the primary factor.

The rapid acceleration of expansion after the 1870s reflected a quantitative rather than a qualitative change. The free trade experiment had been amply vindicated for Britain. Its total trade had leaped from £130 million in 1842 (the year of Peel's first free trade bills) to approximately £600 million in 1876 (the year Russia inaugurated the continental return to protectionism).[9] No wonder that British statesmen were fully committed to the free trade principle. Colonies as such had not been responsible for the increase, and although their trade was important enough to defend, it was not important enough to foster artificially at the risk of Britain's other foreign trade. But world conditions were changing, and if they did not make colonies more important intrinsically, they did make them more important extrinsically.

There was a growing awareness in Britain that other powers, as well as its own white colonies, did not share the same enthusiasm for free trade and were quite prepared to sequester important trading areas for themselves and to subsidize their rising industries in order to undercut British competition. To the British the first was a dog-in-the-manger policy, and the second was simply not cricket. To make matters worse, the trade depression that began in 1873 and reached its nadir in 1878 was the worst of the century, and it was closely followed by another, somewhat less severe, between 1883 and 1886, so that in 1886 Britain's foreign trade was £65 million below the level of 1873. Britain's trade pattern showed some disquieting trends as well, especially with regard to the North American trade. Before 1854 North America customarily took better than 20 percent of Britain's exports. Thereafter it never rose above 20 percent, and the long-term trend was a decline, to a low of 6.5 percent in 1919.[10] The emergence of an aggressive industrialism in Germany and France after 1870 promised a similar decline in Britain's share of those markets in the near future. Although that decline did not in fact occur, there seemed no reason in the 1870s not to expect Western Europe to follow the North American example.

Simultaneously, exports to Africa and Asia experienced a commensurate rise. Moreover it was precisely in those places that

France launched a campaign of territorial acquisition in the late 1870s and 1880s, and in 1883 Germany's Otto von Bismarck allied himself with France's Jules Ferry in what was clearly intended as an effort to reduce Britain's lead and momentum in wo~ld affairs. The equanimity of British statesmen was badly shaken. The old confidence that Britain's influence in Europe and North America would ultimately prevail had been severely undermined. In commercial matters especially, Asia and Africa were gaining stature in British eyes, and statesmen could no longer affect the same nonchalance for those lands as before.

In the words of Sir Robert Giffen, head of the Statistical, Commercial and Labour Department of the Board of Trade from 1876 to 1897, the government "owed something to individuals whose living is threatened by the action of powerful governments."[11] But what was that "something" to be? Committed to free trade, Britain could not indulge in retaliatory protectionism. In the face of the widespread European recourse to protection after 1876 and of the levy of protective tariffs in its own dominions after 1859, Britain resisted this solution until 1932. British tariffs remained revenue tariffs, and although consular agents sometimes used them to bargain with, the bargaining was usually toward reduction, and they were not artificially raised to coerce others into a bargaining position.[12]

This refusal to retaliate in kind left Britain economically defenseless in its trade rivalry with ardently protectionist countries. Unable to persuade rivals to abandon their policies of commercial exclusiveness, Britain's only recourse was to adopt a political solution: to join the Scramble and set aside regions where protectionist policies could not operate. This did not mean that Britain adopted an exclusive commercial policy in retaliation, although inevitably British firms received more cordial treatment than did foreigners in areas under British control. Nor did it mean that the government abandoned the old policy of aiding trade in general rather than traders in particular. Pressure on the government from British industrialists, merchants, and shippers eager to have the protection of the flag was customarily met by a cool reception, if not outright rejection. What it did mean—the sum and substance of the altered official attitude—was a slightly greater inclination to intervene officially, with the minimum force necessary to make intervention effective, in parts of the world where foreign pressure or local conditions made it difficult for British trade to operate in a "fair field with no favor."[13] The result was an acceleration of British imperial expansion: in Malaya in the 1870s, in Burma in the 1880s, in Bechuanaland, the Rhodesias, and Nyasaland after 1884, in the Northern Territories of the Gold Coast in the 1890s, in northern Nigeria in the 1880s and 1890s, in Egypt in the late 1870s and early 1880s, and in the Sudan and Uganda in the late 1880s, all, directly or indirectly, for purposes of trade.

Salisbury was anything but a jingo. He was nonetheless fully aware of the problems created by German, French, and American protectionism and was quite prepared to counteract it by political expansion. He voiced this at least as early as 1884 when criticizing Gladstone's foreign policy and as late as 1895 when urging a forward policy in Uganda. And he used the Brussels Conference of 1889-1890 for ends that were mainly commercial.[14]

Salisbury and his contemporaries and predecessors also talked at length about empire security, but what they really meant was security for trade routes. Many of Britain's acquisitions of the nineteenth century in fact serve to trace out these routes. The long route to India, the one really profitable part of the Empire, was secured by Ascension Island (1815), St. Helena (1651), Walfish Bay (1878), Capetown (1814), Port Natal (1843), St. Lucia Bay (1884), Kosi Bay (1887), Mauritius and Rodriguez islands (1810), the Seychelles (1794), the Maldives (1802), and Ceylon (1796). The short route was safe enough before the opening of the Suez Canal for Britain to be content with the stations at Gibraltar (1704), Malta (1800), and Aden (1839). After the canal's opening, it was thought prudent to acquire Cyprus (1878) and to occupy Egypt itself (1882), eventually to remain there, and later to secure Egypt by occupying the Sudan and Uganda. The Far Eastern trade route was secured by the Andaman Islands (1792), Penang (1786), Malacca (1824), Singapore (1819), Labuan (1846), and Hong Kong (1842).[15] These acquisitions had no geographical relevance, no territorial logic, aside from their position astride three of Britain's major arteries of commerce. The freedom and security of trade, therefore, was the almost universally operable principle behind British expansion throughout the century.

PHILANTHROPY

As compelling as was the commercial motive, in selected places philanthropy was even more important before mid-century. This was especially true of that aspect of philanthropy referred to as aborigines protection and its most specific application, slave trade abolition. Faber contends that aborigines protection was the only aspect of the civilizing mission that served as a primary motive for nineteenth-century British expansion.[16]

This was not the case before the 1830s when the philanthropists thought of empire mainly in terms of Caribbean slaveowning plantations. In that period the abolitionists were ardently anti-imperialist. They became equally ardent imperialists shortly thereafter, however, when they began to seek the government's intervention in southern, western, and eastern Africa in order to cut off the slave trade at its source.

Although it is risky to link cause with effect by statistics, there is no denying the coincidence of slave trade treaty making with Britain's early involvement in West Africa, or of its later involvement in eastern Africa with the successful beginnings of slave trade suppression in that area. More than coincidence was involved. The extensive Slave Trade correspondence found in the Foreign Office records leaves no doubt that its abolition was a major factor in the extension of British control over the Gold Coast in the 1840s, southern Nigeria in the 1850s and 1860s, and Nyasaland, northeastern Rhodesia, and the Sudan in the 1880s. It was not enough to interdict European slaving operations. The indigenous slavers of those regions found the trade much too profitable to abandon unless forced to do so by direct British intervention in their affairs.

In South Africa the target was not so much the abolition of slavery—that was successfully accomplished at one stroke shortly after 1833—as the protection of the aborigines from mistreatment by white settlers, Boer and British alike. There was no way to prevent such mistreatment other than to follow the settlers wherever they went and impose a measure of restraint on their behavior. Protection of the Khoikhoi, Griqua, Basuto, and "Kaffir" was easily the foremost consideration in the first phase of British expansion in South Africa in the 1840s, which included the coast as far as Mozambique and the whole Orange River area.[17]

After mid-century the philanthropic impulse waned, but it never wholly perished, and in the 1880s it revived as an important factor in expansion when it was revealed that the slave trade was still widespread in East Africa and that bonded labor was reviving in West Africa with the connivance of other European powers. Although there was plentiful evidence that British settlers were guilty enough of maltreating Africans, Britons firmly believed that continental Europeans were worse by far. Accordingly aborigines protection was as good a reason as free trade for denying exclusive control of certain areas to continental governments. Cynics continue to deride the sincerity of the British philanthropic impulse, but the evidence is overwhelmingly against them. We know too much about the motivations of pragmatists like Salisbury and Palmerston and of Colonial Secretaries like Russell, Stanley, and Grey to question their honest commitment to this cause.

GOOD GOVERNMENT

If trade and aborigines protection were the seminal motives, they dramatized the need for a climate of security and just, stable government in which to operate. Juxtaposition was one factor that connected the three. Once initial contacts were made in pursuit of trade and slavery abolition, once a relatively efficient, highly rationalized society was juxtaposed to a weaker, more primitive society, further encroachments on the latter by the former were inevitable because of the obvious power differential between the two.

The impulse for colonial good government also had roots at home. It originated in the eighteenth century with Edmund Burke and the younger Pitt and was embodied in legislation for the colonies before it was at home. It began with Pitt's India Act of 1784 and subsequent Charter Acts for the East India Company. It was reinforced by the general climate of reform, free trade, and evangelical humanitarianism that revived in the post-Napoleonic era. From the 1830s onward, the British were preening themselves on the accomplishments of the Great Reform Era and had acquired an almost religious faith in the superiority of liberal British government and in the beneficent effects it must have on all who came in contact with it.

South and east of England this conviction translated itself into a mission to exercise this talent upon peoples who, in British eyes, were obviously badly governed. The French pursued a similar mission by trying to assimilate Africans and Asians into French culture. The Victorian British, equally convinced of the uniqueness of their culture but more prone to racial aloofness, were not at all certain that assimilation was possible. Contact with African societies had confirmed the British in their preconceived image of Africa— that African barbarity must be a function of race—and most of them subscribed to an untutored and unquestioned belief in a more or less permanent African inferiority or at least a limited capacity for improvement.[18] Unhampered by the Gallic dream of cultural universality, the British were convinced that neither Asians nor Africans could be educated to be English, much as they wished to acquire selected trappings of European civilization. In this intellectual climate, dreams of assimilation seemed absurd. Far better to keep order and impose peace and justice; that is, to bestow good government on peoples who could not seem to manage it themselves. In this sense good government was the British alternative to the French principle of assimilation and served as an equally powerful stimulus to, or rationale for, overseas expansion. To what extent it did or did not also serve as a rationalization, I deal with in the case studies in this book.

Local circumstance ensured that the reasons for imposing good government differed widely from place to place. In one place the British were moved to preserve peace and order on a turbulent frontier, which was making life difficult for administrators and settlers. In another they were seeking to maintain the security of coastal stations against attack from the hinterland. Here they intervened to put down piracy; there to force an African chief to abide by his slave trading treaty. They sometimes interceded to prevent harassment of British subjects by native despots, to ensure that British subjects received legal redress for wrongs done them by native governments or others, or even to prevent the maltreatment of Africans and Asians by their own rulers. Often British officials stepped in to protect native peoples from white settlers, or vice-versa. Intervention was not uncommon to forestall an occupation by a rival European power less committed to maintaining high standards of government, free trade, and slavery abolition.

Impelled by their invincible belief in the beneficent effects of good government, British statesmen from Castlereagh onward were prepared to intervene in places like Portugal, Spain, Greece, Belgium, Turkey, Brazil, and elsewhere to induce these badly governed states to take corrective measures in the interests of peace, trade, or slavery abolition. Palmerston justified his intervention in Greece in 1841 on the ground that the Greek constitution should be a genuine guarantee of rights rather than the sham it had turned out to be. Intervention was called for to reestablish controls over royal absolutism and mismanagement. The confident self-righteousness with which the British pursued this self-appointed task seems quaint and arrogant today, but no one can deny its grip on Victorian thinking.

The case studies in part II illustrate the effects of this attitude in regions that eventually became part of the British Empire. In India, from Burke's time until the conquest of the Punjab—when all of India came under British control—there was to be no more corruption of public office, no more indulgence of the cruelties and mismanagement of the native princes. It played a role in all three phases of the annexation of Burma as well as in Malaya. In South Africa it drew the British eastward along the coast to Natal and Zululand and northward into the Boer republics. It motivated all phases of expansion in Nigeria and the Gold Coast from the 1840s to the end of the century, and the same can be said of the acquisition of the entire Nile Valley in the twenty years following 1876.

The Victorians believed deeply in progress, in the superiority of English values and institutions, and in their duty to achieve the former by imposing the latter on "lesser breeds" throughout Africa and Asia. Thus the imperatives of trade, philanthropy, and good government, which dominated foreign policy, dominated imperial expansion as well.

NOTES

1. Leon Levi, *History of British Commerce and of the Economic Progress of the British Nation, 1763-1870* (London, 1872).

2. Ibid., 562-63.

3. Ibid.; Sir John H. Clapham, *An Economic History of Modern Britain* (Cambridge, 1926-1938), 1:482, 486-87; Arthur L. Bowley, *A Short Account of England's Foreign Trade in the 19th Century: Its Economic*

and Social Results (New York, 1905), 72, 120, 132; Samuel B. Saul, *Studies in British Overseas Trade, 1870-1914* (Liverpool, 1960), 11-12.

4. Werner Schlote, *British Overseas Trade from 1700 to the 1930's* (Oxford, 1952), 156-59; Levi, *History of British Commerce*, 562-63.

5. Ronald Hyam corroborates this official concern. See *Britain's Imperial Century, 1815-1914* (New York, 1976), 68.

6. Morier to Derby, May 15, 1877, quoted in Roger Anstey, *Britain in the Congo in the 19th Century* (New York, 1962), 85-86.

7. Quoted in Richard Faber, *The Vision and the Need: Late Victorian Imperialist Aims* (London, 1966), 35.

8. Ronald Robinson and J. Gallagher, *Africa and the Victorians: The Official Mind of Imperialism* (London, 1961), 10.

9. Schlote, *British Overseas Trade*, 129-30.

10. Ibid., 158-60; D. C. M. Platt, *Finance, Trade and Politics in British Foreign Policy, 1815-1914* (Oxford, 1968), 70-73, 83-84.

11. Platt, *Finance, Trade*, 103.

12. Ibid., 145-47.

13. Ibid., xxxiv, 99, 146.

14. See Platt, "Economic Factors in British Policy during the 'New Imperialism,'" *Past and Present* (April 1968):128, and S. Miers, "The Brussels Conference," in P. Gifford and W. R. Louis, *Britain and Germany in Africa: Imperial Rivalry and Colonial Rule* (New Haven, 1967), 83-118.

15. See C. N. Parkinson, *British Intervention in Malaya, 1867-77* (Singapore, 1960), xiii.

16. Faber, *Vision and the Need*, 38.

17. The Orange River area has been omitted for reasons of space, but my study of the region, using chiefly the Colonial Office papers, the private papers of Sir George Napier in the British Museum, and John Chase, *The Natal Papers . . . 1498-1843* (repr., Cape Town, 1968), confirms the conclusions reached in this book about the coastal regions in the same period.

18. See Philip Curtin, *The Image of Africa: British Ideas and Action, 1780-1850* (Madison, Wis., 1964), passim.

4

PARAMOUNTCY

Because British control was imposed gradually, almost imperceptibly in some cases, over long periods of time, it seems advisable to try to isolate the point at which control became effective and the exercise of imperialism began. If we can find this moment in history, we can perhaps identify more accurately the reasons for British expansion before they become muddled by the later demands of administering what was already under control or corrupted by ex post facto rationalizations defending the assumption of control. In a sense, motives for expansion at this moment, as far as they can be discerned, are more likely to have remained pure.

To describe the condition achieved at this moment, I have used the term *paramountcy*. I consider it preferable to the term *informal empire* because nineteenth-century British statesmen did not think in terms of formal or informal empires. They did think in terms of paramountcy and in fact habitually used the word. Moreover whether empire was formal or informal is not important. Whether it was effective is important because only when it became effective can it be called imperialism, and paramountcy connotes effectiveness. It tells us what the British were trying to do in a way that the words formal and informal do not.

More importantly paramountcy draws our attention to the moment when critical decisions were made. Imperialism differs from other major historical phenomena in at least one other cardinal aspect: unlike the Industrial Revolution or the rise of nation-states, Western imperialism was essentially a matter of choice. To discover its roots, we must stop concentrating exclusively on the Scramble, which was largely an acceleration of preexisting trends in which European powers were caught up almost despite themselves. We must look as well to earlier decades—and this applies particularly to the British government—when governments still had a choice whether to occupy or dominate a coast or a hinterland or whether to commit themselves to do so.

This last point raises the question whether paramountcy can be said to exist in some cases simply because the British had decided to exercise it, as well as the larger question of the criteria for judging when paramountcy exists. The first question can be answered in the affirmative because in all cases of this type examined, the British had been reluctant to commit themselves to permanent intervention, and once the decision was (belatedly) made, the exercise of influence had already proceeded so far that control either existed in fact or was seen by all concerned to be inevitable in the near future. An example is the British sphere of influence established over the Upper Nile by the Anglo-German Treaty of 1890, which effectively pegged out the region for future British expansion by squaring Britain's only formidable rival in the region. Once a choice or commitment of this sort was made, a diplomatic paramountcy can be said to exist because thereafter it was politically impossible (and in this case strategically impossible) to retreat, and later expansion proceeded almost organically. This type of paramountcy also applies to the Northern Territories of the Gold Coast and Nigeria where Anglo-French treaties of 1889 and 1890 put other powers on notice that British occupation of those regions was only a matter of time.

A more concrete form of paramountcy can be seen in the control of a country's external relations. While defending the Pretoria Convention of 1881, the Lord Chancellor explained that "the control of Foreign and Frontier relations essentially distinguishes a paramount power."[1] Where local governments had lost control of their foreign relations, where they could no longer act beyond their frontiers for very long in a manner hostile to British interests, whatever latitude remained to them in their domestic affairs, British paramountcy clearly existed. Here we have the type of the British protectorates of the pre-Scramble era.

The clearest criterion is the control over internal affairs. Paramountcy existed under conditions of military occupation, even if formal annexation did not result, as was the case in Egypt after 1882 and in Zululand in 1879. In some places it was acknowledged by a local chief or a rival European power apart from any trial of strength or with no more than a symbolic occupation, such as occurred along the Orange River in the early 1840s. In this book, therefore, paramountcy has a triple connotation; it can mean internal control, external control, or diplomatic hegemony.

It has been suggested that a more refined model of power expansion than that of paramountcy be applied to the cases studied in this book in order to reflect the fact that the growth of empire is a process of the slow growth of effective power rather than the achievement of control at a particular moment, and that something like D. A. Low's model might serve the purpose.[2] Low's analysis offers some interesting insights as he conducts the British (in Uganda) through stages of Impact, Influence, Sway, Ascendancy, Predominance, Mastery, and Dictation, but I have resisted using this or other refined models for several reasons.

While not denying that effective imperial control grows slowly, this book is not primarily a study of the growth of British power overseas. For purposes of identifying reasons for expansion, one can isolate a comparatively short period or even a moment when the imperial factor became dominant in a given place, and this at a relatively early date. Nor is it necessary to extend the study into the period of colonial administration, as Low does; indeed it is better to terminate it before that period if pure motives for expansion are what we seek.

Second, while Low's model informs us with greater precision how the British exercised power and records more accurately the substance and progress of that power, it applies more neatly to internal affairs or administration than to foreign affairs. But paramountcy could consist as well of control over foreign affairs or, in some cases, merely of a sphere of influence. Low's model does not apply here.

Third, the effect of control more than its nature is important here. We do not need to know which details of administration Britain controlled but only whether chiefs or princes were able to frustrate the pursuit of British interests. It mattered not whether these interests were pursued by controlling internal or external affairs or by diplomatic hegemony or whether control was accepted peaceably or fiercely resisted, and all of these alternatives can be seen. It mattered only that some sort of control was achieved at some point as the effective means of reaching British goals. Owing to these reasons and to the great diversity of local conditions in which paramountcy was exercised, it seemed wiser not to try to refine further the criteria by which paramountcy is to be recognized.

REGIONS INCLUDED AND EXCLUDED

Because paramountcy often existed long before formal empire, the emphasis in this book is on early rather than late nineteenth-century expansion although the Upper Nile is included to demonstrate continuity in British motives throughout the century. The countries treated in the case studies are not comprehensive for the early period, but they constitute far more than what statisticians would regard as a representative sample: the periphery of India (Sind, the Punjab, and Burma), Malaya, the South African coast up to Mozambique, the southern tiers of the Gold Coast (now Ghana) and Nigeria, altogether the most important areas of early nineteenth-century British imperialism, if one excludes the dominions that were not examples of imperialism over alien peoples but of colonization. Several important regions have been omitted (although I have completed studies on most of them, which bear out the conclusions reached here) partly to reduce the size of the book and partly because they are continuations of earlier expansion: the interior of South Africa up to Lake Tanganyika, the northern territories of the Gold Coast and Nigeria, as well as Kenya and Egypt, although the last is treated briefly in this book. The West Indies were excluded because they are examples of pre-nineteenth century expansion. Quasi-dependencies such as Persia, Afghanistan, and China and even more tenuous spheres of influence such as Turkey, Argentina, and Venezuela have been left out because, although British paramountcy may have been exerted from time to time, in the long run it did not stick. It is said that this was so because international rivalries led to a stand off, but international rivalry alone did not save the Sudan or Morocco. In my view these grey areas bear out the contention that paramountcy was successful in inverse ratio to the level of rationalization.

In the Latin America republics, for example, Britain's main interests were economic, which meant that before the 1850s Britain looked on them mainly as trading partners and as recipients of manufactured goods rather than of capital.[3] Only after 1860 did

British capital flow into Latin America in quantity, but in neither era did the British government often intervene imperialistically to protect these interests. British merchants learned to get along without their government's help because the republics, though often chaotic, were sufficiently Westernized and powerful to protect their own interests and to have the last word in any conflict with European merchants.[4] Such being the case, the British ordinarily had to achieve their ends by negotiation, whether private, on the part of large, expatriate companies, or officially diplomatic. Only in cases of flagrant violation of the rights of British subjects or in the enforcement of slave trade treaties was Her Majesty's Government willing to intervene. When it did so, it could exert a good deal of pressure to win compliance with its views, and ordinarily the republics bowed to this pressure because it was in their economic interest to do so. But such cases were infrequent and isolated instances and even when taken together do not constitute a pattern of intervention that can be called imperialist in the sense of achieving any sort of permanent paramountcy over the Latin American republics.[5]

What first brought the British into contact with China was commerce, and the intervention that led to the Opium War occurred for commercial reasons far broader than the opium trade alone. It was to settle "the greatest of all questions as to how and where the trade of British subjects is henceforth to be conducted in China."[6] It was commerce that led to the Treaty of Nanking in 1842, placing the relations between China and the West on a new footing for the next century. Palmerston's comment on the treaty was that "there is no doubt that this event, which will form an epoch in the progress of the civilization of the human races, must be attended with the most important advantages to the commercial interest of England."[7] It was only later that European capital began to flow into China for railroads, cotton mills, and other enterprises for which China lacked the necessary capitalization.[8]

But the British never acquired the paramountcy over China that they did in India, Malaya, or Africa because they were able to achieve their ends by means of "Palmerstonian blows" such as the Opium War. Such blows made it possible to open up the China trade without having to burden themselves with controlling the imperial government by means of advisers or residents. As weak as China was, it was more stable than the chaotic or moribund regimes of southern Asia, and it was able to avoid total subversion partly by playing off the European companies and governments against one another and partly because of the relative sophistication of the Chinese economy compared to those of southern Asia. British merchants like Jardine, Matheson & Company were able to operate successfully with the collaboration of their Chinese counterparts either by evading the restrictive regulations of the Ch'ing bureaucracy or by adapting themselves to the idiosyncrasies of the Chinese economy.[9]

It is demonstrable therefore that Britain pursued the same foreign policy objectives in these grey areas as elsewhere, although the philanthropic impulse had far less influence in Asia than in Latin America where the African slave trade was still alive. But paramountcy could not be made to stick in such countries largely because their governments managed to rationalize themselves sufficiently to fend off what might be called full-fledged imperialism.

NOTES

1. Hansard, *Parliamentary Debates*, 3d ser., vol. 260, p. 309.

2. D. A. Low, *Lion Rampant* (London, 1973), pp. 30ff.

3. D. C. M. Platt, *Business Imperialism, 1840-1930: An Inquiry Based on British Experience in Latin America* (Oxford, 1977), 11 and his "Economic Imperialism and the Businessman: Britain and Latin America before 1914," in Roger Owen and Bob Sutcliffe, *Studies in the Theory of Imperialism* (London, 1972), 308.

4. Platt, *Business Imperialism*, 8.

5. See Platt, "Economic Imperialism," 295-311.

6. Michael Greenberg, *British Trade and the Opening of China, 1800-42* (Cambridge, 1957), 212.

7. Ibid., 214-15.

8. Ibid., ix.

9. See Edward Le Fevour, *Western Enterprise in Late Ch'ing China: A Selective Survey of Jardine, Matheson and Company's Operations, 1842-1895* (Cambridge, Mass., 1968), chap. 4, p. 130.

PART II

CASE STUDIES IN ASIA AND AFRICA

5

PROLOGUE TO ASIA:
THE TORSO OF INDIA

PARAMOUNTCY

As of 1820 British rule in India extended over Bengal, Bihar, parts of Oudh, and the imperial cities of Agra and Delhi in the north; over the Circars, the Carnatic, and the Malabar coast in the south; and over Bombay Island, Surat, and the littoral of the Gulf of Cambay in the west. These territories constituted "British India," properly so called. Over much of the rest of India, still nominally independent, varying degrees of control were exercised by virtue of protectorate treaties or subsidiary alliances. Travancore and Coorg came under British protection in 1788 and 1792, respectively. Mysore was broken up and allotted to client rulers in 1799 after Tippu had announced his alliance with Napoleon, and subsidiary treaties were forced on the Nizam of Hyderabad in 1800 and on what was left of Oudh in 1802. In 1809 Ranjit Singh, the Maharaja of the Punjab, signed over the Sikh states south of the Sutlej to British protection. Perhaps the greatest challenge to the Company's supremacy in these years was overcome in two hotly contested wars with one or another of the Maratha chiefs and their sometime allies, the plundering hordes of the Pindaris. By 1818 the latter had been dispersed, and the Maratha confederacy had ceased to exist as a political force. In the same year, nineteen of the Rajput states, long in fear of the Marathas, willingly placed themselves under the protection of the conquerors of their ancient enemies.

Before 1820, then, the British were clearly paramount in the torso of the Indian subcontinent.[1] The later annexations of Mysore and Oudh simply formalized the accomplished fact, as did the numerous minor annexations of Dalhousie's time. Sir Percival Griffiths could say of 1803 that thereafter it was "impossible for any Indian ruler to become the focal point of an Indian political

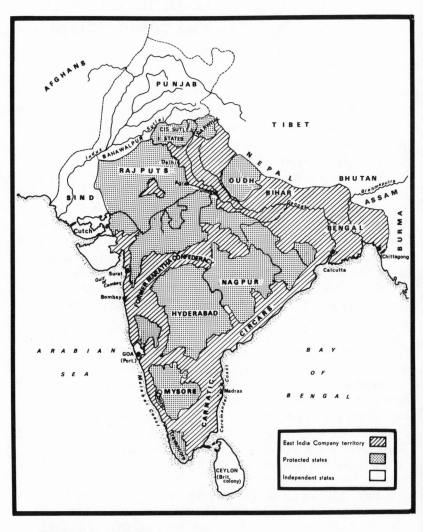

INDIA, c. 1820

system."[2] Whether the Maratha outbreak in 1817-1818 belied that statement, it certainly was true after 1818. When Lord Amherst sailed for India as Governor-General in 1823, his instructions contained the following from Charles Wynn, President of the Board of Control: "No power or combination of powers can make head against us or furnish reasonable ground for attack. No further acquisition of territory can be desirable. The extent of empire which you have to govern...is such that it could not only be unwise but hardly safe to exceed."[3]

Assured as Wynn may have been about the folly of further expansion, the question facing the British was not so much whether it was wise but whether they had any choice. Because they were now paramount power in the torso of India, it was difficult for them not to be concerned about disturbances of the peace in neighboring states where British interests might be affected. This meant Assam and Burma on the east and Sind and the Punjab in the northwest. And because of the China trade, it also meant Malaya.

GROWTH OF THE PRIVATE TRADE

In what direction were British interests, attitudes, and policies moving in India in the years before 1820?

Whatever the political concerns of Robert Clive and Lord Richard Wellesley, who fought and destroyed French influence in India and together bestowed an Indian empire on Britain, it must never be forgotten that the British were in India first and foremost to trade. After Clive acquired the *diwani* (tax collection franchise) of Bengal in 1764, tribute in the form of surplus revenue began to augment the profits from trade. But this did not cause the Company to seek further territories, for the expenses involved in territorial conquest and administration threatened to exceed the revenues and encroach on the profits from trade itself. Until the day it was deprived of all trading rights whatever, the Court of Directors was unalterably opposed to territorial expansion, was constantly at odds with expansive governors like Wellesley, and ultimately exercised its privilege to cashier governors who ignored its views. Bearce points out that succeeding chairmen of the Company, such as David Scott (1796 and 1801), Sir Francis Baring after him, and Charles Grant, several times chairman between 1794 and

1823, were all principally concerned with expanding the Company's trade, not its territories.[4] Until the first decade of the nineteenth century, only exceptional people such as Sir Joshua Child and Clive and Wellesley had any interest in a British empire in India, and few were aware that one was being created. When the truth began to be realized, it was held to be justified only for commercial reasons.[5]

The Court of Directors, however, failed to grasp the historical forces that were shaping Indian affairs and especially the economy. Although the Indian trade greatly increased in volume during the Napoleonic years, it was not very profitable, owing mainly to Napoleon's continental blockade, which virtually closed off the re-export trade to Europe. At the same time the costs of war and administration had consumed the surplus revenues of British India and created a large deficit. Only the proceeds of the profitable China trade enabled the Company to avoid calling upon Parliament for a subsidy, and even this was resorted to on one or two occasions. It had become apparent that neither the Company's jealously guarded trade monopoly nor the bureaucracy devised to oversee it were functioning efficiently. The British government was under pressure from not only the old Burkeian types who had attacked the corruption of Company servants but from a combination of mercantile, industrial, and political interests, which were beginning to champion the cause of free trade vigorously. Lancashire cotton manufacturing especially had grown to maturity during the Napoleonic era and played a leading role in causing the government to abolish the Company's monopoly in 1813.

The trade that now motivated Englishmen was not an obsolete, seventeenth-century monopoly trade but a new sort of trade produced by the Industrial Revolution. It no longer called for the importation of high-quality manufactured goods from India but the reverse: the importation of raw materials from the East and the cultivation of Oriental outlets for British manufactures. To this change the Company had shown itself less adaptable than the private traders, partly because of the restrictions of its charter and partly because of its entrenched bureaucracy. But the Company was fighting a losing battle against the new conditions and at the end of the eighteenth century had virtually surrendered the Indian Ocean trade to aggressive private traders, continuing to enforce its monopoly only on the direct trade to and from Britain. By 1813 most of India's Asian trade, save with China, was conducted by private traders who were optimistic about the prospects of free trade.

The abolition of the Company's monopoly signified a shift in government policy from support of the Company, which had customarily sought to encourage Indian manufacturing, to support of the British cotton manufacturer who wanted to flood the East with the new, cheaper, factory-made textiles. The change took place rapidly, mostly within the long ministry of Lord Liverpool (1812-1827). By the mid-1820s Indian hand loom manufacturing had virtually disappeared. The change was aided by tariff duties that taxed Indian piece goods entering Britain at a high rate (50 to 70 percent) but admitted British cottons into India at a nominal rate of 2.5 percent. By the time the rate for India cottons entering Britain was reduced to 12.5 percent in 1825, Indian hand loom cotton manufacturing had been ruined.

The result was a boon to the private trade and a further decline in Company profits. Although the total Indian trade rose from about £3.5 million in 1811-1812 to approximately £10 million in 1828, the Company's share of that trade diminished from £808,975 in 1812-1813 to £398,469 in 1828-1829.[6] How is it, then, that the Company's directors continued to be interested in fostering trade after the abolition of their monopoly? Partly because the China trade continued to be lucrative but primarily because the private trade interest, acting through the score or so of East India Agency Houses in London, used its growing fortunes to capture the direction of the East India Company. By 1826 eight of the thirty directors (including the six out by rotation) represented the private interest; by 1831 it was seventeen. The sentiments of this group were reflected in and influenced by the thinking of James Mill who became an examiner of correspondence for the Company in 1819 (largely on the strength of this *History of British India* published in 1817) and rose to the eminence of head examiner before his death in 1836. This position made him virtually an under secretary of state for India, for although he was not situated to control policy, the respect with which his views were held made him influential in the Indian administration of his time. Thus it was that the directors were willing in 1826 to abandon the Company's export trade to India and to consider the future loss of the import trade while still lobbying hard in the interests of free trade with India. After 1813 the Company's main function was no longer profitable trade or the rendering of Indian tribute to England but the maintenance of conditions in India conducive to the trade of the private sector. George Canning, when President of the Board of Control (1816-1820), was convinced that Britain's interest in India was still mainly commercial.[7] And the taproot of Mill's philosophy as it applied to India was that India existed not to enhance British military power or to provide tribute but for the opportunity it offered for trade, by which he meant free trade. It was trade that dominated liberal thought at this time, and liberal thought had begun to dominate the minds of those who influenced or controlled British Indian policy. Even after the Charter Act of 1813, therefore, trade remained an important, if not the primary, reason for maintaining and improving the connection with India.

THE LOW ESTIMATE OF INDIAN SOCIETY

The gradual transfer of authority from the Company to the Board of Control also reflected the growing conviction that under the new conditions the promotion of trade required government intervention. Furnivall has pointed out that where the European interest was limited to obtaining tropical produce at low cost, the native economic system could still prevail and the operation could be directed satisfactorily by independent Asian rulers. But where a country was viewed as a market for the sale of European goods, the native economy had to give way to Western commercial law and procedures, and some form of European rule was required.[8] For this reason, and owing to the belief of utilitarians like James Mill and Lord William Bentinck (Governor-General, 1828-1835) that the material interests would naturally foster improvement, trade was inextricably linked with good government in the minds of the rulers of India.[9]

The intent behind the Regulating Act of 1773 and the India Act of 1784 had been to correct the abuses in the Company's administration of India. The second act established a cabinet-level office, the Board of Control, to monitor these affairs, and it was out of the controversy between the Board and the Court of Directors that good government emerged as a guiding principle of the British *raj*.

It originated in the philosophical conservatism of Edmund Burke, which held that Britain's imperial role was to provide the fabric of peace and order upon which the pattern of Indian culture, society, and institutions could be rewoven. But it did not for long retain Burkeian conservatism as its guide, save his insistence that Indian policy be founded on responsibility and high principles. Instead its methods were to be liberal and utilitarian; its goal the reformation and modernization of India in keeping with Western conceptions of progress, not with Indian traditions.

One element of the new doctrine was administrative efficiency. At the moment the Company was being deprived of its trading privileges and converted into a sovereign Asian power, its revenues from commerce were declining as its revenues from taxes and tribute rose. In the interests of its stockholders, therefore, it began in the late eighteenth century to display a growing concern for reforms in the Indian government, which would eliminate corruption and increase efficiency. Indian rulers resisted these at every step, and it was partly for this reason that the Company increasingly intervened in their domestic administrations and imposed Company advisers upon them. This development led to the bureaucratization of Company administration under Cornwallis and to his Permanent Settlement of the revenue collection in Bengal.

The second element was the liberal doctrine of free trade. With the appearance of Lancashire cottons in India at the turn of the century, British merchants acquired a vested interest in the welfare of Indians. A prosperous India, using money, engaging in free trade, and observing the Western law of contracts, was not only a practical necessity, it jibed with the doctrines of economic liberalism then becoming fashionable in Britain. The spread of these doctrines coincided with the government's assumption of control over the East India Company, and once the Company's servants were persuaded that their monopoly was about to end, they too became infected with the liberal tenets of economic freedom. It was now assumed that good government and economic progress must go hand in hand and together would serve the general welfare of Indian and Englishmen alike. But this was going to require a great deal more of government intervention because "commercial interest and liberal philosophy, no less than the conquest of oppression and corruption, required a system of direct rule on Western lines under the immediate supervision of British officials.'' This view was being pressed by James Mill from 1819 onward at India House and being taught by Sir James Mackenzie at Haileybury College, the Company's training school founded in 1806. With lapses and exceptions it prevailed in the government of India from 1815 or 1820 onward.[10]

The third element was evangelical humanitarianism. Both the evangelical and utilitarian movements fostered the humanitarianism that shaped Indian policy in the early nineteenth century, owing to the growing influence of the "Saints" (evangelical humanitarians) in the Court of Directors and the Parliament. Men like Charles Grant, Bengal civilian and several times Chairman of the Court of Directors, who argued that unless the Indian government were based on moral principles Britain might find it hard to justify its control, created in the minds of Company servants "an uneasy conscience about the very existence of British rule in India."[11] William Wilberforce was chief of the evangelical contingent in the Commons, which pressed for the opening of India to missionary activity at the time of the charter renewal in 1813. It succeeded both in gaining entry for missionaries and in the insertion of clause 33 in the Charter Act, which declared that it was the duty of the government "to promote the interest and the happiness of the native inhabitants of India." India provided the evangelicals with a challenging field of endeavor and the utilitarians with an opportunity to test their legal and judicial theories and to rationalize the civil service. Together they helped to modernize India through education, the printing press, and the spread of medical and agricultural technology. For Mill and the liberal utilitarians as for Wilberforce and the evangelicals, commerce and good government were to be the twin foundations of British policy in India.[12]

It is not to be thought that these views were held out of a high regard for Indian society. Quite the opposite was true. They grew out of the generally low estimate of Hindu and Muslim society and of its capacity for self-rule. To the enlightened English ruling class of the time, Oriental government and good government were antithetical; Oriental economic and social systems were incompatible with the tenets of economic freedom and human rights. Oriental rule could be nothing but inept, corrupt, and oppressive, and whatever abuses might creep into Company rule, the far greater malignancy of Indian government fully justified a British raj that bestowed on the Indians peace, order, justice, education, and Christianity. The attitude is described by Henry Prinsep in his well-known account of Hastings' administration published in 1825:

Of all human contrivances for the perpetuation of . . . misrule, there is none so effectual as to throw together a number of independent tribes, each under a separate patriarchal or feudal government, and urged, therefore, by every motive of passion and policy to seek the destruction of its neighbor for its own aggrandizement. It is this state of things that has kept the interior of Africa in perpetual barbarity, . . . and rendered the once happy and polished Arabia the most savage and inhospitable country on the face of the globe. The only remedy and preventive of such evils consists in the establishment of a general controlling government, to restrain the passions of tribes and individuals, to promote mutual confidence, and teach the population to seek wealth and distinction by cultivating the arts of peace instead of looking on one another, like wild beasts, as legitimate objects of prey. . . .

If these considerations have any weight, that is, if any circumstances can warrant an encroachment on the independence of tribes for the purpose of introducing general government, the state of things in Rajpootana at this period [1815-1819] was such as to justify, and indeed imperiously to call for, an interposition by the British Government for that purpose.[13]

The disdainful attitude of even the most high-minded of British officials somewhat tainted their sincere efforts to compensate for Britain's eighteenth-century plundering of India. Nevertheless this generation of Company servants stands out above all others in its genuine concern for the welfare of the Indian: Sir Stamford Raffles in Singapore (1819-1823), Sir Thomas Munro in Madras (1820-1827), Mountstuart Elphinstone in Bombay (1819-1827), and most strikingly, Lord William Bentinck who exercised supreme authority after 1828.

From 1820 onward, then, trade remained, and good government became the foremost objectives of British rule in India. Good government made for smoother administration and more prosperous trade, and it eased the humanitarian conscience. And just as the British had intervened for these purposes in the torso of India, they were prepared to intervene to correct bad governments beyond the borders: along the Indus and in Burma and Malaya, where trade was suffering and political conditions were offensive to English liberalism.

NOTES

1. Ingram states that Britain became paramount power in India after 1818. Edward Ingram, *The Beginning of the Great Game in Asia, 1828-1834* (Oxford, 1979), 4.

2. Sir Percival Griffiths, *The British Impact on India* (London, 1952), 92.

3. Sir Cyril H. Philips, *The East India Company, 1784-1834*, 2d ed. (Manchester, 1961), 240, quoting Register, Secret Committee, # 504, March 10, 1823.

4. George D. Bearce, *British Attitudes towards India, 1784-1858* (London, 1961), 52-54.

5. See Holden Furber, "The Theme of Imperialism and Colonialism in Modern Historical Writing on India," in C. H. Philips, *Historians of India, Pakistan and Ceylon* (London, 1961), 334-37.

6. Philips, *East India Company*, 190-92; Robert M. Martin, *The Indian Empire* (London, 1858), 1:560-63.

7. Wendy Hinde, *George Canning* (London, 1973), 288.

8. J. S. Furnivall, *Colonial Policy and Practice: A Comparative Study of Burma and Netherlands-India* (New York, 1956), 276-77.

9. J. Rosselli, *Lord William Bentinck: The Making of a Liberal Imperialist, 1774-1839* (Berkeley, Calif., 1974), 272.

10. Furnivall, *Colonial Policy*, 28-29, 282-83.

11. Ainslee T. Embree, *Charles Grant and British Rule in India* (New York, 1962), 287.

12. S. A. Low supports my contention that good government was a prime mover in India in the 1820s and 1830s. The evangelical-liberal-humanitarian point of view, convinced of the superiority and benevolence of British intentions (therefore, "anglicist"), won out over the "orientalist" point of view represented by Elphinstone, Malcolm, Metcalfe, and John Lawrence. The "anglicists," of which Bentham and James Mill were the leading intellectual lights and Charles Grant, Bentinck, T. B. Macaulay, and Dalhousie among their greatest disciples, were determined on a root and branch renovation of Indian society to the end that British rule should, in Mill's words, "best minister the public wealth and happiness of the people of India." See Low, *Lion Rampant* (London, 1973), 41-53.

13. Henry T. Prinsep, *History of the Political and Military Transactions in India during the Administration of the Marquess of Hastings, 1813-1823* (London, 1825), 345-46.

The most commonly accepted views of British penetration in Burma[1] have attributed it to the Company's insatiable appetite for expansion,[2] to the expansionist lust of particular Governors-General, especially Dalhousie,[3] or to the requirements of military security on an unstable frontier,[4] and nearly everyone has agreed that a decadent, corrupt, chaotic, and economically stagnant society, such as the precolonial Burmese kingdom was seen to be, must inevitably have fallen prey to its dynamic Western neighbor.

Recent scholarship has tried to revise these views with mixed success. Laurence Kitzan, while acknowledging the role played by frontier security, attributes the first Anglo-Burmese War primarily to wounded British dignity.[5] It was the insolence and arrogance of the Burmese replies to British remonstrances over border forays that caused Amherst to lose patience and declare war.[6] Although Amherst was a judicious man who sincerely wished to avoid war with Burma, his career ambitions, especially because he had not shone in previous assignments in Sicily and China, were sufficiently critical that "he could not afford to be made to look ridiculous" by a troublesome third-rate power on his border.[7]

Oliver Pollak accepts the conventional view of British aims in the first war: that they sought "to obtain an advantageous adjustment of the eastern boundary, and to preclude the recurrence of similar insults and aggressions in the future."[8] But he attributes Anglo-Burmese hostility throughout the century to a fundamental, and inevitable, clash of different cultures exploited by special interests. This was the long-term reason. The "immediate" causes of the second war, upon which Pollak's focus is directed and which led to the annexation of Pegu and the landlocking of the remnant of the Burmese kingdom, were somewhat different. It was provoked by vested missionary and commercial interests who misled Company officials and was declared reluctantly by a Governor-General who "found it more difficult to rebuke and censure a single naval offi-

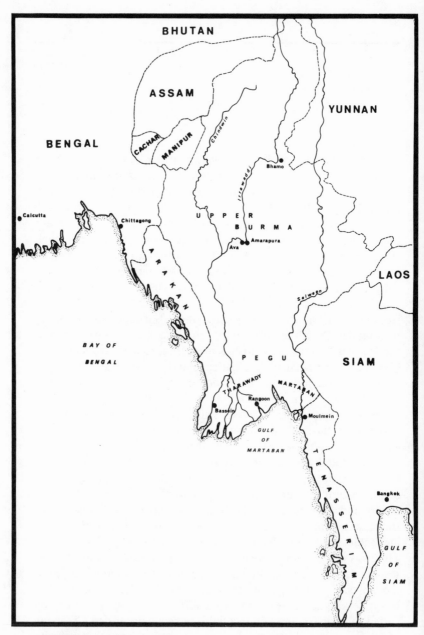

BURMA, 1824–1826

cer than to go to war with a foreign nation." It resulted from men on the spot deliberately exploiting cultural differences and misunderstandings in their own interest.[9]

Neither Kitzan nor Pollak regards the maintenance of trade relations as an important factor. Kitzan confines himself to the undocumented statement,[10] while Pollak portrays the British trading community in Rangoon and Moulmein (in the 1830s and 1840s) as extremely bothersome and irritating to Calcutta, which repeatedly refused to intervene on its behalf to prevent "oppression" by the Burmese authorities. "Oppression" in fact amounted to official restraint of the high-handed behavior and sometimes shady operations of the British traders. Pollak concludes that the Company was not actively interested in protecting or promoting Anglo-Burmese trade.[11]

Pollak nevertheless points out that Calcutta's interest in Burma revived in the 1850s when it became apparent that reasserting control over Burma would help to develop the teak trade and the Rangoon and Siamese trades, would restore control over British merchants who evaded British duties, and would help to restore law and order on a disrupted frontier as well as help the missionaries.[12] Here we have arguments closer to those advanced in this book and which I think both Kitzan and Pollak underrate. Pollak moreover has not closely examined the causes of the first war, which I believe to be the crucial war in the establishment of British paramountcy over Burma. While British dignity, Lord Amherst's personal ambitions, culture conflict, and Pollak's immediate causes cannot be denied as contributing factors, I hope to show that the maintenance of free and peaceful trade was the seminal factor and that frontier security should be seen in the broader and more positive context of the aim of good government.

GROWTH OF TRADE AND BURMESE HOSTILITY

British merchants had traded sporadically in Burma throughout the seventeenth and eighteenth centuries, but the trade was not large and constantly had to overcome the suspicions and rigid control of the Court of Ava. In an effort to develop the trade, the East India Company obtained royal permission to establish a factory on the island of Bassein in 1757, but two years later it was attacked by the Burmese, who killed several of the Company's servants and demolished the factory. From 1759 until 1824 the British had no permanent outposts or factories on the Burmese coast, and trade was left largely in the hands of private adventurers who carried on a precarious existence in Rangoon at the sufferance of the local governor.

Nonetheless trade gradually increased and by 1795 exports from Bengal to Burma (actually to the three provinces of Ava, Pegu, and Arakan only) amounted annually to £10,000, consisting of piece goods, cotton, iron and naval stores, while imports into Bengal from Pegu, consisting mainly of teak but also some tin, wax, ivory, and lac, were valued at approximately £15,500.[13] The trade had whetted sufficient interest by this time to cause the Governor-General, Sir John Shore, to dispatch Captain Michael Symes on a mission to the Court of Ava in 1795. Symes reported enthusiastically on the potential for Burmese trade and was sent again in 1802, but nothing in the form of trade concessions was extracted from the Burmese court beyond a verbal agreement allowing British merchants freedom of movement, and even this was greatly hampered by the sullen distrust of the Burmese officials. Nevertheless English optimism persisted, and Anglo-Burmese trade grew steadily if slowly.

Again in 1809 a mission whose aims were somewhat unclear was sent to Burma with John Canning at its head. The main reason appears to be the anxiety felt by the Company owing to its (mistaken) belief that a large trade was being carried on between Burma and the French islands of Mauritius and Bourbon. The truth was that Burmese foreign (maritime) trade was at that time virtually monopolized by British dependencies and was important to the Company. The Bengal shipbuilding industry was wholly dependent on Burma for its supply of teak.[14] By 1811 about fifty thousand pieces of cotton goods were being imported annually by Burma, and total imports were valued at about £93,600 per annum. The comparable figures for 1817-1822 were one hundred thousand pieces and £191,250, and by the last year total imports reached £282,000 and Indian cottons had been largely supplanted by British. Despite obstinate resistance, Burmese trade had risen 500-600% in twelve years. Calcutta had every reason to be hopeful about it, and the increase in that trade had become its main purpose in cultivating relations with its eastern neighbor.

The eastern neighbor, however, was anything but neighborly. Under the great king Bo-daw-pa-ya (1782-1819), Burma had thrown off Chinese suzerainty and had become an expanding empire. Having occupied the Arakan coastline in 1784, the Burmese found themselves confronting the British at Chittagong at about the same time British traders were beginning to take the Burmese trade seriously. Thus political and economic relations between the two countries commenced simultaneously, and because of the nature of relations between states of widely different levels of development, if the feudal economy and political structure of Burma would prove to be inflexible, European intervention would become inevitable.

From 1784 until 1824 the frontier was repeatedly disturbed by refugees from Arakan who were pursued by detachments of the Burmese army and who themselves took to raiding back across the border. Calcutta irritated the Burmese by refusing to extradite these rebels en masse, although it did cooperate in 1813-1814 to compass the destruction of a particularly troublesome guerrilla, Chan Byan. Meanwhile to the north the Burmese had occupied Manipur (1812) and in 1817 began the occupation of Assam. In 1823 they imprisoned peace negotiators sent by Amherst who threatened war unless they were released. The Burmese replied by amassing an army on the frontier, by completing the occupation of Assam, and by invading Cachar where the actual fighting began in January 1824. Next month Amherst officially declared war after months of fruitless efforts to negotiate peace.

What were Amherst's purposes in going to war? One might conclude that it was largely a matter of self-defense. Amherst wrote that he hoped the lesson to be taught the Burmese would "prevent the interruption in the future of those friendly relations which it is in the interest of both states to maintain."[15] But for what purposes did he wish to maintain friendly relations? In a memorandum of February 20, 1824, after discussing the territorial demands to be made on Burma at the war's end in order to secure the eastern frontier against future aggression, Amherst says he presumes it will "be expedient to stipulate for the permanent residence of a Consul and Political Agent at Rangoon . . . and likewise for several commercial advantages, and freedom from existing restrictions on Trade."[16] A fortnight later, in the declaration that accompanied the proclamation of war, Amherst wrote that the chief relationship established over the years between the Company and Burma was for "the mutually beneficial intercourse of Trade and Commerce." It had never ceased to be the Company's desire to "cement and improve" that relationship. But the Burmese had indulged in repeated aggression and had taken no notice of a series of British initiatives to negotiate their differences.[17]

Amherst by now was persuaded that "bad government" was endemic with the Burmese. He reported privately to Wynn in June:

We have learned enough of the Birmese [sic] to know that the whole system of government is carried out by the exercise of the most barbarous and unrelenting cruelty that was ever yet used to enforce obedience, and the panic which their name spreads through their weak and passive neighbors in Bengal is scarcely to be credited.[18]

Whatever special pleading to justify the war might be read into these remarks, it was the intent of the British government to limit the territorial demands made in Burma at the termination of hostilities to what was necessary to secure the frontier and to weaken the King of Ava as little as possible.[19] At about this same time, Amherst laid down the principles that were to guide the administration of the recently occupied province of Tenasserim. With regard to justice, the Burmese personnel were not to be removed, and the rules and forms in force were to be observed as closely as possible, deviating only where it was necessary to discontinue "practices at variance with natural reason and justice and for the suppression of cruel punishments repugnant to the principles of humanity." Revenue collections were to adhere to existing usage, discontinuing such exactions as appear "unjust, oppressive and destructive of the prosperity of the country." Any necessary political changes in respect to the chiefs were to be carried out with the utmost caution in order "to preserve friendly relations as long as it can be done without submitting to actual hostility or insult to the British Gov't."[20]

Logistically the war was botched by the Company. Little was actually known of the country in which it was fighting, and as the war dragged on for two years, the troops suffered more from the climate and disease than from the Burmese armies who were easily defeated. Arakan and Tenasserim were occupied as well as Pegu and, finally, even much of Upper Burma. The Court of Ava refused to yield, however, until the British armies reached Yandabo, a four days' march from the capital. There, on February 24, 1826, the Burmese emissaries signed a dictated peace, which ceded Arakan, Tenasserim, Assam, Manipur, and other bits to the Company and provided for an indemnity of one crore of rupees (approximately £1 million), about one-fifth of what the war had cost the Company. The treaty also obliged the Burmese to accept a British Resident in Ava, a surrender even more distasteful to them than the loss of territory. A Resident was a colonial official acting as an advisor to the ruler of a protected state, often exercising quasi-gubernatorial powers. The Burmese were also obligated to negotiate in the near future a commercial treaty based upon "principles of reciprocal advantage." Assam and Manipur were declared British protectorates, although they were not immediately occupied. The British armies withdrew from Upper Burma and Pegu, leaving the entire valley of the Irrawaddi in Burmese hands.[21]

The Burmese had been soundly defeated and understood that fact thoroughly. In the spring of 1826, John Crawfurd, the British Civil Commissioner assigned to Ava and Pegu for purposes of implementing the peace treaty and negotiating the commercial treaty, took depositions from a number of Europeans long resident in Burma. According to Adoniram Judson, the American missionary who had lived in Burma since 1813 and was imprisoned during the war, the war had convinced the Burmese of British military superiority. And Judson later asserted, "The Burmese have been conquered, and know it." Others as well testified to the Burmese awareness of British military supremacy.[22]

Once the dust of war had settled, the British returned to their long-term goal of developing the Burmese trade, and the prospects appeared even brighter now that Ava's potential for trade disruption had been weakened. Depositions taken by Crawfurd in the spring of 1826 tended to reinforce this optimism. Henry Gouger, a private merchant, testified that the trade in piece goods was capable of great extension and that, in return, Burmese cotton, though short in staple, was fine and silky and brought a higher price in Dacca than ordinary Bengal cotton. John Laird, a former agent of the Prince of Tharawadi, revealed that the forests of Tharawadi produced fine natural teak and alone were capable of as large an annual yield as the marine market demanded. He further testified that the Chinese of Ava manufactured a fine, white sugar, superior to Siamese sugar, which manufacture could be greatly extended, wanting only a market and elimination of the Burmese ban on its export. Indigo, he said, was well suited to lower Burma (Pegu) and this was at a time when the European market for indigo was flourishing. Laird also reported that imports of British piece goods had grown rapidly in the previous few years even though virtually unknown to the Burmese before that. Imports of Madras piece goods, on the other hand, had declined because of British competition.

In view of these optimistic reports, the Company pressed the commercial treaty by sending Crawfurd on a special mission for that purpose in September 1826. On November 24 the treaty was signed "on terms of entire equality between the two nations," and Crawfurd claimed that it accomplished no more than to formalize a trade that had long been conducted on sufferance. In actuality the treaty was forced on the Burmese by a paramount power and had the effect of removing the disabilities previously suffered by British subjects trading in Burma. It exempted British vessels under fifty tons burthen from tonnage and port duties and guaranteed free commercial intercourse by permitting British officials and traders the right to enter Burmese territory at any point and proceed anywhere they liked without hindrance. If the Burmese saw fit to honor the treaty, the purposes of the war had been achieved.

A word should be said here about the annexation of Arakan and Tenasserim. According to a recent study of Laurence Kitzan, both provinces were kept owing to "frustration and the necessity for revenge" because the Burmese armies had made the war costly in lives and money.[23] An element of revenge may well have crept into the postwar settlement, but it would not have been consistent with the moderation and justice exercised by Amherst in withdrawing from Pegu and which Kitzan acknowledges in the same article.[24] Other reasons need to be sought.

Neither was annexed for commercial purposes because their commercial potential was unknown or thought to be marginal at the time. It seems likely that Arakan was kept as a buffer zone against future Burmese aggression. Robertson, who became Agent for the South East Frontier, wrote in June 1826: "As a source of

revenue Arakan has never been contemplated as a useful possession, all the advantages anticipated from its annexation to our
empire being comprised in the exclusion of the Burmese from a
province where the local peculiarities enabled them to disturb the
tranquility of the contiguous country.''[25] Burmese aggression was
never considered a serious military threat to Bengal but a nuisance
that kept the frontier in turmoil. It was not Burmese military might
that caused the trouble but rather the misgovernment of the Arakan province.

At the outset Tenasserim was held in the same low regard commercially, but the depositions taken by Crawfurd in March 1826
revealed that the province was abundantly supplied with teak and
sapan wood, invaluable for ship timbers, and that rice had formerly been a major export and was thought capable of great expansion.
Moreover the northern district of Martaban lay astride the Salween
River, which reached northward into Yunnan and had long-estab-
lished trade connections with China, Siam, and Laos. Settled government here, too, would much increase the trade in piece goods
now cascading out of the Lancashire mills.

Nevertheless Amherst was opposed to retaining Tenasserim in
1826 because its expenses would outweigh its advantages, and the
Court of Directors agreed. In 1830 an attempt was made to retrocede it to Burma in return for its administrative costs or an equivalent in territory elsewhere. Ava, dreaming of recovering it by
force, rejected the offer. By now, however, the commercial potential of Tenasserim had become apparent, and the trade route from
Moulmein up the Salween and overland to Siam had been opened
by Dr. Richardson, and British manufactured goods were making
their way into Siam in trade for cattle and other Siamese products.
This development caused the government of India and the Court of
Directors to reconsider, and in March 1933 the Court authorized
Calcutta to retain Tenasserim permanently.

BURMA IN LIMBO, 1826-1853

For the quarter-century following the withdrawal of their armies
from Burma, it was British policy to preserve their paramountcy
without resort to force. Their main instrumentality for doing so

was the British Resident as provided in the Treaty of Yandabo. The arrangement would work if the Burmese honored the treaties, but it soon became clear that they would evade every provision they could short of provoking another British invasion. To the Oriental mind of that time, the reception of a permanent foreign emissary was an exceptional act and an admission of subordination, to be avoided at all costs. Judson had thought a Resident would be unnecessary to preserve the peace because the Burmese were thoroughly cowed militarily, but he might be accepted as a commercial agent and would be "highly useful in maintaining and extending your commercial relations."[26] But even as the agent of the commercial treaty, Crawfurd as first Resident was stoutly refused residence in Ava for more than three years after the signature of the treaties, and rather than force the issue, he set up headquarters in Rangoon. His successor was admitted to Ava in 1829, but he, as well as Crawfurd before him and Benson and McLeod after him, were frustrated by the Burmese determination to evade the treaties.

One of Crawfurd's concerns in late 1826, for example, was to raise the matter of Assamese and Manipuri civilians captured and enslaved by the Burmese. Every obstacle was placed in the way of accounting for these people, and Crawfurd, reminded that his mission was a commercial one, received no satisfaction. Crawfurd's days were made up of this sort of frustration. The government of India apparently had blundered in allowing the military to negotiate a defective peace treaty and again in withdrawing the army from Burma in the fall of 1826 after the second installment of the indemnity was paid but before the Burmese had agreed to the settlement of all outstanding issues. More success, however, attended the payment of the indemnity. After trying to postpone the third and fourth installments for three years, the Burmese envoys sent to Calcutta and Moulmein for this purpose in the spring of 1827 agreed to pay up in six months, and the Court at Ava acceded, apparently fearing that failure to do so would provoke a second British invasion.

By 1829 the British had determined that a shorter leash on the recalcitrant Burmese was required, and under strong pressure Ava grudgingly agreed to receive the Resident. Crawfurd's successor, Major Burney, arrived in Ava in 1830 and remained until 1837.

Burney was occasionally subjected to deliberate affronts by the King and his ministers, but by virtue of his goodwill, tact, and quiet determination, he won their respect and was able to moderate the worst effects of Burmese obstructionism.

He was successful, for example, during his negotiations with the King's ministers in 1830 on the return of the Kubaw Valley to Burma in making it clearly understood that they must rely on him because there was no possibility of recovering it by force. It was Burney too who finally made it clear (in 1832) that Tenasserim would not be restored to Burma, although this cost him a considerable cooling of relations with the Court.

But despite Burney's presence in Ava, the conditions to which British merchants in Rangoon were subjected were sometimes oppressive. Burmese officials capriciously molested them and their ships and levied extortionate fines and duties. In March 1836 the Bengal Chamber of Commerce petitioned the government of India that only an accredited British official assigned to Rangoon could maintain the rights of the British community in such an uncivilized land. This petition, along with the continued appeals of the British resident in Ava, finally persuaded Calcutta in July to appoint Dr. G. T. Bayfield, a member of Burney's staff, as Consul in Rangoon and to reinforce his authority and prestige with a periodic visit of a British man-of-war. Beyond this the government of India was reluctant to go, lest another costly war result in the acquisition of additional territories expensive to govern.

The palace coup of 1837 raised to the throne a far more determined opponent of the Residency. As prince and king, Tharawadi on numerous occasions stated that he had never been conquered by the British but that he would never demand the removal of the Residency. He would simply ignore the British and "not say anything" to the treaties of 1826. Tharawadi was painfully suspicious of every British move. Dr. Richardson's commercial expeditions up the Salween River from Moulmein in 1835 and 1836 and Lieutenant McLeod's similar expedition to the border of China in 1837 increased that suspicion and reinforced his hostility to British influence in Burma. Nevertheless the new king had a far more realistic view of British power than his predecessor. He and the ministers around him were fully aware of British military superiority, and although they felt deeply the humiliation of the Residency and made things as difficult for Burney as they dared, they refrained from any serious provocation.

By this time Burney, exhausted after seven years of relentless hostility and studied contempt, decided on his own initiative to withdraw from Ava and did so in June 1837, just as the Court was moving to the new capital, Amarapura. Officials in Calcutta were indignant, but the Governor-General took a more tolerant view:

Of our power to chastise the insolence of the King there can be no doubt, but it is questionable whether it would be worthwhile to dissipate our resources for so unprofitable, so unworthy an object as asserting our superiority over a people who can do us very little harm, and whom we can always keep in check at, a very small expense, compared with that of an open war.[27]

The only overt British reaction was to return Burney to Rangoon two months later in a British warship.

Tharawadi had been apprehensive over Burney's withdrawal, and British merchants in Burma reported that, upon hearing that a British warship had appeared off Rangoon, the King exclaimed: "What cause of war have I with the English? What have I done? I did not send the Residency away."[28] Tharawadi had no desire to provoke a British invasion because "he had a good appreciation of the British power."[29] The Residency was restored, and Colonel Benson was sent to Amarapura in 1838, although the facilities assigned to the Residency, on land which flooded during every rain, were extremely uncomfortable, and the King and his ministers continued either to ignore the Resident or to treat him with studied insolence. Not the diplomat that Burney was, Benson withdrew in desperation in March 1839. Captain McLeod stayed on as acting Resident until July 1839 when he retired to Rangoon. In January 1840 Calcutta ordered the Residency closed, and it was officially terminated in August of that year.

During the previous two years, a rebellion in Lower Burma had caused Tharawadi to send down a large army, which gradually restored authority over the Mons and Karens who had collaborated with the British during the war. For a while Lord Auckland was apprehensive that Ava contemplated war to recover Tenasserim, but the announcement of the Tripartite Treaty between the Afghan pretender, Shah Shuja, Ranjit Singh, and the Company caused the rumor to die down, precisely the effect Auckland hoped it would have. Tharawadi's army was reinforced in 1842 but more likely as a show of force against potential rebels than as a threat against Tenasserim. If the King were in fact entertaining an ill-advised attack on Moulmein, his insanity, which surfaced at this time, and the growing unrest in Upper Burma may have forestalled the campaign. Furthermore the Burmese army of the 1840s was even less effective than that of 1824-1826, and its commander had little desire to test it against the Indian army.[30]

If the Court of Ava feared to provoke the British overtly, it was quite prepared to let the unruly border tribes divert themselves with attacks on the Company territories. In Lower Burma dacoits (gangs of robbers) operated with impunity, repeatedly attacking British outposts in Arakan and Tenasserim, probably with the encouragement of Burmese officials at Rangoon, until the British occupation of Pegu in 1852 terminated their activities. Before 1852 the British were obliged to conduct punitive raids against their lairs in Burmese territory and could do so without fear of colliding with the Burmese army. In January 1830, for example, Major A. D. Maingy, the British Commissioner in Tenasserim, wrote that his raid upon Martaban had at least stopped dacoity for the time being and that British trading vessels were once more secure on the Salween River.[31] In northwestern Burma as well the border chiefs were out of control, occasionally raiding their enemies in British Assam. Here too the British were obliged to take direct retaliatory action.

But despite studied insult, petty obstructionism, and border harassment from the time of the Commercial Treaty until 1850, no serious complaint was laid before the government of India that the right of free passage was being denied British merchants. Traders continued to operate in Burma with comparative freedom from restrictions, one of them, J. Brown, serving as unofficial consul in Rangoon after McLeod's departure in 1840.

After 1850, however, conditions took a turn for the worse. In that year the Governor of Rangoon was replaced by the Collector of Customs who instituted a new regime of annoyances against British and other traders. Foreign merchants, shipbuilders, and ships' officers were subjected to threats and abuse, extortion, and arbitrary detention. In the summer of 1851 two English captains were charged with murder and fined and imprisoned without trial. When the Burmese government refused restitution, Commodore Lambert was dispatched with two frigates to Rangoon to demand the Governor's removal and the reestablishment of a British agent in Rangoon with fifty troops in accordance with the Treaty of Yandabo. Refusal to comply would lead to a blockade, but Lambert was specifically ordered not to resort to a bombardment or occupation.[32]

The King in fact acquiesced in the removal of the Governor and promised to satisfy the other demands, but negotiations went off track because of the deliberate misrepresentations of two of Lambert's most trusted advisors, his assistant, Captain Thomas Latter, and the American missionary, Eugenio Kincaid. Both sought to provoke hostilities for personal reasons, and Lambert was misled and eventually incited to seize one of the King's ships and to bombard the Burmese shore batteries. Although Dalhousie was furious over Lambert's indiscretions, he could not fail to support a British officer and suggested that war could be avoided if the Governor would apologize for his supposedly insulting treatment of one of Lambert's deputations, compensate Sheppard and Lewis, and accept a British agent in Rangoon. This was delivered as an ultimatum on March 1. Although the Governor agreed to the last two demands, he refused to apologize. Dalhousie could see "no alternative but to extract reparation by force of arms."[33]

British forces occupied Martaban and Rangoon in April and Bassein in May, hoping that this limited form of intimidation would cause the Burmese to back down. Quite the opposite occurred. Burmese troops became active in Pegu in the summer and fall and obliged the British to mount a full-scale offensive. The campaign was far better managed than that of 1825-1826. In December Pegu was declared annexed to British India. By the beginning of 1853, regular Burmese resistance in Pegu had ceased, and in February a palace revolution replaced Pagan with Mindon Min who called the war to a halt and withdrew all regular Burmese forces to the north. Guerrilla bands continued to operate for three or four years and dacoity was not wholly suppressed for nearly twenty. No formal peace treaty was ever signed.

With the occupation of Pegu, Britain controlled the entire seacoast of Burma. The landlocked remnant of the kingdom preserved a nominal independence until 1886 when it was annexed by Britain after the Third Burmese War, which lasted about a month, although guerrilla activity continued for years.

PARAMOUNTCY

What can we conclude about the moment when British paramountcy was achieved in Burma? It seems beyond question that it had been achieved at least by 1853 with the conquest of Pegu and the sealing off of the coast. Salisbury testified to this in 1878.

Dalhousie...did not take the capital or dethrone the King. He simply seized the provinces which he thought financially and strategically the most desirable. To this day we hold Pegu, not by any Treaty cession but by simple occupation. The result has been that we are as much masters of the King of Burmah as if we were at Ava.[34]

Dorothy Woodman writes that the second Anglo-Burmese War was "the beginning of the end of her independence as a sovereign power" and that thereafter Burma "could reach the world only by the sufferance of the British."[35]

But it also seems possible to antedate British paramountcy from the evidence presented in this chapter. The rapid collapse of Burmese military resistance in 1852-1853 can be interpreted to reflect an already existing British paramountcy to which the hawkish but unrealistic party at the Court was blind. Wiser heads had counseled acceptance of Dalhousie's ultimatum in early 1852 because they recognized that the Governor of Rangoon had overstepped the limits beyond which the British could safely be provoked and that it was more prudent to swallow unpalatable concessions than to risk another war.

Wiser heads had also prevailed as early as 1838 when the agitation for war caused by the belligerent elements at Court was quickly squelched by the announcement of the Tripartite Treaty. Tharawadi's behavior prior to his insanity also testifies to British paramountcy. Although he felt deeply the humiliation of the Residency at Ava, disavowed the Treaty of Yandabo, and proclaimed his intention of restoring the antebellum status quo, the fact that he did nothing overtly to achieve that end, that he openly acknowledged that the Residency had been imposed on his predecessor, and that he refrained from demanding its removal are clear indications that he had a realistic estimate of British power and feared that an open breach might precipitate another British invasion.

One might also cite the repeated incursions of British forces into Burmese territory from Assam, Arakan, and Tenasserim between 1826 and 1851 for the purpose of punishing dacoits and unruly Burmese border chiefs. That this could take place with no effective Burmese retaliation shows that if anyone, it was the British raj rather than Ava that prevailed in the outlying territories of what remained of independent Burma. And the acquiescence of the Burmese government in the spring of 1827 to the British demand that the final installments of the war indemnity be paid within six months rather than three years was achieved because the Burmese feared the reprisal that might otherwise follow.

The most compelling argument is that the British imposed a Residency on Burma in 1826 and maintained it until 1840 in the face of extreme Burmese hostility. That the Burmese never had the temerity to demand its removal and that its withdrawal in 1840 was entirely voluntary point to the fact of British paramountcy. It may sometimes appear in the decades after 1826 that the British did little to enforce that paramountcy actively, but they were preoccupied elsewhere: in Sind and the Punjab, in Afghanistan and China. But the more rational of the Burmese realized that as long as the British insisted on maintaining the Residency, it would stay where the British wanted it, in Ava or Amarapura or Rangoon, and there was little the Burmese could do about it except to be as uncooperative as they dared short of provoking British retaliation.

It seems beyond a reasonable doubt that we can pinpoint the achievement of British paramountcy in Burma in the year 1826. Having situated themselves astride Burma's access to the sea and expressed the intention of monitoring the internal affairs of Burma —as they related to trade—by imposing a Resident on the King, the British had clearly infringed on the King's control of his foreign relations and had committed themselves beyond the point of no return. Henceforth neither the British nor the Burmese had much of a choice, for different reasons. In the long run, things had to be done to the satisfaction of the British or they would be obliged to intervene with force once again to counteract any challenge to their paramount position.

One additional dimension of British paramountcy might be noted: the psychological. Cady suggests that the territorial losses and the indemnity suffered by Burma after the first war were less harmful to Burmese authority than the loss of prestige that attended defeat. King Bagyidaw was profoundly humiliated and his successors were never able to recover the dynasty's prestige.[36] This, as well as the threat of renewed British intervention that hung over Burma after 1826, were unquestionably factors in the growing instability of Burmese rule from 1826 to 1852.

SUMMARY OF MOTIVES

How, then, can we summarize the motives behind the establishment of British paramountcy in Burma in the years preceding 1826? My narrative has tried to show that by the mid-1820s the development of trade had become the Company's chief object in Burma—that and an end to Burmese misgovernment, which was inhibiting the growth of trade and disturbing the Bengal frontier. There is little if any indication that the British wanted more territory to govern; indeed the evidence points the other way. Both the Court of Directors and the government of India sought to avoid additional administrative expenses. Assam, Manipur, and Arakan were taken as buffer zones, not because the Company feared another Burmese invasion—that was now out of the question—but to ensure that Burmese misgovernment in those provinces would never again disturb the frontier. Amherst soon had second thoughts about the annexation of Tenasserim because its cost outweighed whatever advantage it brought, and in 1830 he tried to retrocede it to Burma for an equivalent in money or in territory elsewhere. Ava, hoping to recover the territory by force, declined the offer, and soon the growth of its trade and the commercial potential of the trade route up the Salween River to Siam caused the Court of Directors to reverse itself and authorize Calcutta to retain the province permanently, for commercial reasons. Amherst had begun his war reluctantly and withdrew from half of the occupied territory at its end. The brief text of the Treaty of Yandabo is convincing proof that the British were less interested in extracting territory or monetary compensation than in restoring peaceful relations and ensuring the exercise of government good enough to foster trade.

Recent studies have tried to explain the nature of nineteenth-century Burmese government in terms of its cultural foundations, and although these enhance our sympathy and understanding, they do little to change the fact that Burmese government in the first half of the nineteenth century was, in British eyes, unable and unwilling to preserve either law and order in its frontier provinces or the conditions necessary for free and peaceful trade.[37] Rightly or wrongly, the British regarded the Burmese government as an impediment, justifying whatever intervention was deemed necessary. Furnivall reminds us that British interest in Burma was awakened at the moment the Industrial Revolution began calling for expanded markets abroad. Thus perhaps even more important than the teak and rice trade, Burma promised to be a significant market for European goods, and since the Burmese political structure resisted the implications of developing trade, the British were forced to apply methods of direct rule, first on the coast and progressively inland.[38]

NOTES

1. The narrative of this chapter is based mainly on the following sources, although their authors are not responsible for the particular emphasis placed on events: Anil C. Banerjee, *The Eastern Frontier of British India, 1784-1826* (Calcutta, 1943); Dorothy Woodman, *The Making of Burma* (London, 1962); Walter S. Desai, *History of the British Residency in Burma, 1826-1840* (Rangoon, 1939); John F. Cady, *A History of Modern Burma* (New York, 1960); John L. Christian, *Modern Burma: A Survey of Political and Economic Development* (Berkeley, 1942); J. S. Furnivall, *Colonial Policy and Practice: A Comparative Study of Burma and Netherlands—India* (New York, 1956); John Crawfurd, *Journal of an Embassy from the Governor-General of India to the Court of Ava in the year 1827*, 2d ed. (London, 1834); Henry Gouger, *Personal Narrative of Two Years' Imprisonment in Burma, 1824-1826* (London, 1860); Oliver B. Pollak, *Empires in Collision: Anglo-Burmese Relations in the Mid-Nineteenth Century* (Westport, Conn., 1979).

2. K. M. Panikkar, *Asia and Western Dominance* (London, 1959).

3. Maung Htin Aung, *A History of Burma* (New York, 1967), and *The*

Stricken Peacock: Anglo-Burmese Relations, 1752-1948 (The Hague, 1965).

4. D. G. E. Hall, "Anglo-Burmese Conflicts in the 19th Century: A Reassessment," *Asia* 6 (1966), and *Henry Burney, A Political Biography* (London, 1974).

5. Laurence Kitzan, "Lord Amherst and the Declaration of War on Burma, 1824" *Journal of Asian History* 9 (1975): 115-16.

6. Ibid., 123.

7. Ibid., 109, 125.

8. Pollak, *Empires in Collision*, 40.

9. Ibid., 67, 82.

10. Kitzan, "Lord Amherst," 123.

11. Pollak, *Empires in Collision*, 40-58.

12. Ibid., 60.

13. Amales Tripathi, *Trade and Finance in the Bengal Presidency, 1793-1833* (Calcutta, 1956), 37-38. The most recent study of Anglo-Burmese relations by G. P. Ramachandra also testifies to the "large commerce between Burma and the British dependencies" at the time Capt. Symes made his 1795 visit. See "The Canning Mission to Burma of 1809/10," *Journal of Southeast Asian Studies* 1 (1979):119.

14. Ramachandra, "Canning Mission," 120.

15. Brian Gardner, *The East India Company: A History* (New York, 1972), 198.

16. Memorandum by Amherst, Feb. 20, 1824, India Office Records, Proceedings (P), Bengal Secret Consultations, vol. 320.

17. Declaration by Amherst, March 5, 1824, ibid., vol. 321.

18. Amherst to Wynn, June 4, 1824, "Statement Explanatory of the Origin and Progress of the War with the State of Ava," p. 134, India Office Records, Political and Secret, L/P&S/20, Political and Secret Library, vol. 101.

19. Board's Drafts of Secret Letters to India, Aug. 3, 1825, India Office Records, Political and Secret, L/P&S/5, vol. 34.

20. Instructions issued by Robert Fullerton, Governor of Prince of Wales Island, to Commissioner A. D. Maingy, Sept. 16, 1825, India Office Records, Proceedings (P), Bengal Secret Consultations, vol. 333.

21. Text of the Treaty of Yandabo, Feb. 24, 1826, in Desai, 463-67.

22. Crawfurd, *Journal*, Appendix, 57-58.

23. Laurence Kitzan, "Lord Amherst and Pegu: The Annexation Issue, 1824-1826," *Journal of Southeast Asian Studies* 2 (1977):192.

24. Ibid., 194.

25. Banerjee, *Eastern Frontier*, 471-72.

26. Crawfurd, *Journal*, Appendix, 58.

27. Auckland's memorandum, Sept. 8, 1837, no. 9, quoted in Desai, *History*, 313.

28. From a confidential letter from Rangoon, Oct. 27, 1837, quoted in Desai, *History*, 316-17.

29. Desai, *History*, 331.

30. Cady, *History of Modern Burma*, 79-80.

31. Desai, *History*, 37-41.

32. Pollak, *Empires in Collision*, 75.

33. Ibid., 77-80.

34. Salisbury to Gathorne-Hardy, Oct. 6, 1878, Salisbury Papers, D/29/74.

35. Woodman, *Making of Burma*, 153.

36. Cady, *History of Modern Burma*, 67.

37. Pollak's is a sensitive treatment of nineteenth-century Burmese politics, but it begs the question of British intervention because it does not change what the British thought at that time. Michael Adas's article, "Imperialist Rhetoric and Modern Historiography: The Case of Lower Burma before and after the Conquest," *Journal of Southeast Asian Studies* 3 (1972):175-92, while complaining that conventional historians have simply assumed that precolonial kingdoms were decadent, corrupt, chaotic, and economically stagnant, offers little evidence to prove otherwise. He in fact shows that the Konbaung dynasty not only prevented the revival of Burma's earlier commercialism but even inhibited the growth of agriculture.

38. See Furnivall, *Colonial Policy*, 278-79.

SIND AND
THE PUNJAB

PARAMOUNTCY UNSETTLES THE FRONTIER

Long before the Sikh wars of 1845-1846 and 1848-1849 and Napier's annexation of Sind in 1842, British paramountcy had been achieved over the states along the Indus.[1] Some evidence shows that it was recognized in the Punjab as early as August 1830 when the Governor-General of India, Lord William Bentinck, wrote to Lord Ellenborough, then President of the Board of Control, that Ranjit Singh "is too sensible a man to think of attacking the British power, if the superiority [is maintained] of which he has been perfectly sensible."[2] This assessment was confirmed by Lieutenant Alexander Burnes's report on his expedition to Lahore in the spring of 1831 and by Bentinck's meeting with Ranjit Singh in Rupar in October: "Such is the extreme caution which has marked all Ranjit's conduct, and such his thorough conviction of our superiority, that a single word from us will put an end to all serious designs of conquest upon the Sind territory."[3] The next February Ranjit Singh abandoned under protest an invasion of Sind when informed that it would disrupt the commercial plans of the British.[4] This is perhaps better evidence than the earlier testimonies of Bentinck, and it was followed in December by Ranjit Singh's agreement to open the Indus and Sutlej rivers to navigation and to permit the residence of a British official at Mithankot who could be in a position to alert the government of India to any renewal of Sikh aggression against Sind.[5] Thereafter until his death in 1839, the old Lion of Lahore repeatedly testified to his awareness of British power. Until then the threat of that power was sufficient to keep the Sikh state under control. Not until internecine struggles broke out in the 1840s and mercenary Sikh chieftains conspired to destroy the Sikh army, which posed a threat to the indulgence of their feudal privileges by deliberately provoking it into a war with the

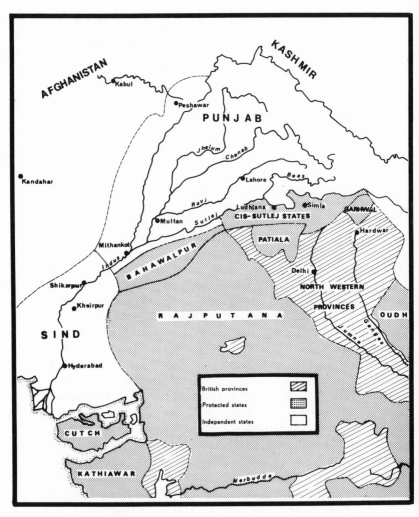

**NORTHWEST INDIA AND AFGHANISTAN,
1830s and 1840s**

British, was direct British military intervention required. The decisive outcome of the two Sikh wars confirmed the preexisting paramountcy.

Farther to the south, the feudal amirs of Sind were highly suspicious of British penetration, with good reason, and they adamantly resisted the first British proposals to open the Indus to trade. Worn down by British persistence and awake to the presence of the Indian army on their frontier, they agreed in April 1832 to commercial treaties granting the minimal concessions that would mollify the British for the moment. To have thrown open the Indus to European commerce and to reduce tolls to levels that the British thought reasonable was a capitulation the amirs would never have made except in the face of an acknowledged British paramountcy. Three years later they confirmed their dependence when they appealed to the government of India for help against the aggressions of Ranjit Singh. Accordingly, by 1835 or before, Britain had become the arbiter of affairs along the Indus.

That British intervention—for whatever motive—did not tranquilize the frontier as hoped soon became evident. Charles Metcalfe, vice-president of the Governor-General's council, was right: it would aggravate rather than diminish the turmoil within the three states. It led to two wars with the Sikhs, the occupation and annexation of Sind, and a disastrous war with Afghanistan. But these events should not mislead us. Long before these disruptions occurred, Britain had already achieved paramountcy in Sind and the Punjab, and the resulting hostilities were the inevitable results of maintaining that paramountcy against uncooperative native governments. Ingram sees the Bentinck period (1828-1835) as one in which British expansion was interrupted as Bentinck sought to consolidate and reform British India.[6] It was, on the contrary, precisely the period when paramountcy was being established beyond the northwest frontier.

ELLENBOROUGH'S INITIATIVE

The question of the defense of India against foreign attack first arose during the Napoleonic occupation of Egypt in 1798, although that particular threat was quickly dissipated by the battle of the Nile. Thereafter the defense problem remained dormant until 1828 when Lord Ellenborough, then President of the Board of Control, sought to revive it. Historically the Indus was the natural highway of trade and conquest into northwestern India. On its right bank lay the passes from central Asia into Hindustan, and Russophobes like Ellenborough, scanning their small-scale maps in London, could imagine a Cossack army sweeping southward into Afghanistan and plunging with little resistance through these passes into the Indus valley. Ellenborough confided his fears to his diary in September, 1829: "The Directors are much afraid of the Russians. So am I ... they announce the presence in Petersburg of an Afghan chief, and of ambassadors from Ranjeet Singh. I feel confident we shall have to fight the Russians on the Indus."[7] Russia's defeat of Turkey in October heightened his fears, as did Colonel G. de Lacy Evans's book, *On the Designs of Russia*, which showed (on faulty assumptions) how Russia with Persian help could attack India through Afghanistan and Sind.[8]

Wellington and Aberdeen, as well as Benjamin Jones, the influential Assistant Secretary of the India Board in charge of the Secret Department, shared these fears but more temperately, owing to reports from Lord Heytesbury, the Ambassador at St. Petersburg, that the Russians were fully aware of the real weakness of their country and of the folly of attempting "so gigantic an enterprise as the invasion of India."[9] The restraint of his colleagues apparently had some effect on Ellenborough, for in the autumn of 1829 he began to revise his extreme view of the nature of the Russian threat. He wrote to Wellington "that Russia will attempt, by conquest or by influence, to secure Persia as a road to the Indus. . . . It is evident that the latter and surer mode, that of influence, is the one she now selects."[10] He nevertheless clung to his belief that Russia constituted a clear and present danger. As the means of counteracting that danger before it was too late, he sought to play the "Great Game in Asia" by turning the India Board into "a second foreign office" that would assume control of Anglo-Russian relations from Teheran eastward.[11]

Ellenborough's opening move in the Great Game was his dispatch to Bentinck of January 1830 in which he outlined the threat of Russian influence as he saw it:

We dread ... not so much actual Invasion by Russia, as the moral effect which would be produced amongst our own Subjects in India and amongst the Princes with whom we are allied by the continued apprehension of that event—We look with dismay on the financial embarrassments in which we should be involved by the necessity of constant military preparation, not only to meet an European Army in the field but to preserve tranquility in our own Provinces and in our Tributary States.[12]

What was needed to counteract that threat was not military action, for that might lead to a collision in Europe, but a "Diplomatick Mission to Bochara," which must be disguised as "purely Commercial" in character, for purposes of obtaining information about central Asia and of substituting British for Russian commercial preponderance in the area as a means of checking any further Russian advance. In order to open the road to central Asia, a gift of horses was being sent to Ranjit Singh, which, it was suggested, knowing Bentinck's fascination with steamboats, might be conveyed up the Indus in a steam vessel, using the opportunity to survey the river and determine its navigability. Should the amirs of Sind object to free passage of the river, it was implied that force could be used: "We are far from desirous of having any collision with the people of Sinde, but we cannot permit any jealous feeling on their parts to close the navigation of the Indus, should it appear to offer results not only Commercially but Politically important which but for them would be attained."[13]

BENTINCK'S RESISTANCE

Bentinck received Ellenborough's dispatch in June with what must have been consternation. He disagreed with his chief's assessment of the Russian threat and his method of meeting it by advancing British influence to Turkistan: "I confess myself to be entirely without interest in the affairs of central Asia and Persia, and even Russia, though from these countries have often sallied forth the past conquerors of India, and will again in all probability... [but] in my time the storm will not gather."[14] Among the several members of his staff to whom he gave Ellenborough's dispatch for comment, Major Josiah Stewart's memorandum confirmed his own reservations about a forward policy in central Asia. Stewart saw no immediate danger of a Russian invasion and warned that sending a diplomatic agent disguised as a merchant to Bokhara "would be more calculated to excite jealousy and alarm than to conciliate friendship'' and that ''if while no preparations are making against us we show an anxiety to adopt preventative measures indicative of weakness, we may provoke the attack we wish to prevent.'' A far greater cause of apprehension, Stewart believed, was the disaffection of the sepoy troops and allies, and in that connection the instability of the states along the Indus was of utmost importance. The government of India could extend its stabilizing influence into these states by means of commerce, but even that was likely to arouse the suspicions of the amirs of Sind and Ranjit Singh who had witnessed British commerce lead to British dominion in neighboring India. If both states refused to open the Indus to free navigation, not even commercial penetration should be attempted. But if Ranjit Singh could be persuaded to agree, coercive measures could more easily be brought to bear on the amirs.[15]

Bentinck concurred with all but the last of Stewart's observations. He was not prepared in mid-1830 to coerce the amirs. He agreed with Stewart that Ellenborough's policy was provocative and had no interest in supporting the campaign to make the India Board a second foreign office. Stewart discerned correctly, he felt, that the real threat to India was the unsettling effect of the turmoil and instability of the states along the Indus, and his answer was ''to create a stable balance of power'' among them. He would play the Great Game in Asia only if it could help him reach that end.[16]

As a devout utilitarian, Bentinck had other ends in view. The East India Company had carried on sporadic trade relations with Sind since the seventeenth century. Company factories were maintained there from 1635 to 1662 and again from 1758 to 1775, but by 1775 the high quality of Sindian cotton textiles had declined, and after the French wars began, British relations with Sind were governed for a time by broader international considerations. An attempt was made in 1799 to establish a commercial mission in Sind in the hope that the British presence would keep the French out and make the Afghans more tractable, but the amirs' Afghan suzerain threatened to invade Sind if the British were not expelled, which they were, in October 1800. Another attempt was made in 1809 to cement friendly relations with the states on the northwest frontier when treaties were made with Sind, Afghanistan, and the Punjab. The amirs of Sind swore eternal friendship with the Company, agreed to exchange ambassadors, and promised to keep ''the tribe of the French" out of the country, but no commercial or political arrangements resulted, and while the treaty was renewed in 1820, Sind sank back into another decade of isolation. It was just at this time that the British trading interest revived.

The year before Bentinck's arrival in India, Dr. James Burnes, the Company surgeon in Bombay, had been invited to Hyderabad to attend the ailing amir, Murad Ali Khan. The report of his journey, published in 1829,[17] reawakened British interest in the commercial potential of Sind and the Indus.

The river Indus might once more become the channel of communication and wealth between the interior of Asia and the peninsula of India; while Sinde herself... would rise renewed to claim a due importance in the scale of nations, and to profit by her benefits which nature has bestowed on her ... A single glance at the Indus will show the easy passage to the very heart of their [the amirs'] dominions, which the river offers to a maritime power.[18]

The book persuaded Bentinck, though he needed little persuading, that the Indus could become a great highway of commerce and a natural waterway for the new steam navigation. To Bentinck the steam engine embodied the essence of the Industrial Revolution, and the promotion of steam navigation became the avocation of the latter half of his life. He looked upon the project of opening the Indus to steam vessels primarily in a utilitarian light—that is, for purely commercial objects—rather than for raison d'état.[19] That Sind was a bleak country with minimal trade potential and that the navigability of the Indus was in fact hindered by shifting sand bars and shallows was not yet realized, and when it was, did not dampen the enthusiasm of utilitarians like Bentinck.

But although Bentinck could assert that his plans for the Indus were purely commercial, his vision actually transcended that. He was imbued with the notion that the transferral of the Industrial Revolution to India would be the main "school of instruction" for the improvement of Indian civilization. "I look to steam navigation," he wrote in 1834, "as the great engine of working this moral improvement."[20] He was fascinated by the civilizing power of trade and the steamship and was more interested in exercising that sort of power than in a new military frontier on the Indus.[21]

Bentinck typified many of the British civil servants who arrived in India in the post-Napoleonic era filled with a mission for evangelical reform and political economy. In their view every Oriental state seemed impossibly corrupt and retrograde, and their impression of Sind in particular was of a people oppressed by unpopular foreign (Baluchi) amirs and who welcomed the first English visitors as the advance guard of a liberating army. Sind was not badly governed in actuality. The Talpur amirs were not unjust or oppressive. They ruled within the laws and traditions and were restrained in taxing their subjects, who were generally content and prosperous. But the English utilitarians could not be expected to view a feudal society and government with anything but distaste, and their views governed their actions.

Given these predilections, Bentinck was more interested in peaceful penetration than in dispatching risky missions to central Asia. Thus Ellenborough's instruction to send an envoy to Bokhara was ignored for the moment. And with the warnings of Major Stewart in mind, Bentinck was no more enthusiastic about the mission to Lahore, but since the horses were already on their way, he gave his approval to Governor Malcolm's plan to ship them up the Indus by steamboat under the command of Lieutenant Alexander Burnes, brother of the doctor who had reported so favorably on the Indus two years before. Burnes began his journey in March 1831 under instructions to proceed slowly so as to permit a full survey of the river. His optimistic report was well received by Bentinck, but his expansionist conclusions were brushed aside.[22] Bentinck wanted more time to study the affairs of the Indus states before approving any further expeditions of any sort, and it was partly with this in mind that he had embarked on his celebrated thirty-month tour of upper India in October 1830. During the first year of this tour his policy for northwestern India matured.

BENTINCK'S POLICY MATURES

Arriving in Delhi in April 1831, Bentinck was much taken by Charles Trevelyan, a young man of twenty-four then assistant to the commissioner at Delhi. Bentinck came to regard him as "the ablest . . . in the service, and the most noble-minded . . . he had ever seen," and the esteem was returned. A close friendship developed and the older man came to rely heavily on the younger's counsel. In Trevelyan were joined the evangelical and utilitarian world view to an extraordinary degree, a turn of mind that appealed greatly to Bentinck.[23] The report on the commercial and military prospects of central Asia that Trevelyan and Lieutenant Arthur Conolly had prepared the previous month confirmed the conclusions Bentinck was reaching at the same time.

Conolly, who had just arrived after an overland journey from St. Petersburg through Persia and Afghanistan and who shared Trevelyan's evangelicalism, was responsible for the military and political portions of the report. He pointed out that the British could never defend India against a Russian attack; a European army would be too costly to maintain, and sepoys were unfit for the task. There was no imminent threat of attack, however, and the best procedure would be to create stable buffer states having mutual interests with Britain. Since Persia was, and would remain, a Russian puppet, only Afghanistan would serve that purpose.[24]

The way to accomplish this, however, was not by military or diplomatic alliances but by penetrating the area with British trade, and at this point Trevelyan picked up the argument. A true believer in the civilizing power of trade, he wrote:

In our negotiations with the Afghans we shall have everything to offer them and nothing to require. . . . We shall offer them peace, security, and independence, the increase of trade and an improvided [sic] condition of social life, and, in return for these advantages we require only their friendship and goodwill. . . .
A connection therefore which enables us to hold out the most important advantages while no sacrifice is require[d] cannot fail to be as easily formed as, when formed, it can be productive of nothing but friendship and goodwill. . . .
They now see that their weakness lies in disunion. . . . Both nobles and people feel themselves degraded . . . and they would accept with feelings of gratitude any assistance we could give them in restoring the integrity of their nation.[25]

Although Bentinck would later concur with Conolly's judgment that Britain was powerless to defend India against a Russian attack at the Indus,[26] at this point he still believed that "British power is invulnerable against every attack.''[27] The threat of any Russian influence in the states neighboring the Indus was so remote that Bentinck relegated it in his mind to the care of the Foreign Office. But Trevelyan's vision of the reforming and stabilizing effects of trade along the Indus was exactly to his taste.

At this juncture Bentinck's views were unexpectedly reinforced from London. The replacement of Ellenborough by Charles Grant in November 1830 had brought to the India Board an evangelical whose view of India matched Bentinck's. Grant disagreed with his bellicose predecessor. He and his fellow board member, Henry Ellis, both wanted to separate India from the balance of power in Europe. The chief threat to India lay not in central Asia but in bankruptcy and rebellion, which unruly states on the frontier could aggravate. Although both men shared Metcalfe's pacifist views, unlike him they were not opposed to intervention of some sort in those states. They had Trevelyan's unshakable faith that Afghans, Sikhs, and Sindians would seize the chance to improve their lot with British help and would then settle down as peaceful, prosperous, independent states friendly to their great benefactor. All this could be achieved by the wonderful instrumentality of commerce,[28] they were certain, but if British overtures were unaccountably rejected, they were reluctant to resort to force.

If . . . it should be found impossible [Grant wrote Bentinck in July 1831] thus to extend our commercial relations, and acquire the free use of the Indus, through the fair influence of persuasion, . . . we have to desire that you will abstain from a resort to any other means . . . our motive is to extend our commerce and *only* our commerce.[29]

Although Grant's instructions reached Bentinck at the end of the year, he had already overcome his former hesitancy and determined on precisely the policy outlined by Grant. With the departure from Bombay of the masterful Malcolm, who had fully agreed with Ellenborough and had jealously guarded Bombay's traditional initiative in the northwest, Bentinck was now able to assume the initiative and direction of policy in that region.[30]

Thus in the summer of 1831 he began to play the Great Game in Asia but for reasons different from those of Ellenborough, Alexander Burnes, and de Lacy Evans. The Great Game, in fact, had been transformed into the Indus Project. Bentinck's growing knowledge of the frontier states had convinced him that both Grant and he had been overly optimistic. He had come around to Trevelyan's view that a judicious use of force, or the threat of it, might be necessary against the amirs of Sind. It would be more effective if Ranjit Singh could be persuaded to cooperate. Bentinck's policy goals were now clearly in mind: trade along the Indus, containment of Ranjit Singh and his employment as a threat against Sind, coercion of the Sindian amirs to protect trade and allow its free passage, the establishment of commercial relations with Afghanistan. He wrote to Campbell in December that "of the means of promoting the commercial prosperity and political security of India, I consider the establishment of our power, as protectors and mediators, upon the Indus, to be of paramount importance."[31] With this in mind Bentinck launched three expeditions to the northwest that fall.

THE INSTRUMENTS OF POLICY

Colonel Henry Pottinger's mission to Sind was to last intermittently for seven years. The first months of negotiations promised an early success, however. In April 1832 the amirs agreed to commercial treaties that opened the rivers and roads of Sind to the merchants of Hindustan and provided for the future reduction and standardization of tolls. As the price of their consent the amirs insisted on the prohibition of armed vessels and the transport of military stores on the river, and Pottinger saw no reason to oppose this. The amirs had salvaged as much as they could under the degree of pressure the British were prepared to exert for the moment. The Indus had been opened to foreign travel much to their distaste, but they had not agreed to receive a British Resident. Bentinck was optimistic about the progress made.

It is impossible to conceive dominion and supremacy so completely acknowledged as that of the British government from one end of India to the other. Our power is irresistable. It is universally declared to be so and I hope it may become actively instrumental in promoting the welfare and improvement of this great society. I have no doubt that we shall succeed in opening the navigation of the Indus.... Col. Pottinger, our able negotiator, writes word that the Indus in depth and general facility to navigation surpasses even the favorable accounts given by Lt. Burnes. This appearance in Sind had, I have every reason to think, prevented the meditated attack of Ranjit upon Shikarpur, the principal emporium of trade on the west of the Indus, situated in the Sind territory.[32]

But Bentinck's optimism was premature. Pottinger labored for six more years in increasing frustration as the amirs temporized on toll reform and steadfastly refused the Resident while intimating periodically that an acceptable quid pro quo might be an ironclad guarantee of British protection against Ranjit Singh, a commitment both Bentinck and his successor, Auckland, wished to avoid.

A tentative regularization of tolls was obtained in 1833, but by early 1834 Pottinger was reaching the end of his patience, and Bentinck found it necessary to counsel forbearance:

You appear to think that I take a different view of all the circumstances belonging to the treaty with the amirs of Sind, to the means of carrying it into execution, and generally to the character of the people and their chiefs, from yourself. I rather believe that we differ upon some of these points, and if there be any difference of opinion at all, it may be not upon the uselessness of forbearance, conciliation and persuasion, but upon the natural fitness at all times, when a strong and enlightened power has to do with a weak and ignorant one, to forbear rather to a fault and only to put forth the effectual argument of your strength as the very last resource, and what is right in itself, is equally required for the satisfaction of the home authorities and the English public. To this proposition I almost think I shall have your assent, although you state that we ought to *dictate*, and not attempt to *persuade*. *Fear*, indeed by a happy concurrence of the circumstances existing at the moment, forced an unwilling assent to a treaty, which it was never intended to execute. The same force will alone obtain an adherence to the treaty, and I have always contemplated as an inevitable consequence, the employment of military force and eventually perhaps, the occupation of the country, to establish the free and uninterrupted navigation of the Indus.[33]

Later that year the amirs agreed to regularize the tolls further and to permit a native agent to reside at the mouth of the river, but

English merchants were not to reside in Sind and the Resident was firmly resisted. In August Pottinger was again urging Bentinck to "change our Requests to Demands and support those demands, increasing the Force in Kutch and blockading the ports of Sinde till everything we wish is fully acceded to."[34] William Macnaghten, head of the Secret and Political Department, replied that if the amirs persisted, action such as Pottinger suggested might well result. Bentinck himself had come to realize that the amirs needed prodding, and he authorized Pottinger in the fall "to intimate to [the amirs] distinctly that unless within a reasonable period . . . they fulfilled the engagements which had been solemnly contracted in the matter of the Treaty, we should be compelled to adopt measures of coercion, as might be necessary to insure their compliance."[35]

During the next two years the amirs appeared to soften as they appealed for British protection against Ranjit Singh who twice threatened to invade Sind in retaliation for raids into Sikh territory. On the second occasion, in late 1836, Auckland, who had now replaced Bentinck, instructed Pottinger to tell the amirs that the government of India was not likely to intervene on their behalf without an inducement: "that they should come fully and heartily into our plans for reestablishing the trade on the Indus."[36] They were to accept one of three alternatives: a protectorate, including a permanent detachment of British troops in Sind; a subsidiary alliance in which the amirs would subsidize a garrison of Company troops; or the mediation of the British government in the Sind-Sikh dispute on condition that the amirs receive a British Resident at Hyderabad and agree to conduct their relations with Lahore through British intermediaries. It is thus apparent that the British occupation of Sind, customarily attributed to the Afghan War, in fact originated in 1836 over a concern that political unrest along the Indus would prevent the expansion of trade. Auckland had no real expectation that the first two alternatives would be acceptable to the amirs. He felt that a Resident at Hyderabad was all that was needed at the moment to promote the Indus project, and he still "sincerely desired that the extension of British influence should be effected by commercial and peaceful objects alone." Pottinger was to apprise the amirs of the danger of their position and to persuade them to strengthen the ties they had with the British.[37] Once it appeared that Ranjit Singh would agree to withdraw, however, the amirs were no longer convinced of their danger or of the need for an extension of British influence, and the Residency was again rejected.

By the end of 1836 the indefatigable Pottinger had badgered the amirs into a promise to receive a Resident at some future date, and Auckland was once again hopeful.[38] On Christmas Day of 1836 he minuted Pottinger's correspondence:

On us the Scindians ought to be led to look as their mutual friends and the best Guardians of their independence. I would make it therefore, a main object of our policy to bring the Government of the Ameers into a more avowed connection with us. The end is one which should not be abruptly pressed, and I have no doubt it will, if not now, at no very distant period, be effected.... Our immediate and declared object is peace upon the Indus.[39]

Eight days later he wrote to the Secret Committee:

our negotiations are now narrowed to two objects—the improvement of our relations with the Ameers of Sinde by stationing a British agent at their capital, and the adjustment, with the consent of both parties of the present differences of the Ameers and Ranjeet Singh—Should these objects be attained of which there is every possibility, the preservation of tranquility along the whole course of the Indus will be the natural consequence.[40]

It was not until after October 1837, when abortive negotiations between the amirs and Ranjit Singh collapsed, that the amirs finally admitted their dependence on Britain. Pottinger was now instructed to warn them that unless they were prepared to concede the Residency without binding obligations on the part of the government of India, the British would refuse to mediate with Ranjit Singh. Having no recourse, they agreed on April 20, 1838, to accept at Hyderabad a British Resident, who could be accompanied by an escort of unspecified size, and to conduct all their relations with the Punjab through British officials. In the face of Ranjit Singh's designs on Sind and the disarray and weakness of Sindian government, there was no way for the British to avoid intervention in the affairs of Sind after 1831 if they wished to pursue their commercial objectives. Although the amirs were not granted their ironclad guarantee, from 1831 to 1838 they owed whatever remained of their independence to British forbearance and a de facto British protectorate.

The Punjab mission was far more satisfactory from the British point of view. In effect Ranjit Singh had already recognized British paramountcy, and however he may have sought to enhance his realm at the expense of his neighbors, he repeatedly abandoned his claims in the face of British objections. This occurred in 1831, 1835, and 1836. In December 1832 he willingly signed a treaty that opened the Indus and Sutlej to navigation, subject to later agreed-upon tolls, and provided for supervision of the trade by a British officer residing at Mithankot near the junction of the two rivers within Sikh-occupied territory. At Lahore there was none of the temporizing or obstructionism that occurred in Sind.

Although the third mission to Afghanistan and Bokhara began auspiciously, it bore nothing but bitter fruit. Leaving Ludhiana in January 1832, Alexander Burnes paused briefly in Lahore, passed the month of May in Kabul, where he was favorably impressed by Dost Mohamed and by the value of an alliance with a country that "lies on the great road by which the manufactures of Britain are imported [to Central Asia]," and arrived in Bokhara in late June. Here he spent nearly a month on an intensive study of the trade routes and the volume and kinds of trade and reported optimistically (and for once, realistically) on the competitive potential of British manufactured articles, especially of cotton and woolen textiles as against Russian goods. Burnes's reports were submitted to London at a time of rapid industrial growth and high commercial optimism, and the conclusions drawn were that the Indus must be fully opened to commerce and that Russian commercial competition in Central Asia could be easily thwarted by a more deliberate exercise of British influence. On a later memorandum prepared by Burnes at Bentinck's request, Bentinck minuted:

I have long been of the opinion that the establishment of a British officer as commercial agent or consul at Kabul, was a very desirable measure. The opening of the Indus must effect, sooner or later, a vast improvement in all the northwestern parts of India, in particular, where the effects will necessarily tell likewise upon our foreign commerce. But to give security to the communications from the Indus westward, and confidence to the merchants and traders, the residence of an agent at Kabul seems almost indispensable, and the enlightened character of Dost Mohamed Khan, and his desire to cultivate a more intimate relation with the British Government will contribute to produce an advantageous impression upon the amirs of Sind.

From an intelligent officer at Kabul we should have a quick and correct intelligence of all events in central Asia as well as of the intrigues and proceedings of Russia in those quarters. Persia is much too far off for the purpose of information. It is not now necessary to anticipate a western invasion, but the opinion of an able officer on the spot, capable of judging of the degree of counteraction that might be excited to such an attempt in those quarters, might be of great value. The suggestion that the agent at Kabul should be authorized by means of natives to extend his enquiries to Bokhara, and towards the Oxus and Russia seems very judicious.

There is, no doubt, this objection to the proposition, that the prince who desires this alliance hopes to make it, in some way or other subservient to the support or aggrandizement of his political power, and if our commercial resident must perforce be converted into a political agent, and made to throw away as many useless millions as in Persia, I should be the last to recommend the measure, but however disposed an agent in general is, to espouse the cause of the durbar at which he resides, still it only depends upon the government by the prudence of its choice and of its instructions to guard against any embarrassment of this kind.

The suggestion of a fair, similar to those held on the borders of Russia, and in our own territories at Hardwar and other places, is deserving of much attention, and it will be proper to consult Colonel Pottinger and our agent in Ludhiana upon the practicability of the project and the sites best adapted for it. There are probably besides Shikarpur, other established places of religious pilgrimage and of great commercial resort, which with some degree of protection might completely answer the purpose.[41]

That Bentinck's interest was primarily commercial is clearly evident here. If there had been any danger that the commercial agency would be diverted into political activities, he would rather not have established it in the first place. The minute has been quoted at length to demonstrate that even beyond the region where British paramountcy prevailed, Bentinck's aims were largely utilitarian.

Unfortunately his aims were diverted by Shah Shuja's abortive invasion of Afghanistan in 1834-1835, by the Afghan-Sikh quarrel over Peshawar in 1836-1837, by the momentary Persian occupation of Herat in 1837, and by the arrival of the Russian agent, Captain Vitkievich, in Kabul in early 1838. Throughout this building crisis, Burnes in Kabul was obliged to operate on instructions that denied him the authority to make any replies whatever to political propositions. The appeals of Dost Mohamed for British aid were met with a steadfast refusal, the only concession being made in late 1837 when Auckland offered to use his good offices with Ranjit Singh if Dost Mohamed would agree to some reasonable compromise with the Sikhs. Dost Mohamed proved stubborn and turned to the Russian envoy for support. Burnes's mission failed, and Auckland momentarily diverted British policy to support Shah Shuja's restoration to the Afghan throne. But this was definitely an aberration in the established policy. Britain's real interests did not lie in that direction, and the Afghan disaster of 1842 was a good lesson in point. The ultimate decision to withdraw from Afghanistan, after the final victorious campaign of 1842 had taught the Afghans themselves a lesson, tends to confirm the contention that British actions in northwestern India were not fundamentally governed by the much exaggerated Russian threat but by concerns closer to home: how matters stood among the three states neighboring the Indus.

SUMMARY OF MOTIVES

There has been a widespread assumption that the British expanded in northern India in response to a Russian threat. In fact an actual Russian invasion was never taken seriously. The influence of Russian agents was undeniably a factor in Britain's forward policy, but it was not the principal factor. Bentinck kept alluding to it in dispatches to appease those in London who were wont to study small-scale maps and to exert leverage on a retrenchment-minded government to supply more troops for the defense of India. Those troops, however, were needed for internal, not external, security: to quell any unrest or rebellion stirred up by the turmoil in which the neighboring states along the Indus were already immersed and in which the influence of Russian agents was only a minor factor. That statement does not hold for Afghanistan in the crisis years following 1834, but by then the British were already paramount in Sind and the Punjab, though no formal occupation or annexation had taken place.

Bentinck was far more interested and confident in trade and its beneficent, civilizing effects than he was in a new military frontier on the Indus. He at first shared the evangelical-utilitarian faith that the Indus people would welcome trade with enthusiasm. When their hostility, suspicion, and tumultuous relations shook that faith and threatened to unsettle neighboring British India as well, he was prepared to violate Grant's instructions and intervene with force. If the three frontier states had been able to resolve their political tensions by themselves and had welcomed British trade, intervention would have been unnecessary, and Bentinck had hoped for this in his initial negotiations with all three states. Fundamentally what he wished to see along the Indus were governments "good" enough, in British terms, to guarantee the tranquility of northwestern India and permit the expansion of trade. Ultimately he found that only British paramountcy—achieved by persuasion, patience, and the threat of force—could create that sort of government in Sind and the Punjab. His successor Auckland discovered, at great cost, the fatal effects of pursuing a more aggressive policy in Afghanistan. Bentinck had achieved his ends by carefully avoiding a military diversion. When the initiative in that "magnificent daydream," the Great Game in Asia, had passed to him after Ellenborough's departure from the India Board, he deliberately sought to blunt Ellenborough's dangerous ambitions by scaling it down to the Indus Project, which was pursued for more realistic, more creative, and more utilitarian ends.[42]

In this period no importance whatever was attached to India as a power base in the eastern seas, as was the case both earlier, during the French wars, and later, in the twentieth century. And there is very little evidence that territorial aggrandizement had any attraction for those at the policy-making level in India. Had that been their goal, the British could easily have swept away the disordered governments of the Sindian amirs at any time and, with little more effort, the leaderless Sikh armies as well. That they did not is additional proof of their true purpose: to avoid as much administrative responsibility along the Indus as was consistent with the promotion of free trade and good government in that region.

NOTES

1. The narrative of this chapter is based mainly on the following sources: Edward Ingram, *The Beginning of the Great Game in Asia, 1828-1834* (Oxford, 1979); Robert A. Huttenback, *British Relations with Sind, 1799-1843: An Anatomy of Imperialism* (Berkeley, Calif., 1962); James A. Norris, *The First Afghan War, 1839-42* (New York, 1967); J. D. Cunningham, *A History of the Sikhs* (London, 1849). *The Affairs of Sinde, Being an Analysis of the Papers Presented to Parliament* (London, 1844); John Rosselli, *Lord William Bentinck: The Making of a Liberal Imperialist, 1774-1839* (Berkeley, Calif., 1974); Gulsham L. Chopra, *The Punjab as a Sovereign State, 1799-1839* (Lahore, 1929); John W. Kaye, *History of the War in Afghanistan* (London, 1851), vol. 1; Ramsay Muir, *The Making of British India, 1756-1858* (London, 1915); Hugh T. Lambrick, *Sir Charles Napier and Sind* (Oxford, 1952); *Cambridge History of India*, vol. V., *British India*, 1497-1858, 3d Indian repr. (Delhi, 1968); H. M. Durand, *The First Afghan War and Its Causes* (London, 1879); Edward J. Thompson and G. T. Garratt, *The Rise and Fulfilment of British Rule in India* (London, 1934); George Anderson and M. Subedhar, *The Expansion of British India, 1818-1858* (London, 1918).

2. Bentinck to Ellenborough, August 2, 1830, in Sir Cyril H. Philips, *The Correspondence of Lord William Bentinck: Governor-General of India, 1828-1835* (Oxford, 1977), vol. 1, 484-85.

3. Bentinck to Campbell, May 11, 1831, in Philips, *Correspondence*, vol. 1, 633; Bentinck to Pottinger, Nov. 3, 1831, in Philips, *Correspondence*, vol. 1, 706.

4. Cunningham, *History of the Sikhs*, 174-77; Chopra, *Punjab*, 45-46.

5. Claude M. Wade, *A Narrative of the Services, Military and Political* (Ryde, Isle of Wight, 1844), 22-23.

6. Ingram, *Beginning of the Great Game*, 333.

7. Norris, *First Afghan War*, 18, quoting Edward Law, *Political Diary*, Sept. 3, 1829.

8. Ingram, *Beginning of the Great Game*, 59.

9. Ibid., 66, quoting Heytesbury to Aberdeen, Jan. 18, 1830.

10. Ibid., 54, quoting Ellenborough to Wellington, Oct. 18, 1829.

11. Ibid., 52.

12. "The East India Company Board of Control to Governor-General in Council," Jan. 12, 1830, in Jacob C. Hurewitz, ed., *The Middle East and North Africa in World Politics*, 2d ed. (New Haven, 1975), 239.

13. Ibid., passim.

14. Quoted in Philips, *Correspondence*, vol. 1, xix.

15. Stewart's memorandum of June 22, 1830, in ibid., 485-89.

16. Ingram, *Beginning of the Great Game*, 73.

17. James A. Burnes, *A Narrative of a Visit to the Court of Sinde* (Bombay, 1829).

18. Huttenback, *British Relations*, 19, quoting Burnes, *Narrative*.

19. John W. Kaye, *The Life and Correspondence of Sir Charles Metcalfe*, 2d ed. (London, 1858), 2:85.

20. George D. Bearce, *British Attitudes towards India, 1784-1858* (London, 1961), 162.

21. Ingram, *Beginning of the Great Game*, 94.

22. Philips, *Correspondence*, vol. 1, xxxiii.

23. Ingram, *Beginning of the Great Game*, 94-95.

24. Ibid., 96-97.

25. "Report Commercial and Military upon the Countries between the Caspian and the Indus by C. E. Trevelyan . . . and Arthur Conolly," March 15-30, 1831, quoted in ibid., 98.

26. See his minute on military policy, March 13, 1835, in Philips, *Correspondence*, vol. 2, 1440-56.

27. Bentinck to Campbell, Dec. 15, 1831, in Philips, *Correspondence*, vol. 1, 730.

28. Ingram, *Beginning of the Great Game*, 84-86, 99.

29. Grant to Bentinck, July 29, 1831, quoted in ibid., 100.

30. Ingram, *Beginning of the Great Game*, 99.

31. Bentinck to Campbell, Dec. 15, 1831, in Philips, *Correspondence*, vol. 1, 730.

32. Bentinck to Grant, May 1, 1832, in Philips, *Correspondence*, vol. 2, 806.

33. Bentinck to Pottinger, Feb. 25, 1834, in Philips, *Correspondence*, vol. 2, 1210.

34. Pottinger to Macnaghten, Aug. 10, 1834, quoted in Huttenback, *British Relations*, 28.

35. Bentinck to Secret Committee, March 5, 1835, quoted in Huttenback, *British Relations*, 28.

36. Colvin to Pottinger, Sept. 1, 1836, Auckland Papers, B.M. Add. Mss. 37690, f.5.

37. *Affairs of Sinde*, 14.

38. Norris, *First Afghan War*, 101.

39. Ibid., 101.

40. Huttenback, *British Relations*, 37, quoting Auckland to Secret Committee, Jan. 2, 1837.

41. Bentinck's minute, June 1, 1833, in Philips, *Correspondence*, vol. 2, 1075-76.

42. Ingram, *Beginning of the Great Game*, 128.

CONTINGENT PARAMOUNTCY, 1824-1874

There seems to be little question that British paramountcy existed on the Malay Peninsula after the establishment of the Residential system in Perak, Selangor, and Sungei Ujong in 1874.[1] While the other states were not incorporated into the system until later— Johore in 1885, the small states of Negri Sembilan between 1886 and 1889, Pahang in 1887-1888, and the northern states, formerly nominal Siamese protectorates, after 1909—some of them had already been subject to considerable British intervention and influence years before. The significance of the 1874 treaties was that they consolidated British influence along the all-important west coast, which, with the help of the Royal Navy, controlled the Straits of Malacca, the corridor that carried most of the world's east-west trade. Because Malaya's geography made it readily accessible from the sea and because Malay and Chinese alike lived along the river banks, the country was vulnerable to a sea power like Britain once it had decided to intervene actively. This occurred in the early 1870s when, far more frequently than before, ships of the Royal Navy began to patrol the straits and gunboats and armed launches the estuaries, rivers, and creeks.[2] Backed up by the navy, British Residents became the de facto governors of their states.

The ease with which the British asserted paramountcy after 1874 —there was very little serious fighting—showed that the job was already half done; the British had established a "moral predominance" over the Malays long before.[3] The question is: how long before and to what extent was it more than moral?

British officials in both London and the straits certainly regarded Britain as paramount before 1874. Colonial Secretary Lord Kimberley's instructions of 1873 to Governor Sir Andrew Clarke included the statement: "we are the paramount power on the Penin-

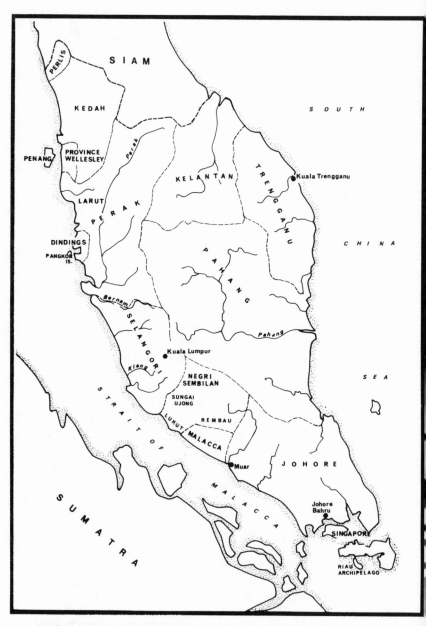

MALAYA, 1824–1874

sula up to the limit of the States tributary to Siam.''⁴ The last India Office Governor, Orfeur Cavenagh, testified to the same belief on several occasions. In 1860 he wrote to Calcutta that political intervention "would seem to be one of the responsibilities attached to our high position as the dominant power in this quarter.''⁵ The following year he asserted that except for "one or two petty Independent states, the possession of the Malay Peninsula is divided between the British and the Siamese.''⁶ But the determination of the British government to cling to its policy of nonintervention drove Cavenagh to distraction. He wrote Calcutta in despair in May 1863 as a civil war in Pahang dragged on:

Without our interference the war . . . may be protracted for months to come . . . there is no doubt that . . . it is at present in our power, with the aid of the naval force in the Straits, to enforce . . . tranquility by bringing the weight of our influence into the scale between the two contending parties.⁷

And five years before Cavenagh's predecessor had warned the Temenggong (the Dato Temenggong was nominally the vassal of the Sultan of Johore but in actuality ruled the state), who proposed to intervene at the outbreak of the Pahang war, that "Your Highness is not the paramount authority in the peninsula but the British India government is such, and as its representative I feel bound to use my utmost influence to prevent the spread of war and of its attendant horrors.''⁸

Official testimony often savors of special pleading, but their assumptions were based on the actual state of affairs. Although not administering any of the Malay States, the East India Company, or its subjects in the Straits Settlements (which comprised the colonies of Singapore, Malacca, Penang, and Province Wellesley and were ruled as a province of British India until 1867 when they were turned over to the Colonial Office) had close economic connections with some of them. The produce of Selangor and Negri Sembilan was marketed through Malacca, which also provided the capital for tin mining in Lukut and Sungei Ujong, while the same reciprocal arrangement was provided by Penang for Perak and Larut.⁹ By virtue of this the Straits Settlements exercised a clear economic predominance over the western states by the late 1850s when tin mining began to come into its own.

This preponderance can be traced back in part to local economic realities but partly as well to the earlier efforts of the British to organize the trade of the west coast and Singapore by treaty arrangements. By the treaty of February 1819, both the Sultan of Johore and the Dato Temenggong had become pensionaries of the East India Company. A further treaty of August 1824 ceded all of Singapore island to the Company, increased the allowances of the Sultan and Temenggong, and obligated them to maintain free trade in Johore and not to engage in any foreign relations without the Company's consent.[10] When a new Temenggong, Ibrahim, came to power in about 1833, he continued to live on Singapore island mainly because it was handier than Johore for the management of his business affairs, including his piratical enterprises. Nevertheless on the island he came increasingly under the thumb of successive Governors who left him to rule Johore without interference as long as he kept his administration in line with the Governors' wishes. He and his successor, Abu Bakar, were able to keep Johore "independent" for so long because they behaved in such a manner as to give the British "no cause for complaint and . . . no excuse for interference." Ibrahim, for example, much against his own predilections, cooperated with the British in suppressing piracy around Singapore after 1840. The economy of Johore and its foreign policy, however, remained firmly in the hands of Singapore.[11] And Governor Blundell could testify in 1852 that Ibrahim was "undoubtedly superior to the young Sultan in the capacity to govern the country in subservience to British interests."[12]

The treaties of 1818 and 1825 with Selangor did not give the British control over that country's foreign relations, but they did, along with the Anglo-Siamese Treaty of 1826, declare Siamese suzerainty at an end and pledge the British to protect the northern boundary against both Siam and Perak. To this extent Selangor was thereafter regarded by the British government as a "British protected state."[13]

The Anglo-Siamese Treaty of 1826 was precipitated by the Siamese occupation of the northern state of Kedah in 1821 when its Sultan and many other refugees fled to Penang pleading for British intervention. Unwilling to do so but wishing to prevent Siamese encroachment in Perak, Governor James Fullerton sent Henry Burney to negotiate terms. Siamese rule in Kedah was recognized in return for the abandonment of Siamese suzerainty over Selangor. The Company agreed not to interfere in the political affairs of the east coast states of Kelantan and Trengganu, over which Siam claimed suzerainty, on condition that Siam not interfere with the Company's trade there. There was a mutual agreement not to interfere in the affairs of Perak.[14] The treaty in effect put Siam on notice that the Company would not permit interference in those parts of the Malay Peninsula that were most important commercially.

The treaty was immediately violated by both parties. In the summer of 1826 Bangkok sent an embassy to Perak, apparently to restore the payment of tribute. When Fullerton heard of this, he dispatched Captain James Low to assure the Sultan of Perak that he was obliged neither to receive the embassy nor to send any tribute to Siam. Low exceeded his instructions, however, by making a treaty with Perak that promised to protect Perak's boundaries against violations from all quarters, writing Fullerton that Perak was now in effect "under the superintendence... of the Honourable East India Company, which must protect it and superintend its government as if it were an English state." Although Fullerton was furious at this infringement of the nonintervention policy, neither he nor his successors repudiated Low's treaty, and it gradually was accepted as the basis of a permanent relationship between Perak and British India.[15]

The effect of the Anglo-Dutch Treaty of 1824 was to grant Dutch recognition to the Malay Peninsula as a British sphere of influence. Until that time the Dutch were more solidly entrenched than the British in the Malay archipelago as a whole, but after 1824 the demarkation between the peninsula and the islands was clear-cut, and the British had a better capability of patroling the straits. And since there were never any serious European challenges to that sphere of influence thereafter, it could be argued that the British were paramount in all of Malaya from 1824 onward.

These shadowy quasi-protectorates, however, were not exercised by the East India Company because it saw no reason to trouble itself as long as the peninsular trade was marginal, and they did not compare with the dependent native states of India where British Residents really exercised control by means of influence or periodic military intervention. But the treaties did provide a theoretical legal basis for future intervention should the authorities have a change of mind.

Although British policy from 1826 to 1873 was steadfastly non-interventionist, there were not a few cases where they intervened either to enforce treaty obligations or where the violation of British interests was so flagrant that it could not be overlooked. On at least two occasions intervention was undertaken to forestall Siamese influence. In 1844 when Siam had ordered the Sultan of Kedah to invade Perak, pressure was brought to bear on Bangkok to obtain his withdrawal.[16] In 1862 Kuala Trengganu was bombarded by British warships after Siamese soldiers and ships had attempted to install Mahmud, ex-Sultan of Lingga, as Sultan of Trengganu. Mahmud seems to have offered to make Pahang a vassal state of Siam in return for these services, but the British intervention discouraged Mongkut, and there were no further Siamese attempts to extend their influence down the east coast. These minor intercessions were sufficient to cause Siamese influence in the northern states to decline as the nineteenth century progressed.[17]

An exceptional case of intervention occurred between 1853 and 1855 when Governors Blundell and Butterworth arbitrated a dispute between the Temenggong Ibrahim and Ali, claimant to the throne. The former ended by recognizing Ali's claim, but the new Sultan in effect relinquished the government of Johore to the Temengong in return for a fixed income from the state's revenues.[18] And there were a number of minor interventions: in 1826 the chief of Muar was forced to withdraw from Malacca territory he had occupied; in 1844-1848 Kedah was compelled to restore the Krian district to Perak; in 1860 the chiefs of Rembau and Sungei Ujong were made to rescind taxes damaging to Malacca's trade; in 1862 Perak was forced to pay awards to Chinese merchants, who were British subjects, to compensate them for their losses; in 1862 the Temenggong of Johore was made to release British subjects he had arrested and to refrain from trying them under Malay law,[19] and four years earlier he had backed away from support of the Bendahara in the Pahang civil war when warned by Governor Blundell to do so.[20]

None of these cases of intervention was of great significance alone, but they demonstrate a pattern of persistent intervention, mainly by influence and advice, which implies a de facto recognition of British paramountcy throughout the peninsula after 1824. There seems to have been little doubt in the minds of those involved, especially of the chiefs who repeatedly invoked British aid or arbitration, that the Company was the dominant power in the area and could have intervened decisively at any time. This was probably not true before 1824 when the Dutch were still present and Singapore was little more than a toehold. Thereafter, however, a contingent British paramountcy can be said to exist, which was intermittently and progressively employed during the next fifty years to settle the affairs of the Malay states.

THE CHINA AND COUNTRY TRADES

In the years immediately preceding 1824, whatever subordinate aims the British had in mind as they scanned the eastern seas, the protection of the China trade overshadowed all. At the beginning of the nineteenth century the trade east of India was of two sorts. The trade with southeast Asia, the "country trade," was largely in the hands of freelance merchants based in India but not associated with the Company. The tea trade between China and Europe was an official monopoly in the hands of the Company and the most profitable part of the Company's operations. It was from the profits of the China trade that the Company paid its dividends and interest between 1813, when its India monopoly was ended, and 1833 when its China monopoly was ended.[21] Thus when the Dutch tried to reassert their former monopoly over the trade of the Malay archipelago after 1814, both the Company and the Board of Control in London were able to overcome their initial disgruntlement over the expense and inconvenience to which Raffles's acquisition of Singapore would put them. Although it is generally held that Raffles exceeded his instructions, his chief in Calcutta, Lord Hastings, had supported the plan to establish another base in the straits and had given Raffles a loophole by warning him that "the object of fixing upon a Port of this nature is not the extension of any territorial influence but strictly limited to the occupation of an advantageous position for the protection of our commerce," which is what Raffles did.[22] And although Canning, as President of the India Board, at first disavowed the acquisition, he withheld action until further information arrived and ultimately authorized the occupation.[23] When Raffles's foresight was justified by the rapid growth of Singapore's trade beyond all expectation, Castlereagh and Canning, who opened the Anglo-Dutch negotiations that culminated in the Treaty of London in 1824, put forward as one of their chief aims the Dutch recognition of Singapore and the British right of free passage through the straits for the China trade.[24]

But as a good liberal utilitarian of his time, Raffles was not without a higher vision. Mary Turnbull describes him in her recent book on Singapore:

Raffles' personal ambitions and concern to boost British trade were backed by a sense of messianic mission. He did not seek territorial aggrandizement for Britain but rather a blend of commercial and moral pre-eminence. Fascinated by the romance of faded civilizations and fired with confidence in British liberal politics and commercial freedom, he saw his country's role in South-East Asia almost as a crusade, to free the peoples of the eastern archipelago from civil war, piracy, slavery and oppression, to restore and revive their old cultures and independence, under the influence of European enlightenment, liberal education, progressive economic prosperity and sound law.[25]

On his last visit to Singapore in 1822-1823 Raffles

set out to ensure Singapore's prosperity as a great port, to abolish slavery and injustice, to devise a way of governing, giving "the utmost possible freedom of trade and equal rights to all, with protection of property and person," and to make Singapore a beautiful and orderly city, the intellectual and educational centre of South-East Asia.[26]

As Turnbull points out, his horror of slavery matched that of Wilberforce, his ideas about law and penal reform those of Bentham, and he made Singapore a thriving free port when England was still protectionist.[27] Here is another example of the motive of good government that pervaded the thinking of many of the East India Company's servants at this time.

Raffles had another more mundane objective as well. Apart from protecting the China trade, he was trying to frustrate Dutch efforts to monopolize the country trade of the archipelago. Hastings supported him in this, complaining that the proceedings of the Netherlands authorities...had been actuated by...a desire to obtain the power of monopolizing the commerce of the eastern archipelago and excluding the English from these advantages which they had long enjoyed, and which they only wished to share in common with the other nations of the earth.[28]

The trade of the archipelago was the earliest trade attracted to the new port. By 1824 it was equal in value to the China trade and not long after would surpass it.[29] The right to free trade in the archipelago became the other major claim of the British negotiators of the Anglo-Dutch Treaty of 1824 insofar as southeast Asia was concerned.[30]

Both Calcutta and London were eager to avoid any additional territorial responsibilities in Malaya. No one spoke of creating a naval base in the eastern seas either to protect trade or for defense against European rivals. If British paramountcy can be said to have been achieved by 1824, almost the sole motive behind it was the encouragement of British trade, although energetic utilitarians like Raffles, who was most responsible for that paramountcy, also entertained visions of the spread of civilization and good government.

THE PENINSULAR TRADE

There are indications that the peninsular trade was becoming important by the 1820s. After Siam's occupation of Kedah in 1821 and the flight of its Sultan to Perak, the Company eventually (1828) used the occasion to force Siam to abandon its suzerainty over Selangor. But its immediate response was to send John Crawfurd on a mission to Siam in 1821 to negotiate the restoration of Perak's trade with Siam.[31] This conformed to the general policy of the Company at that time and of its Governor, Lord Amherst, who believed that "among the states of farther Asia 'a very general fear and distrust of Europeans' predominated to the serious detriment of commerce" and that the first task was to remove it by making it clear that the East India Company sought to establish relations solely for purposes of trade.[32] Thus even in the early years the trade potential of the peninsula played a role in the achievement of the contingent paramountcy of 1824.

If the arguments for paramountcy as of 1824 are not convincing, few will dispute its reality by 1874. During the intervening fifty years, there were repeated cases of intervention on the peninsula, but the Company successfully resisted territorial expansion and even refused to establish naval or military bases on the coasts. After the loss of the China monopoly in 1833 and especially after 1842 when Hong Kong replaced Singapore as the main entrepôt of the China trade, the Straits Settlements became a costly burden for the Company—the annual deficits averaged about $850,000 until as late as 1865—and there was no desire for additional responsibilities.[33] As the country trade became more important, however, and even surpassed the China trade in the 1830s, the Company grudgingly maintained Singapore, where most of the country traders lived, but received little in return for this service because of Singapore's status as a free port. The Company's attitude was that the merchants were doing well enough by themselves with what British protection they had. The Company even refused to furnish a permanent naval force to suppress piracy, although on several occasions it dispatched gunboats and steamers, which proved capable of eradicating piracy in limited areas for short periods of time.[34] The Company was no more enthusiastic about protecting the capital that the straits merchants began to invest in the chaotic interior after mid-century. It was precisely this, however—the increasing tension between trade and turmoil in the peninsula itself —that led to the repeated interventions and to the consolidation of British paramountcy with the establishment of the Residential system in 1874.

Until mid-century the proportion of Singapore's trade with the peninsula to its north was miniscule, amounting to only 3 percent as late as 1860.[35] But in the 1860s several things happened to make the peninsula more attractive to entrepreneurs. The importance of tin in international commerce greatly increased as the canning industry matured. This led to large-scale investment in tin mining in several of the Malay states, as well as a parallel investment in loans to native rulers who found themselves in financial difficulties as a result of the new economic conditions. A general European depression reached the eastern trade in 1867-1868, but during the 1869-1873 period, there was a short-term rise in the price of tin. These developments came at a time when the growth of European and

American competition was beginning to worry the British and when they were confronted by the closing off of many trading areas in southeast Asia by foreign rivals. The Spanish were erecting trade barriers in the Philippines and, along with the Americans, making claims to North Borneo. The French had been moving into Indochina since 1858, erecting tariffs there. The most immediate and important threat lay in Sumatra where the Dutch were extending protectorates and protectionism despite the treaty of 1824. All of this made the potential trade of the Malay peninsula proportionately more attractive and important than it had ever been, and by 1870 the trade was significant enough for the straits merchants to begin to clamor for protection.

Protection was indeed needed because of the breakdown of feudal Malayan governments under the impact of the new economic conditions and Chinese immigration. The breakdown often began as a dispute over the succession, as it did in Perak, Selangor, and Pahang, later complicated by the involvement of rival Malay and Chinese factions. Chiefs whom the sultans could not control preyed on the miners. The Chinese tongs engaged in civil wars in which the Malay chiefs inevitably took sides. The chiefs of the nine states of Negri Sembilan lived in a state of intermittent warfare. During the two decades preceding 1870 the Malay states seemed to be "hard at work committing political *hara-kiri*." When the fighting spread and intensified in the early 1870s, the tin mines all but closed down, and the export of tin and the growing peninsular trade virtually ceased.[36]

From the early 1860s on, the governments at Calcutta and London were pressed to intervene by straits merchants and sympathetic governors on the spot, all of whom understood better than those back home that the traditional Malay governments were incapable of maintaining the peace and order necessary for economic development. Both Calcutta and London resolutely turned a blind eye to these appeals until about 1868 when the policy of nonintervention began to break down. In 1870 London still sought to avoid direct intervention by negotiating a détente with the Dutch to ease off tariff restrictions in Sumatra, one of the straits' best markets. The next year, however, an act of piracy in Selangor finally convinced Kimberley that intervention of some sort was unavoidable.[37]

Parkinson points out that Kimberley and his associates were also influenced by the rising fashionability of imperial expansion and by altruistic sentiments as well. Although Victorian statesmen and their agents abroad were no more honorable in their actions than those of any other age, their aims were in striking contrast to their means. They

honestly desired to bring justice instead of misrule, prosperity instead of want, health instead of sickness, confidence instead of fear.... In their desire to abolish debt-slavery, they were disinterested, enlightened and kind. Nor would it be fair to conclude that the merchants were intent only on trade. They had more than economic reasons for desiring to see their customers at peace.[38]

Thus a breakdown of government in a region of rising commercial importance at a time when "Little Englandism" was going out of fashion combined with altruistic motives to alter the old policy of nonintervention. Although Sir Andrew Clarke exceeded the letter of his instructions, Kimberley himself had foreseen the possibility that British residents might be necessary.[39] Thus began the Residential system, which converted the Malay states into British protectorates.

Some attention must here be given to the strong case made by C. D. Cowan that the key motive behind the intervention of 1874 was not the protection of trade or the demands of the straits merchants but "the fear that some other Power might profit from the situation in the Peninsula to secure a footing there."[40] Although Cowan's case is carefully argued, it is possible to place a different interpretation upon the evidence he presents.

When Kimberley was drafting Clarke's instructions in August 1873, he wrote a passage that was omitted in the final dispatch and that, Cowan claims, reveals the "unstated motive behind the decision to intervene": "we could not see with indifference interference of foreign Powers in the affairs of the Peninsula, on the other hand it is difficult to see how we should be justified in objecting to the native States seeking aid elsewhere if we refuse to take any steps to remedy the evils complained of."[41] And ten days later Gladstone received a letter from Kimberley justifying the proposed intervention:

The condition of the Malay Peninsula is becoming very serious. It is the old story of misgovernment of Asiatic States. This might go on without any very serious consequences except the stoppage of trade, were it not that European and Chinese capitalists, stimulated by the great riches in tin mines which exist in some of the Malay States are suggesting to the native Princes that they should seek the aid of Europeans to enable them to put down the disorders which prevail. We are the paramount power on the Peninsula up to the limit of the States, tributary to Siam, and looking to the vicinity of India and our whole position in the East. I apprehend that it would be a serious matter if any European Power were to obtain a footing in the Peninsula.[42]

In Cowan's view this reveals Kimberley's secret fear and prime motivation. But we should ask why he feared foreign intervention. The letter might be interpreted differently to mean that the disruption of the peninsular trade is a serious matter, that the closing off of trade by protectionist European rivals is endangering "our whole position in the east," and that as paramount power in the peninsula we cannot jeopardize what remains of free trade in the east by allowing any of these rivals to encroach there. That the threat to trade was the fundamental factor is borne out by the rest of Clarke's instructions:

the interests of the British Settlements require that we shall exert our influence to put an end to the state of anarchy and disorder which prevails in several of the States, and which if not checked will probably extend through that part of the Peninsula which is independent of Siam, and will ruin these fertile and productive countries.

Clarke therefore was

carefully to examine the facts, and to report in the case of each state with reference to the present conditions of its affairs and its relations with the British Govt. what mode of proceeding should in his opinion be adopted with a view to restore peace and order, to secure protection to British subjects who may trade with the States, or embark in commercial undertakings in the native territories, and generally to promote the improvement and good Govt. of the native states with which we are connected.[43]

This letter reveals a concern for the peninsular trade somewhat greater than Cowan seems willing to concede, and it reflects the interests of the straits mercantile community and recent straits governors who had been pressing their views on Kimberley, as well as of Clarke who finally consolidated British paramountcy in advance of instructions to do so.

Since there is nowhere any implication of strategic concerns—that anyone seriously feared, for instance, the establishment of a German naval base in Malaya—and since territorial aggrandizement was as repugnant as ever to Kimberley, it is not unreasonable to conclude that he was thinking in the broad context of the freedom of the eastern trade. Given rising protectionism elsewhere, the Malay peninsula offered "suitable alternative trading opportunities," which no European rival should be permitted to jeopardize. Thus the threat of a German protectorate on the peninsula, a nonexistent bogey tossed up by the straits merchants to frighten the Colonial Office into action, was merely the last straw which broke Kimberley's resistance. The fundamental reason underlying intervention was the gradual swelling of pressure from the straits merchants and sympathetic governors for the protection of the peninsular trade from the turbulent political conditions in the interior and from the piracy that those conditions permitted. Kimberley was fearful that foreign intervention would aggravate those conditions, as well as close off yet another region to British trade. Thus "fear of foreign intervention" eventually comes back to trade and the preservation of stable native governments.

Whether one agrees that British paramountcy was established by 1824 or insists on a later date, British interests nevertheless formed a continuum from one period to the next. From the end of the Napoleonic Wars until at least the 1870s Britain's interest in Malaya—what little it displayed—was primarily in commerce and good government: first to protect and foster the China trade, then to exploit the sea trade of the eastern archipelago, and finally to develop the tin mines and the attendant trade of the peninsula and to ensure that the governments of the Malay states abetted rather than hindered these ends.

NOTES

1. The narrative of this chapter is based mainly on the following sources: C. D. Cowan, *Nineteenth Century Malaya: The Origins of British Control* (London, 1961); Joseph Kennedy, *A History of Malaya, A.D. 1400-1959*

(London, 1962); L. A. Mills, *British Malaya 1824-67* (Singapore, 1925); N. J. Ryan, *A History of Malaysia and Singapore* (Kuala Lumpur, 1976); C. M. Turnbull, *The Straits Settlements, 1826-67: Indian Presidency to Crown Colony* (London, 1972); W. D. McIntyre, *The Imperial Frontier in the Tropics, 1865-75* (London, 1967); F. A. Swettenham, *British Malaya* (London, 1929).

2. C. N. Parkinson, *British Intervention in Malaya 1867-1877* (Singapore, 1960), xvii.

3. Mills, *British Malaya*, 187.

4. Cowan, *Nineteenth Century Malaya*, 169.

5. Turnbull, *Straits Settlements*, 307.

6. McIntyre, *Imperial Frontier*, 154.

7. Turnbull, *Straits Settlements*, 310.

8. Ibid., 307.

9. Ryan, *History*, 116-17.

10. Turnbull, *Straits Settlements*, 275.

11. Ibid., 287-90.

12. Mills, *British Malaya*, 185.

13. Cowan, *Nineteenth Century Malaya*, 160.

14. Turnbull, *Straits Settlements*, 256; Ryan, *History*, 112.

15. Turnbull, *Straits Settlements*, 258.

16. Ryan, *History*, 113.

17. Ibid., 115-16; Turnbull, *Straits Settlements*, 290-98.

18. Ryan, *History*, 115. Mills, *British Malaya*, 185-86.

19. Mills, *British Malaya*, 179-81.

20. Turnbull, *Straits Settlements*, 307.

21. Ryan, *History*, 90.

22. Amales Tripathi, *Trade and Finance in the Bengal Presidency, 1793-1833* (Calcutta, 1956), 181.

23. Sir Cyril H. Philips, *The East India Company, 1784-1834*, 2d ed. (Manchester, 1961), 230-32. Charles A. Petrie, *George Canning* (London, 1930), 146.

24. Philips, *East India Company*, 232.

25. C. M. Turnbull, *A History of Singapore, 1819-1975* (Kuala Lumpur, 1977), 7.

26. Ibid., 21.

27. Ibid., 32.

28. J. Ross of Bladensburg, *The Marquess of Hastings* (Oxford, 1893), 185.

29. Cowan, *Nineteenth Century Malaya*, 21; Turnbull, *Straits Settlements*, 162.

30. Philips, *East India Company*, 232.

31. D. G. E. Hall, *Henry Burney: A Political Biography* (London, 1974), 17.

32. Ibid., 16.

33. Ryan, *History*, 110-11.

34. See Turnbull, *Straits Settlements*, 242-55.

35. Cowan, *Nineteenth Century Malaya*, 21.

36. Mills, *British Malaya*, 174. Turnbull, *Straits Settlements*, 83; Ryan, *History*, 149-50.

37. W. D. McIntyre "Britain's Intervention in Malaya: The Origin of Lord Kimberley's Instructions to Sir Andrew Clarke in 1873," in John Bastin and R. Winks, *Malaysia: Selected Historical Readings* (Kuala Lumpur, 1966), 201.

38. Parkinson, *British Intervention*, xx.

39. Cowan, *Nineteenth Century Malaya*, 175.

40. Ibid., 144.

41. Quoted in ibid., 166.

42. Ibid., 169.

43. Ibid., 165.

SOUTH AFRICA:
THE EASTERN COAST

Britain's Cape Colony was a legacy of the Napoleonic Wars. Very likely it would not have been occupied had it not been situated on the route to India, and there is no doubt that it was kept after 1814 to guard that route. But after the Napoleonic era, the route to India came to be valued by liberal officials more for its commercial than for its strategic advantages. It was first and foremost a trade route.

The following account demonstrates that paramountcy was established along the entire South African coast from the Cape Colony to Mozambique by the summer of 1842, and in some places, such as Xhosaland, somewhat before that, and that British motives in South Africa were consistent with those observed elsewhere in this period.

THE FRONTIER TRADE

Once the British were settled at Table Bay, the interior trade of the colony, which provisioned passing ships as well as the colony itself, became important to them, as it had been to the Dutch.[1] From the outset one of the chief concerns of the governors had been to maintain the supply of meat, most of which came from the frontiers. That peace and order reigned on the frontier was of prime importance. Frontier wars between the eastward trekking settlers and the native population could not be countenanced, but they seemed to break out despite efforts to bring the trekkers to heel by cutting off their ammunition supply at the ports. The trekkers of the 1820s and 1830s proved to be almost as troublesome as the later Trekboers who sought to escape British rule by moving into the Orange River territory or Natal.

The older view that the trekkers wandered off into the wilderness, cut themselves off from the Cape and evolved a self-sufficient economy so that the frontier trade was of little consequence to the

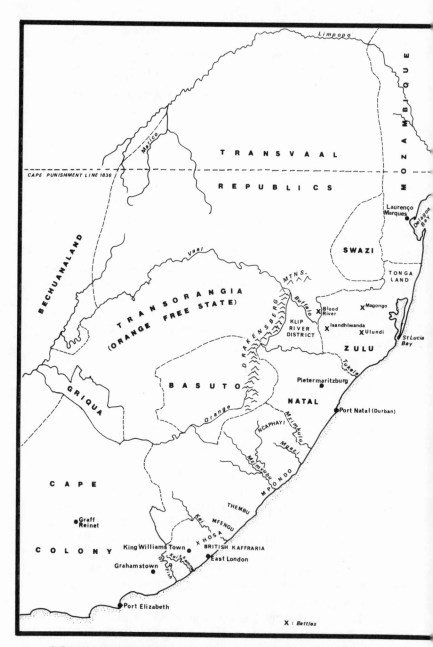

SOUTHEASTERN AFRICA, 1830s and 1840s

British government, has been greatly altered by later scholarship. The frontier was far from being self-supporting. In some areas farmers derived most of their income from the sale of produce, either to Cape Town in the early eighteenth century, or to the advancing line of frontier market towns in the late eighteenth and early nineteenth centuries. In the 1820s and 1830s, trade with Kaffraria was rapidly expanding, and many traders settled there after 1830. Both frontiersmen and Cape dwellers depended on each other, the former for arms, ammunition, wagons, cloth, and other necessities, the latter for meat, hides, soap, and other frontier products of which the Cape was in short supply. Accordingly in addition to the live animal market, there was a small but continuous and growing internal trade in South Africa upon which a healthy colony depended.[2] Because haulage by ox wagon between the frontier and the Cape was the most costly element of this trade, coastwise shipping came to supply the market towns that sprang up on the eastern frontier, towns like Graff Reinet and Grahamstown, which were growing rapidly by the 1820s. This development led in turn to the further expansion of the frontier because the farmers were now freed from the long haul from Cape Town to provide their needs. Advancing markets supplied and made possible the advancing frontiers.[3]

The frontier trade, moreover, supported the foreign trade. From the outset and well into the nineteenth century, the Cape Colony was primarily a victualing station for the East India traffic. It had to produce a surplus to provision passing ships, to supply their crews while in port, and to supply the military garrisons. The demand was mainly for fresh food such as meat, butter, fruits, and vegetables, of which meat was the most important, and until the time of the Great Trek, which began in 1835 when large numbers of Boers moved north of the Orange River, meat was supplied in quantity only by the cattle and sheep graziers on the eastern frontier. Other animal products in short supply at the Cape, such as butter, fat, tallow, soap, hides, skins, and horns, were also supplied by the frontier, as were the highly valued products of hunting such as venison, pelts, ivory, and ostrich feathers. The foreign demand for these products was a significant factor in the growth of South African trade in the 1820s and 1830s and in the prosperity and expansion of the frontiers. Between 1825 and 1835 the number and tonnage of vessels passing through the Cape ports trebled, from approximately 250 ships and 90,000 tons to 950 ships and 270,000 tons, the most rapid rise occurring after 1827. The total exports of the Cape began to rise significantly in the same period. Between 1826 and 1830 they averaged £218,412, of which £120,750 was wine from the colony and £37,454 hides and skins from the frontier. Five years later (1831-1835) the average was £243,640, of which only £84,028 was wine and £62,829 hides and skins. By the late 1820s hides and skins ranked second only to wine on the list of Cape exports, and most of them came from the frontier.[4]

Accordingly in the late 1820s and early 1830s the frontier was becoming a significant factor in the total trade of the Cape Colony. Even if the absolute volume was unimpressive, many of the products were indispensable for the passing ships and only slightly less so for the residents of the Cape itself. Hence a dependable commerce with the frontier was of crucial importance to Cape administrators, and while there seems to be very little testimony to this effect on the part of British officials, there can be little doubt that they felt compelled to intervene in the strife beyond the formal frontiers partly, at least, because it threatened to hamper this trade.

PARAMOUNTCY IN XHOSALAND

By the mid-1820s the frontiers of settlement had reached Kaffraria on the east and the Orange River drifts in the north, and in both places Boer or English cattlemen were living close to Bantu, Griqua, or Khoikhoi graziers who were also involved in the frontier trade.[5] On the eastern frontier the advancing settlers were met by vigorous resistance, mainly on the part of the Xhosa who occupied the territory between the Fish and Kei rivers and the Gcaleka clan of that tribe, which lived beyond the Kei. Before 1819 four frontier wars had been fought with these people, and five more would be fought between 1819 and 1878, each ending in their defeat and the imposition of progressively tighter restraints on their behavior.

Before 1819 control over the Zuurveld, the region west of the Fish River, had been decided in favor of the whites. During the Fifth Frontier War of 1819, Governor Lord Charles Somerset's forces crossed the Fish River and advanced easily to the Kei, traversing all of what later became British Kaffraria and mopping up Xhosa resistance in about one month. The chiefs responsible for the raids that precipitated the war were made to accept Gaika as their paramount chief, and a verbal agreement was forced on Gaika by which the district between the Fish and Keiskamma rivers, named Victoria East, was declared neutral, to be occupied only by British military patrols. Although little was actually done to extrude the entire Xhosa population of Victoria East, certain troublesome chiefs and their followers were periodically expelled in the 1820s and 1830s, and white settlers were allowed to filter in. Under these circumstances strife was inevitable, and the vacillations of British policy, which at one point (1833) prohibited the settlers from calling out commandos to recover stolen cattle, convinced the chiefs that the British were too weak to uphold their rights and led to the war of 1834-1835.

This time the British were caught off guard and the frontier settlements were ravaged for about three months by Xhosa armies numbering twelve thousand to fifteen thousand men. Once the retaliating force of about three thousand men had been assembled, however, in March 1835, only thirty days were required to sweep through Xhosaland and squelch all resistance. In 1835 all the territory to the Kei River was annexed by Governor Sir Benjamin D'Urban as Queen Adelaide Province and the administration of the country placed in the hands of British civil commissioners and a military commandant at King Williams Town.

The fact that the Colonial Office did its best to divest itself of the new responsibility thereafter did not alter the realities of power, but Colonial Secretary Lord Glenelg's celebrated dispatch of December 1835, instructing D'Urban to annul the annexation and the treaty system inaugurated by the Lieutenant Governor Andries Stockenstrom, of the Eastern Province, under direct orders from Glenelg, placed too much faith in the gratitude and peaceful inclinations of the Xhosa chiefs, and their increasing boldness led once again to war in 1846.

After the War of the Axe, Governor Sir Harry Smith annexed Xhosaland again, renamed it British Kaffraria, and appointed assistant commissioners to regulate the affairs of each clan backed by a British commandant with two thousand troops at his disposal. British paramountcy was to be challenged by two more Frontier Wars (1850-1852 and 1877-1878), but although the first of these challenges was serious, each was in the nature of an insurrection against an already established British paramountcy.

Paramountcy, then, was achieved in Xhosaland by 1835 and possibly as early as 1819. Before 1819 the British had contented themselves with defensive action, driving the Xhosa back across the Fish River frontier but never crossing that frontier themselves. Thereafter despite evacuations and withdrawals, the ease with which the British occupied Xhosaland and enforced a temporary obedience demonstrates that they enjoyed a paramountcy, which could be enforced any time they chose. Thus British paramountcy was achieved just when the frontier trade was becoming a significant factor in the total trade of the Cape, and governors felt called upon to put a stop to cattle lifting and the retaliatory commando raids that disrupted that trade.

ABORIGINES PROTECTION

Simultaneously a new factor appeared, which was first to influence the treatment of aborigines in the Colony and later Natal but had little effect in Xhosaland. British administration at the Cape commenced just as the forces of liberalism and the evangelical revival were gaining momentum in English political life. They appeared in South Africa in the attitudes of British Army officers and civil servants and, most notably, of the missionaries who began to live among the Khoikhoi and to witness their mistreatment at first hand. From the start British governors took steps to ameliorate their condition. In 1800 Governor Francis Dundas undertook

to convince the Hottentots [Khoikhoi] and Caffres that it was the intention of his Britannic Majesty's Government to alleviate the sufferings of the former, and to prevent in the future the injustice which upon many occasions has been done the latter on the part of the farmers in their dealings with them. [Further, the landdrosts were ordered] not to suffer with impunity any acts of violence or cruelty as have been usual on the parts of the farmers towards the Hottentots.[6]

After 1801 all Khoikhoi labor contracts were to be in writing. Dundas's orders, of course, were not sufficient to alter the ingrained habits of the Boers, and the mistreatment of Khoikhoi servants continued, but Dundas at least had established the precedent of British intervention on their behalf.

After 1809, however, there was a period of retrogression. In that year the Governor, the Earl Caledon, issued a proclamation defining the legal status of the Khoikhoi, which came to be known as the Caledon code. While the code proposed to regularize and secure Khoikhoi wages and service, its other aspects, especially the requirement for a "fixed place of abode" and the carrying of passes, counteracted whatever good was intended. This was the case because the enforcement of the code was left largely to the field cornets who, as "farmers among farmers," were far more interested in applying the vagrancy provisions and in enforcing the pass laws and promoting apprenticeship than in enforcing the provisions that protected the Khoikhoi from abusive treatment. From 1809 until 1828 the condition of the Khoikhoi deteriorated, despite several governmental attempts, inspired by missionary complaints, to reverse the trend.

Conditions changed only after the celebrated missionary, John Philip, gave the Khoikhoi scandal a complete airing in the press and Parliament. Philip's researches and revelations finally persuaded the Cape government to take effective action, and on July 17, 1828, it issued the celebrated Fiftieth Ordinance. The ordinance took precedence over all previous legislation and gave the Khoikhoi all but complete equality with whites in terms of service, treatment, mobility, landownership, and litigation.

The suffering of the Khoikhoi did not end overnight, however, and during Sir Lowry Cole's governorship an attempt was made to restore the former regime. The Draft Vagrancy Law, passed by the Cape Legislative Council in 1834, would have restored the old restrictions on Khoikhoi movement and placed them once again at the mercy of the local farmers, but the Legislative Council had not bargained on the reaction of His Majesty's Government. The commencement of the Great Reform Era in England ushered in a new dispensation in the colonies as well. The disciples of reform and evangelical humanitarianism believed that they had discovered the secret of enlightened government, that governments could, and should, intervene where before they had not, and they were determined to govern the colonies according to the new principles, which included equal justice for the native populations. The Vagrancy Law was therefore disallowed by Lord Aberdeen in March 1835. The outraged farmers began to trek out of the colony in mass, and from this time forward the lot of the Khoikhoi gradually improved, and the "Hottentot problem" ceased to plague Cape politics until it was revived by the nationalists after World War II.

At the moment when the disallowance of the Vagrancy Law caused the proliferation of South Africa's frontier problems by precipitating the Great Trek, aborigines protection was becoming a tenet of British colonial policy. It had only a marginal effect on Xhosaland where troublesome farmers and warriors made life miserable for the magistrates. Its chief influence was felt within the colony, where colonists could be more easily controlled, and in Natal, which was sufficiently distant to evoke British idealism.

THE LEAPFROG TO NATAL

Far along the coast, beyond the Xhosas and the Transkei tribes, lay Natal, a land greatly disturbed by the depredations of the great Zulu king, Shaka. British traders nonetheless had been drifting in and settling at Port Natal since the 1820s, and in 1836 the leading settler, Captain Allan Gardiner, petitioned Governor D'Urban to recognize the environs of the Port as the District of Victoria. D'Urban was supportive, but the petition was lost in London. Meanwhile the Trekboers had marched over the Drakensberg into the interior of Natal under Piet Retief and had reached an agreement with Shaka's successor, Dingane. By 1837 Natal consisted of approximately a hundred English settlers at the Port, an indeterminate number of Boers inland, and perhaps ten thousand Africans, most of whom were either Zulu refugees from Dingane's despotism or remnants of tribes decimated by the Zulu and who had placed themselves under a precarious European protection.

As of 1837 Dingane claimed for the Zulu all of the territory as far as the Mzimvubu River—about half of the modern Transkei—and those Europeans who lived in Natal were there at Dingane's sufferance. Retief's agreement with the chief proved to be valueless because the defeat of the Ndebele by Andries Potgieter and Pieter Uys at the Marico River in November 1837 alarmed Dingane who determined to rid himself of the white threat. Luring Retief into his kraal on the pretense of treaty making, he slaughtered the entire party and simultaneously launched an all-out offensive against the whites in Natal. During February and March 1838 the Zulu armies laid waste to the country and in April occupied and destroyed the Port, from which all the Europeans had fled. In May the remaining Boers under Potgieter withdrew beyond the Drakensberg, while Dingane, having achieved his ends, pulled back beyond the Tukela.

The departing Boers, however, were almost immediately replaced by new arrivals. By June there were again about 650 male Europeans in Natal, and more trickled in during the remainder of the year. Dingane attacked their camps in August but this time had to withdraw with heavy losses. By December a commando nearly five hundred strong under Andries Pretorius was ready to take action against the Zulu, and on December 16 it encountered Dingane's army of ten thousand near a small tributary of the Tukela. In a sharp, three-hour battle three thousand Zulu were killed with no loss of life on the Boer side, a carnage that so discolored the adjacent stream that it was rechristened the Blood River. "Dingane's Day" encouraged the Boers to renew their settlement of Natal, and they now hastened to organize a republic before the British could intervene.

The Abortive Occupation

The British meanwhile were expressing concern over these developments, and at this time all their sympathies were on the side of the Zulu. The new Governor of the Cape Colony, Sir George Napier, viewed the line of Trekboers that arched through Transorangia and down into Natal as a burning fuse that at any moment and at any point could ignite another frontier war. Stockenstrom had warned him in March 1838 that a small British detachment should be dispatched to Natal "before the emigrants gain a permanent footing there, and embroil themselves with the natives,—a collision which, once begun, can only end in extermination."[7] Napier forwarded this with his endorsement to Glenelg and by May was himself advocating the occupation of Port Natal as the only effective way "to protect the natives . . . from extermination or slavery by the Boers who are already there and commencing a war with Dingaan, which, end as it may, must be the cause of great slaughter and bloodshed."[8]

Glenelg found himself in a dilemma. The least expansionist and most philanthropic of Colonial Secretaries, he was torn between limiting British sovereignty and putting a stop to the aggressions of the Boers and their continued practice of bonded labor, word of which reached his desk from Stockenstrom and Napier in the form of highly colored and disturbing missionary reports. Responding to the dispatch of March, he instructed Napier in May to issue a stern warning to the Boers:

It is important that the natives should be aware that Her Majesty's Government are determined to discountenance and punish by all lawful means the acts of aggression and plunder which, there is too much reason to believe, it is the practice of the emigrants to perpetrate; and the latter must be made to understand that such is the determination of your Government.[9]

Further reports that emigrant farmers were forcibly carrying off apprentices and former slaves[10] overcame his distaste for a forward policy to the extent that he authorized a small detachment of troops, if necessary, on the understanding that there was no intention on the part of Her Majesty's Government to occupy the Port permanently.[11]

Although not insensitive to the philanthropic impulse, Napier, like most other British governors who had to deal with trouble on the spot, was less affected by concern for the aborigines than for peace and order on the frontiers.[12] The raids mounted by the emigrant Boers in Natal against their cattle-lifting neighbors drove refugees southwestward and in turn disrupted the peace of the eastern frontier. His answer to the problem of cattle lifting and other frontier disturbances, however, was not the commando system, which had been prohibited by the Colonial Office in 1833, but to mediate between the contending parties and to try to protect each party against the marauding of the other.[13] In September he prohibited the export of arms and munitions to Natal.[14] In October he sent Field Cornet Gideon Joubert with a stern warning to the emigrating farmers to return all former slaves taken with them:

You will also impress upon their minds that the Government is still inclined to do all that is possible to prevent the emigrants becoming the victims of the inland tribes by whom they are surrounded; while the same Government will certainly not suffer to go unpunished any acts of violence or assault on the part of the emigrants upon the aborigines or their possessions. In short, you will assure them that Government is animated with the most friendly affection towards the aborigines, and that it is the most ardent wish of Government to preserve peace between the sons of Africa, of whatever order or condition they may be.[15]

At the same time Napier informed his chief that he expected to send off the troops within three weeks, adding that since the emigrants could not be forcibly returned to the colony, or be allowed to establish an independent government at Port Natal, or be driven back into the interior where they would either exterminate the Africans or be exterminated themselves, the only feasible alternative appeared to be the establishment of British sovereignty over Port Natal under a lieutenant-governor.[16] On November 14 Napier proclaimed the Port seized in the name of Her Majesty's Government, and on November 20 a company of the Seventy-second Highlanders and some artillery sailed from Cape Town under orders to confiscate all the arms and ammunition they could find to prevent it from falling into the hands of the Boers and to order the Boers not to cross the Tukela again to attack the Zulu.

Glenelg belatedly authorized the occupation of the Port in January 1839 after Stockenstrom, home on leave, had written him that the occupation would be "the first step towards further arrangements for arresting a system of encroachments, usurpation, oppression, and bloodshed, which, though familiar in the history of South Africa, was even there unparalleled in atrocity and extent."[17] Glenelg's successor, Lord Normanby, confirmed it in April, strictly for purposes of cutting off ammunition supplies and checking emigration from the Cape and on condition that it was not to be construed as an extension of British sovereignty.

The year 1839 was relatively quiet in South Africa. The British occupation of Port Natal may have had a damping effect on the warlike enthusiasms of Boer and Zulu, but a more effective truce arose out of the realities of power as they now existed. Blood River had dealt a serious blow to Dingane and had encouraged the Boers to establish the first of their trekker republics. Fixing their capital at Pietermaritzburg, they elected a landdrost (chief judicial officer) and assembled their Volksraad, or legislature, pointedly ignoring the small band of Highlanders stationed at Port Natal. The sole function that the British commander, Captain Jervis, was able to perform was to mediate between the defeated Zulu and the victorious Boers. In May Dingane agreed to return the guns and horses he had captured, to relinquish a large herd of cattle as indemnity, and to cede to the new republic the southern half of Zululand, including, unbeknown to Captain Jervis, St. Lucia Bay. In September Dingane was ousted by his brother, Mpande (1838-1872), and in October the new chief signed a treaty with the Republic in which he accepted status as a vassal chief in return for Boer assistance against his brother, who was still at large. The submission of the Zulu quieted affairs in Natal to the extent that Napier felt there was no further point in keeping a costly garrison at the Port, and it was withdrawn in December.

Change of Heart, 1839-1842

No sooner had the troops departed, however, than the Boers sent a large commando to assist in Mpande's destruction of Dingane. The two armies met on January 30, 1840, at Magongo where two-thirds of Dingane's forces were annihilated and the rest deserted to the enemy. The slaughter of Zulu on both sides was so enormous, however, that in conjunction with Blood River, Magongo put an end to Zulu aggressive power for many years to come. On February 10 the Volksraad recognized Mpande as King of the Zulu, while the chief in turn confirmed the cession of southern Zululand to the republic and his status as a vassal chief in charge of Zulu administration in the ceded territory.

In September the new republic formally requested British recognition of its independence, but by this time the attitude of the Colonial Office had undergone a change. Lord John Russell, who had replaced Normanby in September 1839, was far more sympathetic to intervention. Disturbed by the independent line of the Boers, he had already instructed Napier in December 1839 to maintain the occupation of Port Natal or some other strategic location nearby, unaware that Napier had already withdrawn the troops.

Another factor now appeared to reinforce his inclinations. In April 1840, at a time when steam navigation was much on people's minds, reports of high-quality coal in Natal began to appear in the Colonial Office along with memoranda by James Stephen and others to the effect that it might become a useful coaling station on the route to India. The possibility that such a station might come under foreign domination unless it were preempted by Britain seemed not unlikely, since Dutch, American, and other vessels were appearing with rising frequency on the southeast coast. With both commercial and strategic possibilities in mind, Russell was now more than ever inclined to intervene, on condition that no flagrant injustice be done to the Africans and that the new colony pay its own expenses. When he learned in June 1840 that Napier had actually withdrawn the garrison, he immediately instructed the Governor to reoccupy the Port.[18]

Despite these developments, neither trade nor strategy seems to have been foremost in British thinking about Natal in these years when paramountcy was being achieved. D'Urban, presented with a merchants' petition in 1834 urging annexation of the Port, had rejected it as too costly,[19] and Napier does not seem to have noticed any trade potential in Natal. Russell himself, while undoubtedly mindful of its commercial and strategic potential, was probably influenced more by other factors.[20] There is more evidence to suggest that protection of the aborigines continued to be the principal British objective on the frontiers of the Cape Colony, and this brings us to the Ncaphayi affair and the Zulu resettlement project.

Napier had not obeyed Russell's instructions of December 1839 because all the troops he could move were then guarding the Xhosa frontier, and he could not foresee reoccupying the Port without a fight, the Boers having planted the flag after the British departure. He was delighted, however, to be supported at last by a Colonial Secretary who understood the realities as he saw them himself, and he could now prepare to act in Natal when the opportune moment arrived.

The Natalians provided that opportunity. By now they were reviving the old regime of pass laws, forced labor, and cattle-recovering commandos, which the British had so recently suppressed in territories under their jurisdiction. The precipitating event was the Ncaphayi affair. In September 1840 some seven hundred head of cattle and fifty horses were stolen from Natal and traced to the kraals of the Bhaca chief Ncaphayi across the Mzimkulu River. A commando organized in December attacked Ncaphayi by surprise, made off with three thousand cattle and seventeen apprentices and killed about forty Bhaca in the process. Ncaphayi's neighbor, the Mpondo Chief Faku, appealed to Napier for protection, while missionaries in the area protested the brutal reprisal, asserting incorrectly that it was "wanton and unprovoked." Napier's reaction was that the Boers were imperiling the stability of the frontier by increasing the pressure of the Xhosa on the Cape Colony. He now had all the excuse he needed, and acting on Russell's instructions of June, which he had now received, he dispatched Captain Thomas C. Smith in January 1841 with two companies of the Twenty-seventh Regiment and some Cape Mounted Rifles and artillery overland from Fort Peddie to camp on the Mgazi River, technically within the boundaries claimed by the Republic of Natal. He also wrote Russell for further instructions. When the Volksraad protested that the expedition was uncalled for because no harm was meant to the Mpondo, Napier ignored them until June 10 when he replied that he could not communicate or negotiate with them unless they acknowledged their allegiance to the Queen and agreed to submit to British authority.

This impasse might have been maintained indefinitely had the Volksraad not decided in August to settle some Zulu refugees on land just north of the Mzimvubu River in Mpondo territory. This would crowd the Xhosa frontier all the more and in Napier's view was to be avoided. By now Napier had received Russell's letter of April:

If . . . any of the Kafir tribes which are threatened by the emigrant farmers should offer to place themselves under the Queen's protection, you are authorized to promise it to them, but not to annex their territory to the colony under your government. It will be proper in that case to send a special agent to reside at the chief seat of the Kafirs to whom you shall have promised Her Majesty's protection.

It will be your policy to draw closer the connection between the colony and the Kafir tribes: to influence the latter by means of the missionaries and resident agents, and to punish any colonist who may do them injury, so that they may look up to the British power as their friend and protector.[21]

Acting on this and on the earlier instruction to reoccupy, Napier announced to the Boers on December 2 that the Africans "were established at Port Natal long previous to its occupation by the Emigrant Farmers . . . and living at peace with all of Her Majesty's Subjects" and that this "unjust and illegal proceeding" (the Zulu resettlement plan) was very likely to occasion "warfare and bloodshed.'' The Boer declaration of independence was proclaimed null and void, Port Natal was to be reoccupied, and anyone who tried to prevent it would place himself beyond the law.[22] Reinforcements were sent to the camp on the Mgazi, and Captain Smith set out with some 250 troops and three artillery pieces to occupy Port Natal, under orders to treat the Boers courteously but to refer to them constantly as Her Majesty's subjects and to keep peace between the Boers and Africans. Justifying his actions to Russell, Napier wrote on December 6 that the resettlement project, if allowed to proceed, would have disrupted an already congested frontier and that the Natalians were too disunited to form a stable government capable of dealing equitably with the Africans.[23]

Smith reached the Port on May 4, lowered the Republican flag, and hoisted the Union Jack. When Pretorius's repeated protests were ignored, a Boer commando of about six hundred men invested Smith's makeshift fort, not very effectively, until June 26 when they were routed by the guns of the frigate *Southampton* and a small British landing party under Colonel A. J. Cloete. The Boers quickly broke camp and either dispersed or returned to Pieter-maritzburg, the militant hard-liners under the Jan Mocke returning in disgust to their homes beyond the Drakensberg. Such unity as the Boers had displayed now broke down. After a stormy session the Volksraad invited Colonel Cloete to Pietermaritzburg under safe conduct to present his terms. These included submission to the Queen's authority, in return for a general amnesty for all the Boers who had been under arms, and the assurance that the British had no intention of interfering with Republican administration or civil institutions until a final settlement could be negotiated with the British government. The terms were accepted on July 14, and on July 21 Cloete embarked on the *Southampton* with most of the troops, leaving only 361 officers and men at Port Natal under the command of Smith, now promoted to Major.

Decision to Annex, 1841-1845

By now Napier had decided that annexation was the only solution to the turmoil in Natal, and when he wrote the Colonial Office in December 1841 that he had ordered Captain Smith to reoccupy the Port, he requested authority to annex it. Russell's successor,

Lord Stanley, was not convinced. He believed no more than his predecessors that the commercial prospects justified annexation, nor was he apparently much concerned about rumors of French or Dutch intervention on behalf of the Boers.[24] He was, in fact, decidedly opposed to intervention and not the least impressed by Napier's assurance that Smith had been instructed to avoid "any interference with the internal arrangements of the Emigrant Farmers, unless the Troops, or the Colonists, or the Native Tribes are attacked."[25] Replying on April 10, 1842, Stanley instructed Napier to withdraw Smith's force on the grounds that the government was already hard pressed financially and wished to avoid any further costly adventures, which the administration of Natal would surely be. But he was not sure of his ground because to some extent he had been moved by the reports of African mistreatment, which came to him in official dispatches and from the Aborigines Protection Society.[26] His instructions of April 10 opened with a lengthy policy statement on the subject:

I cannot but infer that you were mainly influenced in your decision [to occupy the Port] . . . by the apparent necessity of meeting in some way the embarrassment occasioned by the emigration of the Dutch Colonists to the vicinity of Port Natal. I understand you consider the colonization of that country not as in itself a desirable measure [Stanley had just described it as worthless], but as desirable because affording the best, or rather the only, remedy against an evil in which it is impossible any longer to acquiesce in [sic] . . .

H.M.[S] Govt. are fully impressed with the magnitude of the mischiefs which have arisen, and which are likely to result from the emigration of the Dutch Colonists to the neighborhood of Port Natal, and from their settlement there . . . nor can they regard without lively indignation the slaughter and oppressions to which, in the prosecution of their enterprise they have subjected the native tribes. If your apprehensions should be realized and the tribes with whom we have made Treaties should become the victims of the injustice of the Emigrants, it would not be enough to lament the evil. We must in that case take active measures for the redress or the prevention of it.

With this in view it is necessary that you should . . . inform them that H.M.[S] Govt. regard as altogether inadmissable . . . the pretention they make to be regarded as an independent State . . . and that if they should presume to molest, invade or injure the Caffre tribes with which Her M. is in alliance, H.M.[S] Forces will support these tribes in resisting such aggressions, and that any of the emigrants who might be found in arms against the Forces of their Sovereign, whether beyond or within the Precincts of the Colony, would be regarded by the Queen as Rebels, and would be liable to be dealt with accordingly.

The only "active measures" he was prepared to endorse, however, were to place an embargo on the Boers' trade with the Cape Colony and to deny them access to the seaports along the eastern coast.[27]

Against these unsatisfactory instructions Napier protested vehemently, arguing that withdrawal of the expedition would precipitate the evils Stanley sought to avoid. He reiterated his arguments for annexation and assured Stanley that occupying Port Natal and annexing the whole coast between the Mzimkulu and Tukela was the only way to interdict the supply of arms to rebellious Boers and the only way to forestall warfare between the emigrant farmers and the blacks.[28]

Meanwhile Captain Smith's control over the farmers was somewhat precarious and depended largely on their acquiescence. Napier decided to ignore Stanley's order and replied to Smith's anxious communiqués that he should sit tight, keep the peace, and feign unawareness of any Boer republic until Napier could get more satisfactory instructions from home. Smith was to

adopt towards the people every conciliation consistent with the dignity of the British Government, but at the same time accord them no official sanction or recognition as an independent people. . . .

The Volksraad and other administrative institutions are to remain uninterfered with so long as no flagrant outrage on justice is committed. The people . . . are to be protected against the assaults and aggressions of the Natives, while on the other hand, no commandos are to be permitted to go against them without your consent and cooperation.[29]

In London receipt of Napier's urgings and the reports of the fighting of May and June confronted Stanley with the alternatives of annexation or the recognition of Boer sovereignty, the undoubted consequences of the latter being endless strife between Boers and Africans unrestrained by British jurisdiction. In October he wrote Napier that he was half-persuaded, that he approved of the temporary occupation of the Port, and would sound the cabinet about annexation. By December he had reluctantly decided that annexation would be less costly in the end and so instructed Napier, but the terms of government were to be very carefully drawn. Adherence to abstract British forms of government was less important than the "contentment of the Emigrants." A special commissioner was to be sent to Natal to ask the Boers what sort of arrangement they would accept under the umbrella of British rule. The Boers were to understand, however, that British sovereignty prevailed, and all revenues were to be under British control. The Commissioner was to insist on three further conditions: no distinctions or disqualifications under law were to be made for differences of "color, origin, language, or creed"; "no aggression shall be sanctioned upon the Natives residing beyond the limits of the Colony, under any plea whatever"; and "slavery, in any shape . . . is absolutely unlawful."[30] As eager as the British were to mollify the Natal Boers and to prevent further trekking, they would not have insisted on these conditions, which were known to be unacceptable to the majority of the emigrants, unless they meant to enforce them.

Receiving Stanley's dispatch on April 23, 1843, Napier proclaimed the Queen's sovereignty on May 12 and selected as first Commissioner of Natal Henry Cloete (brother of the colonel), a well-respected Boer who understood and sympathized with the problems of both African and emigrant farmer. Judge Cloete disembarked at Port Natal on June 5 and proceeded immediately to Pietermaritzburg where he read Napier's proclamation on June 9 to a hostile and disrespectful audience. In the long run, however, the majority of Natalians were disposed to submit to British rule despite the encouragement to resist by large numbers of their compatriots from north of the Drakensberg who had arrived under Jan Mocke for the August meeting of the Volksraad. The speech of Andries Pretorius reflected the mood of the majority:

Every reasonable person must ask himself if a continuation of hostilities does not mean self-destruction. . . . Thousands of hostile natives have penetrated among us. What is to become of our families while we fight the English? Then too our supply of ammunition has been cut off. What chances do we stand against the English and the Zulus?[31]

In this mood the Volksraad sent a deputation to Cloete on the afternoon of August 18 accepting the Queen's sovereignty on condition that British insistence on absolute equality for colored people be modified. Cloete refused the condition and the Volksraad gave way. Next day Mocke and his militants again marched back over the Drakensberg thoroughly embittered by the pusillanimity of the Natalians. On August 31 Major Smith occupied a hill west of Pietermaritzburg with two hundred men and two guns, and on September 28 Napier proclaimed Natal a Crown Colony.

The submission of the Boers did not mean that they intended to remain forever under British rule. Some swore allegiance to the Queen, and others started almost immediately to trek northward into Transorangia and the Transvaal. It was not British rule that drove all of them out. A factor equally important was the tidal wave of Zulu refugees, eventually almost one hundred thousand, mentioned in Pretorius's speech. Engulfing Natal in the early 1840s as they escaped from the wrath of Mpande, they stole, pillaged, and burned, despite the preventive measures taken by British troops, and made so many Boer farms untenable that the farmers trekked in droves, having less faith in British troops than in their own, now-prohibited commandos.

Negotiations for replacing the Republican institutions with a settled British government dragged on for two more years, not because the British were powerless to dictate terms but because they wished to arrive at an arrangement as acceptable as possible to the Boers in order to forestall any further trekking. They failed. Ultimately only sixty Boer families remained in Natal, which became the most British of the South African colonies. As Potgieter bitterly observed, since the English were masters of the sea, it was inevitable that they would control all the seacoast.

Paramountcy in Natal

It seems clear that British paramountcy over Natal was effective at a moment somewhat before the formal annexation of September 1843. That moment would appear to be June 26, 1842, when the landing of a small British force under Colonel Cloete raised the siege of Port Natal and dispersed a Boer commando at least twice its size. Mentioning this episode in a letter to Napier of December 13, 1842, Stanley referred to "the supremacy of the British Crown having been established."[32]

The temporary occupation of Port Natal in 1839 did not infringe significantly on Boer sovereignty because the republicans continued to conduct their affairs as usual, and their momentary peace with the Zulu was more the result of local conditions than of pressure exerted by the British at the Port. Before June 1842, then, the Natalian Boers had behaved as they wished toward their Bantu neighbors and among themselves. After that date they repeatedly acquiesced in the various British maneuvers designed to control their relations with the Africans.

NATAL'S NEIGHBORS: THE TRANSKEI AND ZULULAND

The fate of the Transkei lands was a function of events in Natal. Between the Kei and the Mzimkulu, which eventually became the southern boundary of Natal, lay tribes of which the Mfengu, Thembu, and Mpondo were the foremost. None of them ever seriously contested the encroachment of Europeans on their borders. Their warriors shamelessly lifted cattle from the frontier settlements, but with the exception of some so-called emigrant Thembu, they did not go to war with the British; indeed they occasionally fought as British allies against their traditional enemies, the Xhosa. The major British concern in their regard was that they refrain from their endless internecine warfare, which disturbed the whole frontier by driving their neighbors down onto the Colony.

Prior to the Trekboer occupation of Natal there was little European, other than missionary, contact with these people and certainly no attempt by the British to establish a paramountcy. But the occupation of Natal cast a new light on the Transkei. By the 1830s philanthropy was running strong in English hearts and the Boer treatment of their Bantu neighbors was correspondingly deplored. For this reason Napier sent Captain Smith in January 1841 to camp on the Mgazi River in response to Faku's appeal for protection against threatening Boer commandos.

Faku's call for help and Captain Smith's year-long encampment in Pondoland marks the establishment of British paramountcy in the Transkei, and the achievement of British control over Natal in 1842 merely confirmed it. Thereafter any threat to British interests on the frontiers of the Colony or Natal was sure to bring British intervention. In 1843 Faku was forced to agree to submit all disputes with neighboring tribes to British arbitration, and while the British sometimes refrained from intervention, there is no question that they had the ready power to do so and that the tribes between the Kei and Mzimkulu knew it. Accordingly British paramountcy in the Transkei was established but a moment before that in Natal and for the same reasons.

Beyond Natal, from the Tukela River to the borders of Portuguese Mozambique, the coastal lands remained independent until the annexation of Zululand in 1887. The question arises whether British paramountcy can be said to exist beyond the Tukela before that date. Without question it existed in 1879. The opening battle of the Zulu War, Isandhlwana, dealt a blow to British prestige, but it was only a technical defeat for the British and it was a Pyrrhic victory for Cetshwayo because the Zulu lost three thousand of their best troops. The rest of the war went entirely in favor of the British, and the battle of Ulundi, only five months after Isandhlwana, broke Zulu power forever. Ulundi, and Wolseley's subsequent division of Zululand into thirteen districts, each under a British Resident, were unmistakable signs of British paramountcy.

Zulu power had been destroyed once before, however—forty years earlier at Magongo—and Mpande had become the vassal, first of the Republic of Natal and then, briefly, of the British government. The latter had occurred in October 1843 when Mpande, recalling Dingane's fate, had agreed to cede the Klip River area to Natal, to renounce all authority over Zulu living in Natal, and to cede the shores of St. Lucia Bay to the Queen that the British might cut off the Transvaal's access to ammunition from abroad. Two years later the British formally abandoned their claims of suzerainty beyond the Tukela and Buffalo rivers and left their claim to St. Lucia Bay in abeyance for forty years, but they retained the Klip River district, and on two occasions in the 1860s they momentarily revived the St. Lucia Bay claim to forestall control of the bay by the Transvaal. During this period Mpande carefully avoided war with the whites, consolidated and strengthened Zulu government, and bequeathed to Cetshwayo a once more viable Zulu state.

Cetshwayo himself tried to preserve peace after his accession in 1872, but he was struggling against the natural inclinations of the Zulu army, once again nearly fifty thousand strong. Chafing under Cetshwayo's restraining hand, the younger regiments sought occasions to qualify for marriage by "washing their spears" in the blood of their traditional enemies. Frustrated by their own king and by the refusal of Theophilus Shepstone, Lieutenant-Governor of Natal, to allow them even "one small swoop" against the Swazi, the Zulu army did in fact constitute a dangerously unstable element in the peace of the frontier and a challenge to British paramountcy. One can argue, however, that it did not override that paramountcy, if only for the reason that when the confrontation came the Zulu forces collapsed in short order.

British paramountcy over Zululand is a somewhat peripheral question for this study. The key to that paramountcy was the British establishment in Natal in 1842. From that moment onward, paramountcy over the Zulu was implicit in the obvious power differential, and the crushing finality of the Zulu defeat in 1879 simply confirmed its preexistence. If the foregoing argument is convincing, we can conclude that British paramountcy over Zululand was established about the same time as in Natal and for the same reasons that prevailed there.

SUMMARY OF MOTIVES

Trade, especially in the early years, was a larger factor in South African expansion than has generally been recognized. The Cape was indispensable as a port of call on the route to India, which was significant primarily as a trade route. From the beginning of the British occupation, the internal trade not only served the passing traffic but was vital to the Colony itself. During the 1820s and 1830s the Xhosa were regarded as troublesome by the government primarily because they disrupted the frontier trade, upon which the Colony depended, and made life difficult for administrators. Except among the missionaries they evoked little of the philanthropic sentiment displayed a few years later in Natal. Good government was the main consideration here, for the purpose of raising a protective umbrella over the frontier trade. Although officials deplored the settlers' commando raids, their chief concern was to prevent the cattle-lifting incursions of the Xhosa, which were seen as the source of the trouble.

It was otherwise in Natal where the Boers were regarded as the main problem. There can be little doubt that the common goal of Russell, Stanley, and Napier was to install the type of government in Natal that would serve the welfare of Boer and Bantu alike while curbing their mutual aggressions. They all would have preferred to leave the Boers self-governing had they been able to maintain a just order, which they demonstrably could not. Many of the Boers themselves admitted that their short experiment in self-government was a failure from every point of view: a failure in leadership, a failure in native policy, and an economic and financial failure.[33]

The evidence seems to say that the joint purpose behind the achievement of British paramountcy in Natal and the adjacent parts of Kaffraria and Zululand was the protection of the aborigines and the establishment of a government that would achieve that end and maintain peace. All of the officials involved were prodded into action by a succession of events that thwarted those ends: the slaughter at Blood River, the commando raids on Pondoland, the Zulu resettlement plan, and the continuing reports of slavery and forced labor among the emigrant farmers. Napier sought to impose restraints upon the Boers whose inability either to govern or restrain themselves kept the frontier in turmoil, and Faku's appeal for help, the allegations of slavery in Natal, and the missionary accounts of the Ncaphayi affair justified this view and persuaded Russell and Stanley as well.[34]

If Britain's purpose had been to keep the Boers landlocked in order to prevent their contact or alliance with other European powers, Napier would not have withdrawn the garrison in December 1839, nor would Stanley have ordered a new withdrawal in April 1842. The fear of foreign intervention and the commercial potential of coal deposits may have been contributing factors, but they appear to have carried less weight than the condition of society and government within Natal itself, shaped in these years principally by the Great Trek.[35] It was not foreign intervention in Natal that the British feared but Boer intervention. By thrusting large numbers of whites into the midst of Griqua and Bantu populations, the Trek aggravated all the existing frontier problems of South Africa at the very moment when the fervor for aborigines protection swept into British colonial policy. The Great Trek tied philanthropy to British expansion.

The occupation of Port Natal, accordingly, was largely for political reasons. It would keep the British settlers in line and by landlocking the Boers into economic dependence, it was hoped, would render them more amenable to the liberal policy that the British wished to prevail throughout South Africa. Given the administrative vacuum existing on the South African frontiers from 1815 to the 1840s—the Cape government could control the trekking Boers and English settlers no more than the American government could control its frontiersmen—the British government reluctantly but ineluctably moved in. By the 1840s when British officials and emigrant farmers met head on, good government had become the clear and present duty of the former, with Boer cooperation if possible, without it if necessary. Napier neatly summed up the official attitude in a letter to his brother on New Year's Day, 1843:

The Dutch Boers and Dutch colonists hate me because I am favorable to the colored races (all of whom I am happy to say like me and have often proved it) and will not allow them to injure them. And the English detest me because I will not let them have their own way, nor let them plunder the government by their extortions and cupidity.[36]

EPILOGUE: THE ROAD NORTH

The coast was the key to Britain's later domination of the rest of Southern Africa. Once the coast was under control and the Trekboers began to draw British bureaucrats into the Free State and the Transvaal, and the economic potential of Central Africa beckoned, nothing could stop British expansion until it came up against its European rivals in Central Africa.

The same motives can be seen operating in the Transvaal as had operated earlier in Natal. The successful efforts to quarantine the Transvaal from 1861 onward, while avoiding intervention in its unruly internal affairs, was motivated chiefly by the wish to prevent its turbulent politics from infecting the rest of South Africa. This was partly to protect the tribes who lived on its borders, partly to influence its treatment of its "own" natives, and partly to cater to the commercial ambitions of the "British party" at the Cape, which wanted to control the ports and monopolize the trade potential of Bechuanaland and Matabeleland. While not effectively imposing good government on the Transvaal, this policy at least helped to isolate bad government, and it was effective enough to constitute a form of paramountcy from 1861 until the century's end, despite momentary lapses.[37]

In Central Africa the conventional assumption has been that

British expansion resulted from the initiatives of Cecil Rhodes and associated European capitalists, and in some respects this is true. But an exhaustive recent study of South African gold mining finance by Robert Kubicek has shown that although a large amount of European finance capital was invested in South African mines, it did not control the mining enterprises, nor did these chaotic and competing companies successfully resist or manipulate the imperial factor there.[38] Although Kubicek deals primarily with the period after 1890 in the goldfields, he bears out my findings that in the Rhodesias and Nyasaland, the imperial factor and not European finance capital or Rhodes's group prevailed at the time paramountcy was being achieved: between August 1887 and July 1889.[39] And what drove the imperial factor?

Salisbury cordoned off Northern and Southern Rhodesia in 1887 to protect what promised to be a lucrative trading area, and he saw to it that imperial policy prevailed when Rhodes got his charter in 1889, in order to prevent the overriding of African rights and to ensure the preservation of free trade from Rhodes's monopolizing tendencies, as well as a minimum standard of good government. And when Salisbury warned Portugal off Nyasaland in the summer of 1887, he was acting to protect commercial and missionary enterprises on the lake. In Central Africa, therefore, the British continued to be moved, as they were earlier, by a mixture of commercial and philanthropic concerns and the felt need to impose a measure of justice and stability in its governance, although it can be said that the trading interest predominated in the Rhodesias, the missionary interest in Nyasaland.

NOTES

1. The narrative of this chapter is based primarily on the following sources: George M. Theal, *History of South Africa, 1795-1872*, 5 vols. (London, 1919-1927); John S. Galbraith, *Reluctant Empire: British Policy on the South African Frontier, 1834-1854* (Berkeley, Calif., 1963); S. Daniel Neumark, *Economic Influences on the South African Frontier, 1652-1836* (Stanford, 1957); John Bird, ed. *The Annals of Natal, 1495 to 1845*, 2 vols., (Pietermaritzburg, 1888; repr., Cape Town, C. Struik, 1965); Edgar H. Brookes and Colin deB. Webb, *A History of Natal* (Pietermaritzburg, 1965); Johannes Meintjes, *The Voortrekkers: The Story of the Great Trek and the Making of South Africa* (London, 1973); Alan F.

Hattersley, *The British Settlement of Natal: A Study in Imperial Migration* (Cambridge, 1950); Donald R. Morris, *The Washing of the Spears* (New York, 1965); Cornelius W. De Kiewiet, *A History of South Africa: Social and Economic*, 2d ed. (London, 1950).

The spelling of South African names generally follows the usage in Monica Wilson & L. Thompson, *The Oxford History of South Africa*, 2 v. (Oxford, 1969-71).

2. Neumark, *Economic Influences*, 59, 136-37, 165.

3. Ibid., 140-51.

4. Ibid., 58, 156-57. Theal, *History*, 2:38, 42-43.

5. Neumark, *Economic Influences*, 94, 106, 121.

6. Ibid., 113-14, quoting George M. Theal, (ed.), *Records of the Cape Colony* (London, 1897) 3:53.

7. Bird, *Annals of Natal*, 1:391.

8. Napier to Glenelg, May 18, 1838, in ibid., 397.

9. Glenelg to Napier, May 9, 1838, in ibid., 391-93.

10. Hattersley, *British Settlement*, 36.

11. Glenelg to Napier, June 8, 1838, in Bird, *Annals of Natal*, 1:399.

12. Galbraith, *Reluctant Empire*, 50; T. R. H. Davenport, *South Africa: A Modern History* (London, 1977), 86.

13. Galbraith, *Reluctant Empire*, 51.

14. Bird, *Annals of Natal*, 1:414.

15. Napier to Joubert, Oct. 16, 1838, in ibid., 417.

16. Napier to Glenelg, Oct. 16, 1838, in ibid., 420.

17. Theal, *History of South Africa*, 2:383-84.

18. Russell to Napier, June 18, 1840, in Bird, *Annals of Natal*, 1:605.

19. Hattersley, *British Settlement*, 15.

20. That coal deposits or cotton were reasons for the British acquisition of Natal, Davenport regards as improbable. Davenport, *South Africa*, 86.

21. Bird, *Annals of Natal*, 1:640.

22. Napier's proclamation, Dec. 2, 1841, in ibid., 658-60.

23. Napier to Russell, Dec. 6, 1841, cited by Hattersley, *British Settlement*, 48.

24. Galbraith, *Reluctant Empire*, 196.

25. Napier to Stanley, Feb. 4, 1842, C. O. 48/217, f. 382.

26. See, for example, the Aborigines Protection Society memorial of June 26, 1842, Derby Papers, 23/6.

27. Stanley to Napier, April 10, 1842, C.O. 49/34, pp. 359-65.

28. Napier to Stanley, July 25, 1842, in J. S. Bell and W. P. Morrell, eds., *Select Documents on British Colonial Policy, 1830-1860* (Oxford, 1928), 490-95.

29. Meintjes, *Voortrekkers*, 192-93.

30. Stanley to Napier, Dec. 13, 1842, C.O. 49/36, pp. 160-61.

31. Meintjes, *Voortrekkers*, 200.

32. Stanley to Napier, Dec. 13, 1842, C.O. 49/36, p. 145.

33. Brookes and Webb, *History of Natal*, 41.

34. John B. Wright agrees. See his *Bushman Raiders of the Drakensberg, 1840-1870* (Pietermaritzburg, 1971), 38.

35. This view is corroborated by David Welsh, *The Roots of Segregation: Native Policy in Colonial Natal, 1845-1910* (London, 1971), 9.

36. Sir George Napier to William Napier, Jan. 1, 1843, Napier Papers, B.M. Add. Ms. 49168, f. 44.

37. These are the conclusions I have drawn from a study of the Transvaal from 1836 to 1900 based on the Colonial Office papers, the Grey papers in Durham, and the standard documents collections and secondary sources.

38. Robert Kubicek, *Economic Imperialism in Theory and Practice: The Case of South African Gold Mining, 1886-1914* (Durham, N.C., 1979).

39. This conclusion and the remarks that follow are drawn from the Foreign Office, Colonial Office, and Cabinet papers, the Rhodes House Mss. and Salisbury papers, and the usual secondary sources. The period examined was from approximately 1870, when Lobengula came to power in Matabeleland, to 1899, when the Barotseland Order-in-Council created a mixed administration in Northwestern Rhodesia with authority vested in the Crown and patronage left in the hands of the Company.

During the three centuries before 1783, European enterprise on the West African coast was private and on a small scale. It was private (at least the British part was private) because the government was not interested in financing what appeared to be an unprofitable trade. It was on a small scale because the coast was fever ridden and, east of Cape Palmas, geographically forbidding, and companies found that the limited and irregular trade did not justify large-scale enterprise. This was so even with the slave trade, as well as with gold dust, pepper, ivory, and palm oil. It was mainly the small operator, cruising along the coast until he chanced upon a cargo, who found the trade profitable. Large companies, which had to maintain expensive factories, generally did not find it so, and the Company of Merchants Trading to Africa was no exception. (The Company of Merchants Trading to Africa had been chartered, as the Royal African Company, by Charles II in 1672 and administered the Gold Coast factories until 1821.) Because joint stock was not permitted and it was not allowed to operate on the West Coast in a corporate capacity, its members acted more or less independently as individual traders. Moreover, wherever Europeans did set up factories, they were almost entirely dependent on the goodwill of the local chiefs from whom they leased their stations, for Europeans owned little territory in Africa in this period.

In the three decades following 1783, however, three things happened, which changed dramatically European involvement in tropical Africa: the campaign to abolish the slave trade, the exploration of the interior with a view to legitimate trade, and the flowering of the religious missionary spirit. The first was led by Granville Sharpe and William Wilberforce who founded a joint stock company in 1787 to make a home for liberated slaves in Sierra Leone. The second took shape as the African Association in 1788 to pro-

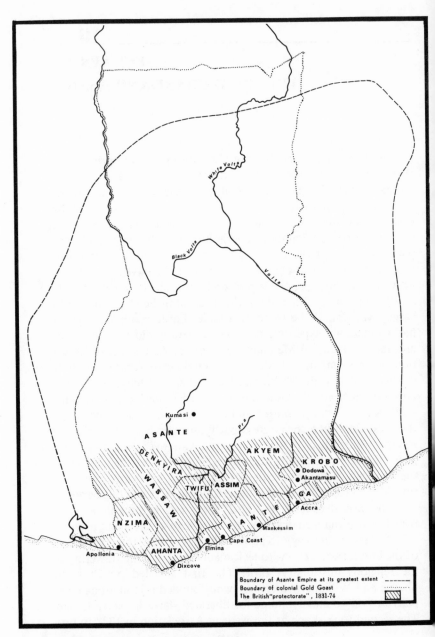

GOLD COAST, 1820s–1840s

mote both exploration and trade. The third was a kind of by-product of the antislavery movement. It was felt that Africans were degenerate because they were denied the benefit of the Gospel, and to correct this deficiency, the London Missionary Society was founded in 1795 and the Church Missionary Society in 1799. Little came of any of these developments until 1807 when the Slavery Abolition Act was passed and the British government decided to make Freetown in Sierra Leone the headquarters of the Preventive Squadron. The transfer of Sierra Leone from the Company to the Crown on January 1, 1808, opened a new era of increasing British intervention in West Africa. During the following half-century, the slave trade showed a disturbing durability despite the efforts of the Preventive Squadron, and British ministers displayed their growing concern by allowing themselves to be drawn into West African politics.

The Company continued as a collection of private merchants until 1821 when it was finally dissolved. Thereafter the merchants were on their own and just as happy to be so except for the occasional help they required from a reluctant government. One hundred and fifty years of British commercial activity had produced very little trade in fact. Flint estimates that as late as 1870 only about 10 percent of the produce of West Africa was involved in the European trade and that whatever expansion had taken place in palm oil and groundnut production for European sale was simply an increment over the basic commerce that these products already enjoyed in the domestic African economy. In the same way European imports before 1870 played a minor role in that economy; only alcoholic liquor, tobacco, guns and ammunition, small quantities of cotton cloth, and some iron agricultural tools were of any importance at all.[1] Nevertheless to a few European merchants this trade seemed to be worthwhile because it was growing rapidly and showed great promise. Between 1810 and 1860 palm oil exports from West Africa to Britain rose from a thousand tons to more than fifty thousand tons, and cotton yard goods imported by West Africa from Britain increased thirty-fold between 1816 and 1850.[2] Hence, by mid-century the prospects for the growth of this trade seemed decidedly good, and British statesmen began to think—in the 1850s on the Niger coast and a bit earlier on the Gold Coast—that perhaps the territory was worth protecting.

THE CONTEST FOR COASTAL SUZERAINTY, 1806-1830

There was no European paramountcy on the Gold Coast before 1826.[3] Prior to that year European traders lived along the coast on the sufferance of the Asante who exerted a form of suzerainty over the coastal Fante. The Europeans sought to develop trade with the interior, while the goals of the Asante, largely misunderstood by the British, were to keep the trade routes open and to gain direct access to the European factories by controlling their vassals who sought to play the role of middlemen. The Asante periodically invaded the coast to reassert their suzerainty, and after 1806 the British allied themselves with the Fante to resist, as well as to pursue a new British objective, the abolition of the slave trade, which the Asante found most lucrative.

As of 1820, however, the fortified European factories—British, Danish, and Dutch—were still the weakest of toeholds, and the surrounding country was entirely at the mercy of Asante war parties. Bowdich asserted in 1819 that Asante was "indisputably the greatest and the rising power of Western Africa,"[4] and while Bowdich proved to be no prophet, his assessment of the status quo was accurate. None of the forts could withstand a concerted attack. All had been forced to acknowledge Asante suzerainty over their coastal allies and to pay an annual rent for the land on which the forts were built.

These unsatisfactory conditions led to rising criticism of the Company's administration, and in 1821 an act of Parliament dissolved the Company and transferred its factories to the Crown. The new governor, Sir Charles MacCarthy, was as blind as his predecessors to the commercial objectives of Asante and, greeted by a chorus of Asantephobia on his arrival, determined that negotiations were pointless and began to prepare for war. To the Asantehene's sincere efforts to reach an accommodation, MacCarthy replied with studied insult and offense, until the Asantehene was faced with a choice of war or abdication.

Hostilities opened in January 1824 and for the first two and a half years the British had the worst of it. During the first seven months of 1826 the Asante ravaged the coast with impunity. August found them encamped north of Accra intending to punish its inhabitants for defecting to the British two years before. There, at the village of Akantamasu, they were met on August 7 by the British and their allies armed with Congreve rockets and were disastrously defeated in the "battle which decided the fate of the Gold Coast."⁵ Prior to this the Fante had not enjoyed a reputation for prowess in battle, but their steadfast performance at Akantamasu, stiffened by a detachment of British troops, did much to retrieve their reputation and to enhance British prestige as well. An immediate result of this victory was to transfer ownership of the land on which the forts stood to the British (and Danes) by right of conquest. Henceforth the British considered the notes held by the Asantehene as cancelled and ceased to pay tribute or to render gifts to that monarch. The upturn in British fortunes on the Gold Coast, which dates from the battle of Akantamasu, marks the beginning of the decline of the Asante empire and the first step in the substitution of British for Asante paramountcy.

Licking their wounded pride in Kumasi, the Asante did not sue for peace until 1827, and several months of diplomatic haggling delayed the opening of negotiations until December of that year. Not until 1831 were the peace terms ultimately ratified, but by the end of 1827 the Asante had agreed to provisions that implicitly acknowledged the superior authority of the British. Asante would abandon its suzerainty over Denkyira, Akyem, Assin, and other coastal vassals who were now to come under British protection, while all parties agreed to submit all "palavers" to arbitration by the British Governor. The Asante promised to keep the trade routes open and to forgo panyarring,⁶ and they agreed to deposit at Cape Coast for a period of six years, as an earnest of their good behavior, an undetermined amount of gold, as well as two young hostages of the royal family. Acquiescence to such far-reaching changes in the political hierarchy of the Gold Coast marked another long step in the achievement of British paramountcy.

Yet on the threshold of success, the British government discarded the fruits of its victory. By the mid-1820s many of those who had promoted West African enterprise, especially the missionaries and philanthropists and many members of Parliament as well, had become disillusioned with the results. Legitimate trade had not developed as expected. It was estimated that the sum total of British manufactures shipped to the Gold Coast between 1822 and 1826 was a meager £108,560.[7] Moreover, the slave trade in 1825 was more active than ever despite the efforts of the Preventive Squadron, and West Africans had displayed a remarkable apathy about being converted and "civilized." When to the depression at home and the need to retrench was added the recent Asante war and its attendant destruction of trade, the costly and profitless forts on the Gold Coast began to look very unattractive indeed. By April 1826, apparently—that is, before the battle of Akantamasu—the British government had already decided to jettison its difficult African allies and withdraw from the Gold Coast forts.

So vehement was the outcry of the merchants and the Fantes, at the prospect of being deserted by the government, however, that the withdrawal was delayed for over two years and a compromise reached that permitted the merchants to remain in occupation of two of the forts (Accra and Cape Coast), to appoint their own administration subject to the oversight of the British government, and to receive a small subsidy to cover administrative expenses. In October 1828 a Committee of London Merchants, unincorporated and unchartered, took possession of the forts from the departing government. The senior merchant on the coast, John Jackson, served as acting President until February 1830 when Captain George Maclean arrived to begin a memorable term of office.

THE MACLEAN ERA, 1830-1843

The attempt to end official control of the Gold Coast forts resulted not in any decline of British influence or jurisdiction but quite the opposite. For two years prior to Maclean's arrival the peace negotiations had foundered on the refusal of Elmina, an Asante ally, to submit to its Fante neighbors. Warfare among the coastal tribes continued, and trade was at a standstill. All parties, including the Asante, were eager for peace, but on their own terms. Maclean had little military power readily at hand, but by the sheer force of his personality and character he dominated the situation. Substituting firm dignity for the blustering and arrogance of his predecessors, mixing adroit and tactful diplomacy with warnings to the Fante to cooperate or be left to their own devices, and suggesting to the Asante that if necessary Britain could repeat the lesson of Akantamasu, he brought the peace negotiations to a successful conclusion in April 1831.

The Maclean Treaty, as it came to be known, formalized the provisions conditionally agreed to in December 1827.[8] By its most significant clauses, the Asantehene "renounced all right or title to any tribute or homage from the Kings of Dinkara, Assin, and others formerly his subjects" and agreed to submit all palavers to the decision of the British Governor or Commander of Cape Coast sitting with two or more chiefs as a council. These clauses were a clear acknowledgment of the supremacy of the British over the Asante and Fante. Henceforth the Asante writ ran only north of the Pra River.

Learning from the mistakes of his predecessors who had flagrantly ignored the treaties of 1816 and 1820, Maclean insisted on a scrupulous observance of his treaty, in spirit as well as in letter. The gold that was deposited at Cape Coast to guarantee the good behavior of the Asante was carefully returned in the same bags in which it had been sent from Kumasi six years earlier. Within a few years of his arrival Maclean had restored the prestige and credibility of Britain eroded by the folly of his predecessors. The Maclean Treaty governed Anglo-Asante relations for the next forty years until the Asante outburst of 1873. Peace did not always prevail in that period, it is true, but the treaty of 1831 served as the norm "on which the affairs of the Gold Coast should stand."[9]

Thereafter the exercise of British influence on the Gold Coast was a matter of consolidating rather than acquiring paramountcy. Maclean's success as a peacemaker was soon equaled by his reputation as an impartial judge. He consistently sought to resolve the palavers among the coastal tribes by persuasion and negotiation, since his military forces were severely limited, but on occasion he did call out and effectively use his small army to coerce recalcitrants. He insisted on even-handed justice and personally supervised not only the magistrates within the British forts but the courts of the coastal chiefs as well. By patient education he gradually eliminated the more barbaric aspects of African law and customs and won acceptance of some of the principles of British justice. Increasingly he was called upon to arbitrate disputes, and his judgments were rarely challenged. But however beneficent all this may have been, Maclean's acts were a definite encroachment on the sovereignty of the chiefs of the Gold Coast.

The effect of this regime on Gold Coast society was salutary. Its main purpose, and its main effect, was to create the peaceful conditions necessary for trade, and in this it was immensely successful, for the decline of hostilities and the rise of security caused trade to revive not only on the coast but in Asante as well. British traders and their agents traveled everywhere in complete security, even in Kumasi, and for the first time in its history, legitimate overseas trade on the Gold Coast became significant. Total imports and exports through Cape Coast alone grew from £221,000 in 1831 to £747,000 in 1840.[10]

Maclean also tried to assist the missionaries, and it was in his administration that the first mission schools were established in the Gold Coast. And although he did not attack domestic slavery, judging it to be too closely tied to the survival of African society (a judgment that eventually cost him his post), he did put an end to the external slave trade along that portion of the coast under his influence.

While Maclean's power must not be exaggerated, his influence was so pervasive that "from this time onwards we must recognize that a considerable area of country had accepted a position in a British sphere of influence."[11] The Select Committee's report of 1842 described that influence:

a kind of irregular jurisdiction has grown up extending itself far beyond the limits of the Forts by the voluntary submission of the Natives themselves, whether chiefs or traders, to British equity; and its decisions, owing to the moral influence, partly of our acknowledged power, and partly of the respect which has been inspired by the fairness with which it has been exercised by Captain Maclean and the Magistrates at the other Forts, have generally, we might say uniformly, been carried into effect without the interposition of force.[12]

The area over which this influence was exercised was bounded on the east by the Volta, extended westward beyond the Pra into Wassaw, Appolonia, and Dixcove (although there were Dutch and Danish enclaves all along), and reached inland as far as the Asante border. It might even be said to penetrate Asante as long as

Maclean held it to the terms of the treaty. In effect, during Maclean's time an informal, extralegal protectorate existed along three-fourths of the coast of modern Ghana. The Select Committee's report acknowledged that the coast peoples owed no formal allegiance to the Crown, nor should they, but as weaker powers they should defer to their "stronger and more enlightened neighbor, whose protection and counsel they seek, and to whom they are bound by certain definite obligations."[13] During Maclean's term of office, then, Britain became the dominant power on the Gold Coast, and British traders controlled the bulk of the trade.

How did Maclean accomplish this metamorphosis with his "miserable pittance of between £3500 and £4000 a year" and his "four ill-provided forts...manned by a few ill-paid black soldiers?"[14] He did it by patience and wisdom, uprightness and impartiality, and a genuine concern for the welfare of the people. Some have held that his influence was entirely the result of his moral stature and repute, implying that the chiefs could have thrown the British out at will if they had united. This may have been true hypothetically. But the chiefs were not united—they were very disunited and quarrelsome, which was their main problem—and Maclean parlayed his moral influence into actual physical supremacy by playing off one against the other. So highly valued was the stability and peace that Maclean brought to the coast that if one chief stepped out of line, others could be counted on to bring him back. Most critical in this respect was Maclean's reliance on the friendship of the new Asantehene, Kwaku Dua I (1834-1867), who, despite the agitation of the hawks in his court, succeeded in staying on friendly terms with the British until the last three years of his reign. Under these circumstances, Maclean could on occasion call out his tiny army of 120 men and use it effectively. The Asante and everyone else knew that if pressed too hard, the British could bring to bear much larger forces than Maclean had immediately at hand; that they could, if necessary, repeat Akantamasu.

The inevitable jealousies aroused by a forceful and successful personality led to criticism and even vicious slanders of Maclean's rule, including the report that he had turned a blind eye to the slave trade. These called forth two inquiries in 1841 and 1842, which ultimately exonerated Maclean but ended in the government's resumption of the Gold Coast forts in 1843.

REOCCUPATION AND PARAMOUNTCY

Governor H. W. Hill arrived in February 1844 with a threefold mandate: to render de jure Maclean's de facto administration of British justice, to replace the Council of Merchants and its committees by a proper British colonial government, and to promote trade and the diffusion of Western civilization.[15]

The initial results of the reoccupation were salutary. Maclean's private treaties were formalized in the "Bond" of 1844 and 1845 by which all the chiefs not in the Dutch or Danish spheres acknowledged British jurisdiction over the protection of property and individuals, the abolition of certain "barbarous customs" such as human sacrifice and panyarring, and the administration of criminal justice.[16] Under the Bond, the states of the Gold Coast constituted a loosely knit British protectorate, marking the advent of Britain's peculiar system of African "protectorates," as well as a forward imperial policy, however spasmodic it may have been for the next two decades.

Ultimately, however, the erosion of chiefly sovereignty, the attempts to impose a poll tax (1852-1862), the consolidation of territory by the acquisition of the Danish and Dutch forts (1850 and 1868), and a fleeting sentiment in London (1864-1865) to abandon the whole affair, which the Asante mistook for a sign of weakness, upset stability and caused rebellion among the Fante and increasing anxiety and restiveness among the Asante. In 1863 the Asante mounted the first of a series of attacks on the coast that kept the British on the defensive for ten years until Lord Kimberley decided to put a stop to the nuisance once and for all by carrying the war to Asante. The result was Garnet Wolseley's celebrated march to Kumasi, which administered the coup de grace to the Asante empire.

In retrospect can the acquisition of British paramountcy be dated precisely? The rapidity with which the Asante political and military organization collapsed in 1874 leads us to believe that Wolseley merely knocked apart a shell and that British paramountcy had been achieved long before. The actions of the government following the reoccupation of 1843 had served to consolidate paramountcy, but it seems likely that it existed even before that. It stemmed, in fact, from the British defeat of Asante in the war of 1824-1826 and from the subsequent acknowledgment of British supremacy by all parties in Maclean's treaty of 1831. Prior to that time, right up through the early stages of the war, the European settlements on the coast existed at the sufferance of the Asante. But the battle of Akantamasu changed all that. It was the turning point in Anglo-Asante relations, which marked the transfer of paramountcy from one to the other. Henceforth the Asante were able to disrupt the coast by brief invasions, when they caught the British unprepared, but they were never again able to enforce their former suzerainty over the coastal peoples who were coming increasingly under British protection.

It may have seemed that British paramountcy wavered when the government officially withdrew from the forts in 1828, but the essential agreement of the Asante and Fante alike to British arbitration as a condition of peace as early as December 1827, an agreement that was embodied in the Maclean Treaty along with other subordinating provisions, certifies that Britain paramountcy was an acknowledged fact by 1827. Thereafter it remained continuously in effect, even though vacillating British behavior deluded Africans at times into believing that they could reassert themselves against it. The official British withdrawal of 1828 did not dissolve it, for Maclean's influence not only maintained but augmented it. The Asante challenges or actual outbursts of the 1850s and 1860s were no more than that; they jeopardized but did not overturn that paramountcy. In conclusion it seems safe to say that British paramountcy was established sometime between the battle of Akantamasu (1826) and the official extension of the Bond in the mid-1840s.

MOTIVES

What motivated the British to take possession of the Gold Coast? In these early years they had no territorial ambitions there. Until the 1880s when the French and Germans began to move in, the British were content to let the various tribes govern themselves to the extent that they could preserve the peace, keep the trade paths open, and eschew the slave trade. Huskisson certainly felt this way during his brief tenure as Colonial Secretary. Having read all the papers on West Africa as a new arrival in the Colonial Office just as the negotiations for the Maclean Treaty were commencing at Cape Coast, he concluded that "we ought not to attempt to form Colonies and Settlements on the Coast of Africa ... and that our ... exertions ought to be limited to the measures necessary first for watching, and as much as possible preventing the Slave Trade and secondly for affording protection and facility to all innocent Commerce with the natives of Africa."[17]

His successor, Sir George Murray, was less interested in trade than in philanthropy. After Maclean had been on the coast for about six months, Murray was unwilling to approve the expense of reoccupying some of the abandoned coastal forts on Maclean's recommendation. If the merchants wished to occupy them at their own risk and expense for purposes of legitimate trade, they could do so, but if they refused to cooperate with the Preventive Squadron in checking the slave trade, the Secretary of State "would not hesitate to authorize the magistrates to claim possession of the abandoned forts."[18] For purposes of trade, then, the merchants could shift for themselves; the government would engage in imperialism only if its philanthropic activities were frustrated.

Maclean did not agree at first. In his early years he was the practical, unromantic representative of business interests whose primary objective, both before and after the Asante War of 1824-1826, was to establish free trade with the interior without the interference of the coastal tribes. At this time Maclean reflected the views of the resident merchants of Cape Coast who asserted in a letter to the Colonial Office in 1831 that "the establishment of the free intercourse was for above half a century the great object both of the Kings of Ashantee and of the late African Committee; but they were always foiled in it by the neighbouring chiefs."[19] These neighboring chiefs seemed to be the stumbling block at this time, and Maclean's strategy, because he was unwilling to sacrifice them to the Asante, was to organize them into a peaceful association and get them to compose their differences with Asante for the benefit of trade and prosperity.[20] Maclean's treaty of April 1831 with Asante had the same goal, and his strategy was highly successful.[21] From 1831 to 1840 the trade of Cape Coast trebled, largely because of the expanding export of palm oil. The other staples (gold, ivory, pepper, coffee, corn, and cam wood) fluctuated considerably, but the total picture was one of solid prosperity.[22]

By 1835, however, Maclean too was being moved by philanthropy, or perhaps by a vested interest in good government. In February of that year he mounted an expedition against King Kwehu Aka of Nzima to enforce the ban against human sacrifice and to put a stop to the kidnapping and robbing of strangers. The rules that Maclean laid down for the future good government of Nzima provided that human sacrifice, slave trading, blockage of the trade paths, and interference with traders would be severely punished.[23] Maclean's philanthropic impulse may well have been stimulated by his concern for the disruption of trade, but the two can hardly be separated in these years. It can probably be said without much question that in the early years when the battle of Akantamasu had marked a transfer of paramountcy to the British and when the merchants first began to assert that paramountcy, the British were moved by a mixture of philanthropic and commercial ends, the former predominating at home, the latter on the spot.

For nearly a decade the Colonial Office was satisfied that the merchants were managing affairs on the Gold Coast in accordance with official guidelines, but its philanthropic conscience was reawakened when reports were received in 1839 that some of the merchants were conniving in the slave trade and that the Governor had willfully ignored it. The report of Dr. Madden, sent by Earl Russell to investigate, was so hostile to Maclean that a Select Committee of the House decided to make its own inquiry. Its report of August 1842 was a watershed in British colonial history, for it recommended a forward policy in West Africa that was never successfully reversed. Formerly Parliament had bridled at the expense of any extension of territory, but the Select Committee came out squarely for a reoccupation of the Gold Coast forts by the British government "for the sake of enlarging the sphere of usefulness of these Settlements ... not for the extension of Territory, but [for] control over the neighboring Chiefs" as well as to regularize the judicial authority then exercised informally by Maclean and to upgrade the schools which the Wesleyan missionaries had founded. The report concluded:

Encouragement and ample protection ... should be given to lawful trade in every shape, and the settlements which we hold ... should be kept open indifferently to all nations as to ourselves, that they may see and be compelled to acknowledge, that in all we are attempting for Africa, we are... seeking... no advantage to ourselves, save that which may fairly fall to our lot from a proportionate share of a more abundant table, spread out for the common benefit of all.[24]

The report was adopted not only by the Parliament but by Lord John Russell and his successor at the Colonial Office, Lord Stanley, and it formed the basis for colonial policy in West Africa for at least the next two decades. Its primary concern for the abolition of the slave trade, and for the good government necessary to that end, is undeniable. The concern for legitimate trade is substantial but secondary, the main point here being that it be kept free.

Even Maclean's dispatches at this time reflect greater concern for abolishing the slave trade than for the legal trade that was progressing well under his guidance. In May 1843 he wrote Stanley in a most optimistic mood of the prospects of abolishing the Dahomean slave trade, one of the most lucrative and persistent of the entire coast. He reported that the King of Dahomey had just expressed to the missionary T. B. Freeman his willingness to abandon slaving immediately for an annual payment of £700 for seven years to indemnify him for his losses until other lines of trade could be developed. Maclean felt that for very little cost the forts at Whydah and Badagry could be reoccupied and outposts stationed at Popo and Lagos, thereby sealing off all coastal slave depots and saving the expense of the three cruisers then needed for patrol.[25] But Maclean was equally concerned for maintaining peaceful, stable government, and to do so he had to leave domestic slavery alone. Any attempt to abolish it would so convulse native society that it would nullify all his success in "maintaining tranquility and order throughout a large extent of country,... ensuring protection to commerce and safety to Travellers, ... and encouragement of those who are engaged in extending the blessings of education and Christianity to the Native population."[26] And the extension of the Bond to all the coastal tribes within the British sphere in 1845, stressing as it did certain principles of good government, was another sign of British intentions in reoccupying the forts.

Without resorting to later testimony, which falls outside the period when British paramountcy was achieved, it seems clear that with Russell and Palmerston and their predecessors, the three motives that form the theme of this book were fully articulated regarding the Gold Coast and played mutually supportive roles in the extension of British paramountcy there. We can conclude that legitimate trade and slave trade abolition were the foremost objectives. But conditions on the Gold Coast did not foster peace. The influx of European ideas and a money economy as well as the political tension caused by the presence of rival Europeans on the coast thoroughly disrupted and demoralized native society, and there came to be no hope for the kind of peace the British needed to conduct their trade and suppress slaving. Consequently although endeavoring to hew to a policy of noninterference, the British found themselves interfering repeatedly. Trying to maintain a low profile, which deceived the Africans about their intentions, the British found it necessary to undeceive them occasionally by imposing good government on them in a variety of forms.

NOTES

1. John E. Flint, "Economic Change in West Africa in the Nineteenth Century," in J. F. A. Ajayi and Michael Crowder, eds., *History of West Africa*, (New York, 1973), 2:397-98.

2. Anthony G. Hopkins, *An Economic History of West Africa* (New York, 1973), 128.

3. The narrative of events in this chapter is based primarily on the following sources: W. E. F. Ward, *A History of Ghana*, 3d ed. (London, 1966); W. W. Claridge, *A History of the Gold Coast and Ashanti*, 2d ed., 2 vols. (New York, 1964); Adu Boahen, "Politics in Ghana, 1800-1874," in J. F. A. Ajayi and Michael Crowder, eds., *History of West Africa* (New York, 1973), 2:167-261; John D. Fage, *A History of West Africa: An Introductory Survey* (Cambridge, 1969); John D. Hargreaves, *Prelude to the Partition of West Africa* (London, 1963); J. B. Webster and A. A. Boahen, *History of West Africa: The Revolutionary Years—1815 to Independence* (New York, 1970); Francis Agbodeka, *African Politics and British Policy in the Gold Coast 1868-1900: A Study in the Forms and Forces of Protest* (London, 1971).

4. J. K. Fynn, "Ghana-Asante," in Michael Crowder, ed., *West African Resistance: The Military Response to Colonial Occupation* (London, 1971), 25.

5. Ward, *History*, 183-84.

6. Panyarring is the practice of kidnapping persons in order to recover a just debt or property unlawfully held. The practice was sometimes abused by selling off as slaves the persons panyarred.

7. Boahen, "Politics," 206.

8. Full text in Claridge, *History of the Gold Coast*, 1:409-11.

9. Ward, *History*, 188.

10. Edward Reynolds, *Trade and Economic Change on the Gold Coast, 1807-1874* (London, 1974), 88; John E. Flint, *Nigeria and Ghana* (Englewood Cliffs, N.J., 1966), 122.

11. Quoted in Ward, *History*, 192.

12. Ibid., 191.

13. Ibid., 193.

14. Claridge, *History of the Gold Coast*, 1:447.

15. Boahen, "Politics," 213.

16. Text in Claridge, *History of the Gold Coast*, 1:452-53.

17. Memorandum by Huskisson, Nov. 3, 1827, Grey Papers, "Colonial."

18. Hays to Committee of London Merchants, Sept. 23, 1830, quoted in George E. Metcalfe, *Maclean of the Gold Coast . . . 1801-1847* (London, 1962), 79.

19. Resident Merchants to R. W. Hay, July 25, 1831, quoted in Vincent Harlow and F. Madden, eds., *British Colonial Developments, 1774-1834* (Oxford, 1952), 503.

20. Metcalfe, *Maclean*, ix.

21. Text in J. J. Crooks, ed. *Records Relating to the Gold Coast Settlements, 1750-1874* (Dublin, 1923), 262-64.

22. Metcalfe, *Maclean*, 115-17.

23. Ibid., 166-67.

24. Report of the Select Committee, in George E. Metcalfe, ed., *Great Britain and Ghana. Documents of Ghana History, 1807-1957* (London, 1964), 179-83.

25. Maclean to Stanley, May 20, 1843, ibid., 190-91.

26. Maclean to Stanley, Aug. 13, 1843, in Colin W. Newbury, ed., *British Policy Towards West Africa: Select Documents, 1786-1874* (Oxford, 1965), 295-96.

11

WEST AFRICA:
THE OIL RIVERS
AND LOWER NIGER

RISE OF THE EQUITABLE TRADE

Although official British involvement on the Niger Coast would occur much later than on the Gold Coast—not until the second quarter of the nineteenth century—even then it would abort twice before becoming permanent.[1] It was to foster the equitable trade and to fight the slave trade that the island of Fernando Po was occupied in 1827 with Spanish acquiescence. Within a few years, however, the hostility of the West Indian interest and of the abolitionists of Sierra Leone, who feared their base in Freetown might be superseded, was sufficient to cause a retrenchment-minded government to abandon the base in 1834.

Simultaneous developments on the mainland, however, would soon lead to a second attempt. The efforts of the Preventive Squadron were driving marginal slavers out of business, and several new firms had been formed to exploit the growing demand for the groundnuts, gum, indigo, and palm oil needed by British industry. Palm oil shipments alone from the Oil Rivers doubled from 1827 to 1830 and by 1830 had surpassed the slave trade in value. By the mid-1830s, the palm oil exports of Bonny, the most powerful of the delta states, were approximating £500,000 a year.[2] Moreover, in 1830 the explorer Richard Lander had proved that the labyrinth of streams long known as the Oil Rivers was in fact the delta of the great Niger, a revelation that promised access to the trade of the populous Muslim emirates of the southern Sudan. Finally, the dismaying discovery in the late 1830s that the slave trade was reviving enabled Thomas Fowell Buxton, at the height of his influence after his victory over the apprenticeship system, to persuade Palmerston and Russell to sponsor his commercial-missionary expedition to Lokoja at the confluence of the Niger and Benué. Stricken by malaria, the Niger expedition of 1841 was an utter failure, and the philanthropic movement suffered a blow from which it never fully

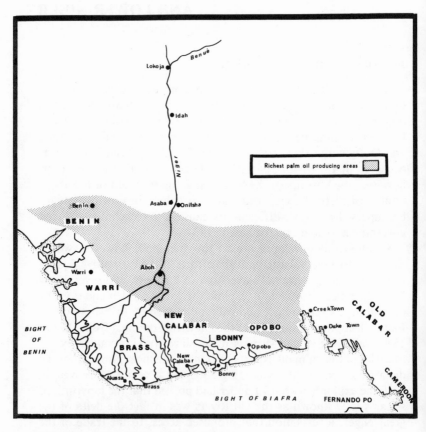

NIGER COAST, 1840s–1860s

recovered. The Peelite government, which took office in September 1841, was wholly opposed to Niger expeditions, and official interest in the Lower Niger remained dormant until the end of the decade when the Whigs returned to office.

CONSULAR ARBITRATION IN THE OIL RIVERS

Retreat from the Niger River, however, did not mean retreat from the coast, and throughout the 1830s and 1840s there was continued activity, official and otherwise. In 1836 and 1837 the Preventive Squadron intervened in Bonny to prevent the mistreatment of British traders and to force treaties first on the Regent Alali, head of the Anna Pepple house and then on the young king, William Pepple, head of the rival Manila house, which had the effect of making Pepple a British client dependent on British protection. After 1839 slave trade treaties were made with Bonny and a number of smaller delta states. A misunderstanding about the Bonny treaty led to rising tension, and in February 1844 a small war broke out between Bonny and the local British merchants. A rising tide of petitions, complaints, and memorials from this quarter gradually converted Palmerston once again to intervention. In December 1847, at his request, the Board of Trade produced a report showing that the amount of property and trade involved in the Bonny conflict was substantial. In January the Preventive Squadron received instructions to arrest those responsible for fomenting the war and to oblige Pepple to accept new commercial and slave trade treaties, the latter according him a subsidy of £2,000 a year for five years in lieu of his slave trade profits.

The endless difficulties of the delta, however, had convinced Palmerston that the intermittent authority of the Preventive Squadron was inadequate to enforce the observance of treaties by either Africans or Europeans. In 1848 he decided to appoint a consul at Whydah and the next year a consul for the Bights of Biafra and Benin "for the purpose of regulating the legal trade between British merchants and the ports of Benin, Brass, New and Old Calabar, Bonny, Bimbia, the Cameroon, and the ports in the territory of the King of Dahomey."[3] The man selected for the Bights was John Beecroft who had traded on the coast since the early 1830s, had served as an ad hoc diplomatic agent on several occasions when the

Preventive Squadron sought to negotiate or implement treaties, and was on friendly terms with many of the chiefs on the coast. From his appointment in June 1849 until his death in 1854, Beecroft extended British influence on the Niger coast much as Maclean had done on the Gold Coast a few years earlier, with the notable difference that in addition to his undoubted abilities, he had the Foreign Office and the British Navy behind him.

Palmerston, perhaps alone among his fellow ministers, understood the implications of events on the Niger coast. The shift from slaving to legitimate trade would necessitate far more intervention than the government had been willing to countenance until now. During 1850 Palmerston repeatedly instructed Beecroft to embark on missions to one part of the coast or another for purposes of gathering commercial information, making treaties, or supporting the projects of British merchants. Palmerston could foresee a vast West African trade the door to which was the Niger coast. He had good reason to feel this way because even under the adverse conditions of the 1840s, the palm oil production of the delta had averaged fifteen thousand to twenty thousand tons a year, valued in the neighborhood of £500,000, while in the peak year of 1845 it reached twenty-five thousand tons valued at £750,000. Palm oil had become the preeminent product of Britain's African trade, all others accounting for less than 10 percent of the total. West Africa in turn absorbed on an average £492,000 of British manufactures during the 1840s, £261,000 of it in cotton goods.[4]

Interventionist by temperament, Beecroft responded readily to Palmerston's lead. The smaller states of the delta and east of it were among the first to recognize British consular authority and to try to cooperate with it. On the occasion of the slave revolt of 1851 in Old Calabar, for example, the British supercargoes whose property and trade were endangered called in the Consul to arbitrate. Beecroft arrived with two men-of-war and imposed a compromise agreement that responded to the slaves' demand to abolish human sacrifice while restoring the authority of the Egbo aristocracy on all other issues. It was little more than a truce, however, and the slaves continued to combine for further demands, but it did demonstrate that the British Consul could impose peace in the interests of British trade, which was Beecroft's chief concern. The following year Beecroft presided over the election of a new king at Old Calabar with the acquiescence of the chiefs, and shortly thereafter he deposed King Aqua of the Cameroons in order to restore peace and revive commerce in that area.

The Consul's policy, regularly carried out, was to depose any African chief who hindered trade or disputed British influence, and his deposition of King Pepple of Bonny is the most celebrated example. The old troubles with Bonny had never been resolved. If anything, the British were more at fault than Pepple and his unruly chiefs, for owing to bureaucratic ineptness in London, the treaty of 1848 had failed to be ratified and the promised subsidy was withheld from Pepple. Understandably he was annoyed and made life difficult for the British supercargoes, who complained to Beecroft. In October 1850 Beecroft met with Pepple in an effort to resolve the issues. When Pepple asked the Consul to cancel the 1848 treaty and revert to the status quo ante 1837, Beecroft accused him of planning to resume the slave trade, although there was no evidence that he planned to do so or that he was still engaged in it. Nothing was accomplished at this time in resolving issues except to impress Pepple with British naval power by giving him a tour of a man-of-war. This may have persuaded him not to resort to violence against British traders as the Regent Alali had foolishly done in 1836.

This unsatisfactory state of affairs lasted for another four years. In 1852 Pepple aggravated the merchants by decreeing that all those trading with the interior must take trusts from the King. This attempt to monopolize trade was detrimental to the interests of the merchants, and as time went on they collaborated with the leader of the Anna Pepple house, the deposed Regent Alali, and clamored for William Pepple's removal by Beecroft. The Consul was sympathetic. Having made Pepple, he could unmake him, but he preferred to wait for a flagrant abuse of power. He got his pretext in 1854 when Pepple threatened to ruin trade by going to war with New Calabar against the advice of many of his chiefs. The Anna Pepple party called in Beecroft to adjudicate, and he did so by means of the Court of Equity, composed of prominent white and black traders and chaired by Beecroft himself. The Court declared Pepple deposed.

The crux of the matter was the King's power to monopolize trade or endanger it by war, and Beecroft now took a step to limit that power. By a treaty imposed on Pepple's successor, Dappo, in

January 1854, the King was forbidden to engage in trade of any kind or to make war without the approval of the British super-cargoes. The Court of Equity was to be the supreme authority in all commercial matters. In effect the King of the most powerful Afri-can state in the Niger delta had been subordinated to the authority of the Court of Equity and the British Consul. In 1856 the other major state of the delta, Brass, signed a treaty agreeing to suppress the slave trade and promote legitimate trade. The most salutary effect of these developments was the virtual disappearance of the slave trade from the Niger delta in the 1850s and the continued expansion of legitimate trade. In 1851 the delta exported twenty-nine thousand tons of palm oil, in 1853 thirty thousand tons, and for the remainder of the decade it continued to provide more than half the entire West African production.[5]

There were other results of Beecroft's activities, less salutary from the African point of view. One of the reasons for the rise of British paramountcy on the Niger coast was the breakdown of tra-ditional authority caused in part by the impact of European culture in its several aspects—economic, religious, and political—and in part by the slave movements demanding freedom and participation in government. Slave rebellions broke out all along the Niger coast in such places as Bonny and Old Calabar in the late 1840s and recurred sporadically until the 1870s because the despotic nature of the traditional political structure did not reflect the realities of power under the new economic conditions where many slaves or ex-slaves had risen to positions of wealth.

In Bonny the slave revolt aggravated the continuing dynastic struggle, and after the premature death of Dappo in 1855, a civil war broke out among the four Regents, lasting sporadically for the next several years much to the detriment of trade. Alali, the undis-puted leader of the Anna Pepple party, agreed to reopen the trade routes if the British would revert to nonintervention. Since the Regent had his hands on some £80,000 of British goods in trust and threatened to use it to rebuild the city if the British destroyed it by gunfire, Consul J. W. B. Lynslager concluded that appeasement would serve better than force and for the time being agreed to Alali's conditions, stating that "no white man had any right to interfere" in the affairs of Bonny.[6]

In other circumstances many of the British traders would have agreed. It was preferable to operate without the constraints and

customs duties imposed in territories under the rule of British consuls so long as African governments provided adequate security,
credit facilities, and redress for bad debts, but in the civil strife of
the delta in the 1850s and 1860s these conditions did not prevail.
The Courts of Equity, which could function well enough in peace-
time, were virtually useless in times of war since their jurisdiction
was traditionally limited to commercial matters. By 1859 the British
were exploring the possibility of extending magisterial authority
over the delta chiefs by an Order-in-Council, similar to what had
been done on the Gold Coast fifteen years earlier under the Foreign
Jurisdiction Acts.[7] The chiefs, however, were puzzled when their
approval was sought, for they had already "come to recognize the
Consul and the warship as the supreme political force in the Bight
of Biafra and were unable to perceive how they, politically the
inferiors of the Consul, could confer fresh powers upon him."[8]

Unable to secure the cooperation of the chiefs, the government
bent to the wishes of the merchants. By 1859 the traders who had
demanded Pepple's exile in 1854 had come to feel that only his
despotic rule could restore order, and they now demanded his return. The government ultimately consented, and Pepple was
restored in October 1861, but the royal house was so hemmed in by
the restrictions of the British Consulate that it never regained its
former influence. In 1864, for example, when Pepple tried to augment his income by granting concessions to non-British companies,
he was restrained from doing so by the Consul.

In 1869 the renewal of the Bonny civil war led to the flight of Ja
Ja, Alali's successor as head of the Anna Pepple house, and to his
foundation of the new state of Opobo. When Opobo displaced
Bonny as the dominant state in southeastern Nigeria, the British
did not interfere. Ja Ja still had to trade on the coast if his new state
were to thrive, and on the coast he had to answer to the British. For
the time being the British were content to let him govern the interior
so long as he behaved himself in the delta.

The endless strife and cutthroat competition in the delta hurt
trade, and under the new circumstances it was only the intervention
of British consuls imposing a measure of peace and order that kept
trade alive at all. The report of the Parliamentary Committee of
1865 may have reflected a desire for retrenchment and withdrawal,
but it had no effect on the Niger delta where the decade from 1865
to 1875 was one of expansion. The officials responsible for West

African affairs, both in London and on the spot, did not share the dogmas of the doctrinaire free traders. They knew that British intervention in the now confused politics of the Niger delta was required for the restoration of peaceful legitimate trade. Accordingly the recommendations of the Committee were not carried out in the delta, so remote were they from the economic and political realities.

GUNBOAT DIPLOMACY ON THE LOWER NIGER

Meanwhile on the Lower Niger from the delta up to its confluence with the Benué, British interest, official and private, had revived after the initial discouragements of the 1830s and early 1840s. In 1849 Macgregor Laird founded the African Steamship Company, which was soon providing scheduled runs along the West African coast. In the same year the government sent out James Richardson, Heinrich Barth, and Adolf Overweg to reach the Niger from the north, hoping thereby to avoid the disastrous effects of fever, which had destroyed earlier expeditions. After Richardson's death, Barth continued his explorations for another five years and in 1857 published the classic five-volume account of his *Travels*, still required reading for any serious student of West Africa. Long before the *Travels* appeared, however, scraps of news about Barth's appearance on the Benué had reached Europe and prompted Laird's offer to provide facilities for another Niger expedition to establish contact with the explorer. Laird received a government contract and the famous Niger Expedition of 1854 was in the making.

Led by Surgeon Commander Dr. William Balfour Baikie (because Beecroft had just died), the expedition was a success in every way and the first to plant British influence in the interior. Baikie reached Hausaland, spent several months exploring the Niger and Benué above their confluence, and returned to the coast without the loss of a single life, owing to the use of quinine. The small amount of trade that was successfully carried on proved to be the beginning of the regular British trade on the Niger. Baikie showed that Macgregor Laird's visions of interior trade were attainable, and he raised great hopes for its future dimensions. He reported that the populations of the Muslim emirates were eager for European goods and would "absorb thousands of cargoes" of

European manufacturers in trade for "their inexhaustible stores ... of highly prized articles."[9] Moreover, he lived at a time when it was still possible to be hopeful that the Africans would readily abandon the slave trade and its attendant warfare once they had been shown how to profit from legitimate trade.

The success of Laird's Steamship Company and of Baikie's expedition was a great stimulus to official activity. Laird was awarded a mail-carrying contract in 1854 and in January 1857 a five-year contract to send at least one annual trading steamer up the Niger to Lokoja and beyond. Provided with a subsidy of £8,000 the first year, diminishing to £6,000 the last, Laird established factories at Aboh (the northernmost town of the delta) and at Onitsha and Lokoja. The total value of produce collected for export was only £1,800 in 1857 and rose to approximately £9,000 in 1859, not enough to pay for the steamer but enough to arouse the determined hostility of the delta middlemen and the European supercargoes on the coast. In 1859 the steamer *Rainbow* returning to the coast fully laden was attacked by armed tribesmen about seventy miles from the sea. Laird's bypassing of the established trade patterns had opened an era of violent conflict in which the delta middlemen, encouraged by the European supercargoes, attacked Laird's steamers and interfered in every way they could with his operations.

By 1860 Laird's enterprise showed sufficient promise and the attacks on his steamers were sufficiently serious for the Foreign Secretary, Lord John Russell, to inquire of the Board of Trade whether the prospects of trade on the Niger justified sending an armed expedition.[10] The Board's reply was so optimistic that Palmerston was inspired to write his celebrated minute on the enforcement of trade by cannon balls, and the Admiralty was requested to provide a gunboat as soon as possible to protect the upriver trade.[11] In June Russell wrote Consul Brand that the government had decided "to establish and develop permanent commercial intercourse by this route [the Niger] with the interior of Africa," and a few days later instructed Baikie to advise the riverain chiefs that British trading vessels would regularly ply the river.[12] Despite the opposition encountered and despite moments of official hesitation, this was to remain the policy of the British government. The promised gunboat did not ascend the river in 1860 because of the vacillation of the British Admiral. As a consequence Laird's steamer could not enter the river that year, and his posts at Aboh and Onitsha were attacked and destroyed. This did not mean that Britain had lost the initiative or the power to retaliate. The gunboat finally arrived in 1861 and with little trouble destroyed the towns responsible for the attacks on British traders during the past two years. From this moment onward until at least 1879 British warships moved annually up the river protecting the trading steamers and taking occasional reprisals on the most troublesome of the towns that sought to resist British upriver trade.[13]

The decision to send gunboats upriver opened a new era on the Niger coast. The fact that steamers manned by white men could now penetrate these malarial lowlands with impunity ended the old monopoly of the African trading houses and their Liverpool confederates. British traders, missionaries, and government officials began to shift their attention to the hinterland, and the government began to rely less on treaties and more on the instruments of power to make the way straight for British traders on the Niger.[14] The struggle to overcome the African middlemen and the Liverpool merchants was a long one, however, and was not fully won until the consolidation of the Lower Niger and the Oil Rivers under a single protectorate was achieved in 1893. Until his death Macgregor Laird was the guiding spirit of that struggle. He, perhaps, more than Sir George Goldie, later head of the Royal Niger Company, laid the foundations for British supremacy in Nigeria, for it was Laird who almost single-handedly dragged the British government into active involvement in the Lower Niger.[15] By the time of his death in 1861, the government was wholly committed on the Niger and could not turn back.

PARAMOUNTCY

Without doubt Britain was the paramount power along the Niger from the ocean to the Benué during the 1860s and 1870s once the decision had been made to protect the trading steamers with gunboats because that decision amounted to a defeat for all the delta states that had sought to contest direct British trade. After the gunboats started in 1861, neither of the two strongest states in the delta area, Bonny in the 1860s and Opobo in the 1870s, could act with impunity in a manner harmful to British enterprise on the Niger.

After his restoration King Pepple of Bonny was clearly a British client, and even Ja Ja's autonomy in the interior east of Opobo did not extend to the coast where he had to trade with the British on British terms and was disciplined when his disturbance of the peace overtaxed British patience. The key decision, never reversed, to intervene effectively in the Oil Rivers and Lower Niger appears to have been that made by Palmerston and Russell in the spring of 1860. The awareness that it lay with Britain to maintain peaceful and legitimate trading conditions and the intent to do so were clearly in their minds, and they were successful to the extent that trade did in fact prosper under the gunboat umbrella. If imperial determination wavered a bit during the momentary withdrawal sentiment of the mid-1860s, the aggressiveness of British consuls on the Niger was not affected. The question is, then, how long before 1861 can we trace British paramountcy?

The Oil Rivers chiefs had apparently acknowledged it in 1859 at the time the British were considering the feasibility of extending magisterial authority over them as had been done earlier on the Gold Coast. The chiefs were puzzled that their approval was needed to confer on the Consul powers that in their view he already exercised. Or if the intermittent interventions of the Consul and his warships constituted political supremacy in the eyes of the chiefs, we might even push paramountcy back to the start of the Consulate in 1849. Paramountcy is surely visible in the most dramatic of those interventions, the deposition of King Pepple in 1854 and the reconstitution of the Bonny monarchy on terms imposed by Beecroft. Dike states that Beecroft's consulate marked the end of the British policy of nonintervention and the beginning of British imperialism in Nigeria, and I am inclined to agree.[16] By this time traditional authority structures were already breaking down under the impact of European incursions in one form or another, and the British had learned that the suppression of the slave trade and the promotion of legitimate trade were not to be accomplished without a measure of political control.

Interventions that infringed on the sovereignty of the Oil Rivers states had already occurred in the 1830s, but to see paramountcy in this period would not be justified in my judgment. The occasional browbeating of a weaker state by a stronger one does not constitute imperialism in the true sense of the word. It appears that we must wait for the period after 1849 when the regularity of intervention by Beecroft and his successors does constitute imperialism. Although they had few legal powers, the consuls were regarded by the Africans as de facto governors, and from Beecroft's time onward, Britain exercised an effective protectorate over the Niger coast.

Because the development of the palm oil trade bound the economy of the Lower Niger as far as Lokoja ever more tightly to the coastal trade, whoever was paramount on the coast exercised an ultimate paramountcy over the hinterland as well.[17] In eastern Nigeria it was not enforced until late in the century, partly because states like the Cameroons and Old Calabar were willing to cooperate with the British and were left alone, but it was imposed on the Lower Niger from 1861 onward and could be foreseen as early as Baikie's expedition of 1854 and the British government's 1857 commitment to subsidize Laird's upriver enterprise.

If it is hard to pinpoint the establishment of British paramountcy in the Oil Rivers and Lower Niger, we can say with some assurance that it occurred between the creation of the Consulate in 1849 and the appearance of the first gunboat upriver in 1861. It is in those years that we shall search for the motives. The dramatis personae are Palmerston, as Foreign Secretary and Prime Minister, Clarendon and Russell as Foreign Secretaries, Beecroft as the aggressive man on the spot, and Macgregor Laird as the entrepreneur.

MOTIVES

The attitude of mid-century Liberal governments toward West Africa is characterized by a confidential memorandum drafted by Palmerston and circulated among the cabinet in February 1839, advocating an expedition up the Niger. It was to be armed and led by competent negotiators but was not to become involved in territorial conquest. The memorandum was accompanied by "Draft Instructions to the Negotiators" whose explanatory preamble stated: "The Negotiators are told, that they must not mix up either themselves or the Government with commercial or agricultural speculations, and that they are not authorized to accept for Great Britain the sovereignty of any foreign state." The instructions themselves began:

Her Majesty's Government being earnestly desirous to put down the traffic in slaves, and to substitute instead thereof a friendly commercial intercourse between Her Majesty's subjects and the natives of Africa, and having recommended to Her Majesty in this view to send persons of trust to open a communication with the native African chiefs, and, where it shall appear proper for Her Majesty's service, to negotiate and to conclude in Her Majesty's name with those chiefs arrangements calculated to attain the salutary objects above declared; Her Majesty has been pleased to approve of an expedition to...the Bights of Benin and Biafra, on or near the mouths of the several rivers which open into the said Bights and up and within the river Quorra [the Niger] as far as to the place at which it shall cease to be navigable for steamers of the size and draft of those which accompany...the expedition.[18]

Although the expedition fell through for the moment and the government took no other action for ten years to establish its presence on the Niger coast, Palmerston's objectives are clear, and his memorandum set the tone for British policy on the coast for the next three decades.

In 1848 Palmerston responded to a petition of the British traders on the Niger coast and to reports (which proved to be inaccurate) that the primary slave trader of the area, King Ghezo of Dahomey, had promised to abstain from the slave trade once cotton culture and legitimate commerce took root, by appointing John Duncan Consul at Whydah and, the next year, John Beecroft as Consul in the Bights. On this occasion he had the backing of a House of Lords committee that recommended that consulates and forts on the West African coast be expanded wherever they were "fitted to become emporiums of trade."[19] It was hoped that the influence that Beecroft had acquired over the coastal chiefs would enable him "to prevent quarrels and misunderstanding between those chiefs and the crews of British ships resorting to those parts for the purposes of Trade, and thereby on the one Hand legal Commerce will be promoted; while on the other Hand, the Slave Trade which can scarcely coexist with legal Commerce will be much discouraged." Although stricken from the final instructions, the following statement appeared in the first draft:

H.M.'s Governm't. in establishing this Consulate in the Bights of Benin and Biafra, have no intention to seek to gain Possession, either by purchase or otherwise, of any portion of the African Continent in those parts, nor of any neighbouring Island. H.M.'s Government merely wish to avail themselves of such means as the natural resources of the Country, the wants of the natives, and the favourable disposition of the Chiefs and Rulers, aided by the protection and influence of the British Government, may afford, to encourage and extend British Commerce, and thereby to displace the Slave Trade.[20]

These instructions were wholly congruent with Beecroft's character, which Dike describes as typically Victorian, governed by general principles and noble causes, which in his case were slavery abolition, legitimate commerce, and the spread of Christianity.[21] None of Beecroft's actions during his five years as Consul deviated from these principles.

Macgregor Laird, if anything, was even more inspired by noble causes, and Lander's discovery of the mouths of the Niger in 1830 fired his youthful imagination. Then working in his father's shipbuilding firm in Birkenhead, Laird was not unlike many other Victorian businessmen who combined philanthropy and five percent. He dreamed of using legitimate commerce to deliver "a mortal blow to that debasing and demoralizing traffic which has for centuries cursed that unhappy land", [and he aspired] "to be the means of rescuing millions of ... fellow men from the miseries of a religion characterized by violence and blood, by imparting to them the truths of Christianity."[22] It was Laird who initiated the first disastrous expedition of 1832, as well as the successful expedition of 1854 whose ramifications led to British paramountcy over the Oil Rivers and Lower Niger.

If trade was a major objective of British policy, it was not to be an exclusive trade. British merchants were not to be allowed to monopolize it, and African traders were to be encouraged. When it was reported in 1856 that some of the supercargoes of Old Calabar had tried to drive the Sierra Leoneans out because they had been trading in palm oil on their own account, Clarendon, then Foreign Secretary, replied that "Her M's Govt. learn with satisfaction the growing disposition of the natives to embark in legitimate Trade, and desire that all due encouragement and protection should be given them ... and you will report in detail any illegal or Arbitrary Acts committed by the Supercargoes and let it be known among them that you are instructed to do so."[23]

In December of the same year Clarendon refused to sanction a commercial code for Old Calabar drawn up by the kings and chiefs and British supercargoes because

viewed as a whole [it] appears to be so framed as to favor and protect the Interests of the Supercargoes at the Expence [*sic*] of all others, whether Natives, British Subjects, or liberated Africans. No sufficient Protection is provided for the Natives against the Supercargoes and no sufficient Process is to be found in this Code either for compelling a Supercargo to pay his Debts to a Native, or for punishing a Supercargo for any fraudulent or improper conduct towards a Native.... The 18th article declaring that any Native Trader who may fail to pay his Debts to a Supercargo may be detained as a Prisoner on board the Supercargo's Ship until his debt is paid, is one which in the opinion of H.M.'s Govt. is altogether unjustifiable, and likely to lead to serious abuses and crimes.

The fact that the Kings and Chiefs of Old Calabar were consenting Parties to that Article, does not alter its very objectionable Character... and I regret that such a Law should have received your Sanction, and should have been enacted at a Meeting held on board one of H.M.'s Ships.[24]

As important an object as trade may have been, it was not to be pursued to the detriment of justice and good government.

Until the late 1850s it was assumed that these objects could be accomplished peacefully and without undue intervention by the government. The Niger Expedition had proved successful in showing "the advantage of legitimate trade over the debasing and demoralizing traffic in slaves," and high hopes had been raised about the river's potential.[25] Laird eagerly accepted Palmerston's offer of a subsidy for an annual commercial mission up the Niger. There was no thought that he needed any government assistance beyond the subsidy, and even as late as 1859, on the occasion of King Pepple's restoration, Consul Hutchinson was informed that "Her M's. Govt. have no wish to interfere in the Domestic Affairs of the Bonny Chiefs further than to encourage Peace and legitimate Commerce and to suppress the Slave Trade within their Territories," and if the people and chiefs of Bonny wished to recall Pepple, Her Majesty's Government would throw no obstacle in the way.[26]

The attacks on Laird's steamers destroyed this optimism and led Russell to inquire of the Admiralty the best way to protect trade on the river, observing that if the Plan of opening up legitimate trade with Africa by the Channel of the Niger can successfully be carried out, it will tend to a great extent to diminish the traffic in Slaves and will thus not only promote an object which this Country has at heart, and which for so long a period had been held to be of the highest importance in the interests of humanity, but will benefit British Commerce and will diminish the coast of maintaining Cruizers on the African Coast.[27]

In the same connection Palmerston wrote his famous minute of April 22, 1860, a classic statement of mid-Victorian British objectives enforced by gunboat diplomacy.

The extension of our Trade on the West Coast of Africa generally and up the Niger in particular is an object which ought to be actively and increasingly pursued, but it cannot be accomplished without physical efforts for the Protection of that Trade. It may be true in one sense that Trade ought not to be enforced by Cannon Balls, but on the other Hand Trade cannot flourish without security, and that security may often be unattainable without the Protection of Physical Force.

It might be said of an European Country that Trade ought not to be enforced by the Cudgels of a Police or the Sabres and Carbines of a Gendarmerie, but those Cudgels and Sabres and Carbines are necessary to keep quiet the ill disposed People whose violence would render Trade insecure and thus prevent its operations.

So it is in Africa; the Slave Traders African and European endeavour by violence to put a stop to, and to drive away Legitimate Commerce in order that it may not interfere with Slave Trade, and if we wish Commerce to prosper we must employ Force or the threat of Force to keep these Enemies of Legitimate Commerce quiet.

For this Purpose some armed vessel ought to go up the Niger at the proper season, for the Purpose of dissuading or forcing those villages whose people have fired on our trading vessels to desist from Interrupting our Commercial Enterprizes and I believe the occupation of Lagos would be a very useful and important step for the suppression of Slave Trade and for the Promotion of Legitimate Commerce.

It is said that Commerce will put an end to Slave Trade, but it is equally true that Slave Trade puts an end to Commerce; and experience tends to show that it is necessary to begin by rooting out the overshadowing weed Slave Trade, before the nourishing Crop of Legitimate Commerce, can rear its head and flourish to useful Purpose.

It is not easy to put a Limit upon the Resources which Africa affords for advantageous Commerce with England. Cotton Palm Oil Ground Nuts

Coffee Ivory may be obtained in immense Quantities, and of course in exchange for the Productions of British Industry. The advantages to be derived from a great Increase of our Trade with Africa, would infinitely counterbalance the small expenditure necessary for protecting that Trade in its Infancy.[28]

These were the sentiments that caused Russell to request Treasury assistance in May "for the development of a regular trade, until such trade has become sufficiently established to be carried on by private enterprise in the ordinary manner."[29] It was thus, for purposes both commercial and philanthropic, that British gunboats made clear who was paramount on the Lower Niger and made it possible for better government to prevail.

CONCLUSION TO WEST AFRICA

Because the slave trade had been the economic mainstay of the more cohesive and powerful West African kingdoms, its suppression by the British after 1807, and especially after the 1830s, seriously disrupted not only African economic structures but political and social structures as well. For this reason the British were able to exert a paramountcy over selected parts of West Africa with comparatively weak military detachments or, in some cases, with no more than moral influence backed up by potential military force. This happened rather early on: in the 1830s and 1840s on the Gold Coast and the 1850s and 1860s in southern Nigeria. After that the British were left with very little choice because coastal paramountcy proved to be the determining factor in the extension of imperialism inland. While a movement to withdraw occasionally welled up, it was never able to overcome the vested interests Britain had acquired by this time in West Africa, interests that were moral as much as commercial. And the nature of government being what it is, tending to dominate inefficient and turbulent neighbors, the spread of paramountcy to the hinterlands was almost inevitable.

Philip Curtin has observed that few Britishers were motivated by power or glory. "The desired ends of British policy were either wealth [trade] or the civilizing mission [philanthropy], or a combination of both. Only the means were political [the derivative factor of good government]."[30] John Flint has replied to the criticism that British West African policy was vacillating by showing that it was surprisingly steady throughout the nineteenth century, founded as it was on the two principles that the slave trade must be abolished and that legitimate trade should be given reasonable support by the government. Ordinarily it was hoped until late in the century that these ends could be achieved without costly and troublesome territorial annexations.[31] Whatever appearance of vacillation attended British actions in this period in West Africa can be attributed to the wish to exert control while avoiding formal administrative entanglements.

Slave trade abolition appears to be the chief motive in the early years on both the Gold and Niger coasts, while legitimate trade, though it had promise, was thought of primarily as a device to squeeze out the slave trade. Only later, when the West Coast slave trade was essentially ended and the promise of legitimate trade began to be realized, did the latter take precedence. This was clearly the case in northern Nigeria during the 1880s.[32]

Because good government rather than territorial control or direct administration was seen as the prerequisite of legal commerce, British statesmen and proconsuls sought not so much to rule as to influence native governments in salutary ways. So long as native rulers were able and willing to suppress slaving and facilitate legal trade, the British were content not to interfere or to limit their intervention. But where slaving persisted, as at Lagos, or where the penetration of British traders was jeopardized by native warfare, as on the Gold Coast or in Yorubaland, or by native hostility, as on the Niger, or by foreign rivalry, as later in northern Nigeria, the British government was prepared to step in and enforce what it regarded as just and equitable rule.

NOTES

1. The narrative parts of this chapter are based primarily on the following works: Kenneth Onwuka Dike, *Trade and Politics in the Niger Delta, 1830-1885: An Introduction to the Economic and Political History of Nigeria* (Oxford, 1956); John E. Flint, *Sir George Goldie and the Making of Nigeria* (London, 1960) and "Economic Change in West Africa in the Nineteenth Century," in J. F. A. Ajayi and M. Crowder, eds., *History of West Africa* (New York, 1973), vol. 2; Alan Burns, *History of Nigeria*, 8th ed. (London, 1972); John D. Hargreaves, *Prelude to the Partition of West Africa* (London, 1963).

2. Dike, *Trade and Politics*, 57-58, 80.

3. Palmerston to Beecroft, June 30, 1849, quoted in Burns, *History*, 114.

4. Dike, *Trade and Politics*, 99-102.

5. Ibid., 100-101.

6. Ibid., 149-52.

7. Malmsbury to Hutchinson, May 23, 1859, F.O. 84/1087, f. 27.

8. Dike, *Trade and Politics*, 200.

9. Flint, *Sir George Goldie*, 19-20, quoting Baikie.

10. Foreign Office to Board of Trade, Jan. 25, 1860, F.O. 2/36, f. 32.

11. Board of Trade to Foreign Office, Feb. 10, 1860, F.O. 2/35, f. 59. Palmerston's minute of April 22, 1860, on report of Capt. John Washington to Foreign Office, same date, F.O. 2/34, ff. 194-96. Foreign Office to Admiralty, May 22, 1860, F.O. 2/34, ff. 238-40.

12. Dike, *Trade and Politics*, 176-77, citing Russell to Brand, June 18, 1860, and Russell to Baikie, June 22, 1860, F.O. 2/34.

13. After 1871 the gunboats did not ordinarily go above the delta, but it was there rather than farther north that the attacks on the upriver trade were mounted.

14. Lewis H. Gann and Peter Duignan, *Burden of Empire: An Appraisal of Western Colonialism in Africa South of the Sahara* (New York, 1967), 173.

15. Dike, *Trade and Politics*, 62-64.

16. Ibid., 128, 147.

17. Anthony G. Hopkins, *An Economic History of West Africa* (New York, 1973), 131.

18. Memorandum on "Bights of Benin and Biafra," Feb. 1, 1839, and "Draft Instructions for the Negotiators," Grey Papers, "Foreign Affairs —Slave Trade."

19. S. O. Biobaku, *The Egba and Their Neighbors, 1842-1872* (Oxford, 1957), 39.

20. Palmerston to Beecroft, Draft Instructions, June 30, 1849, F.O. 84/775, ff. 87-93.

21. Dike, *Trade and Politics*, 130.

22. Flint, *Sir George Goldie*, 13.

23. Clarendon to Hutchinson, Aug. 23, 1856, F.O. 84/1001, f. 60.

24. Ibid., Dec. 20, 1856, F.O. 84/1001, f. 82-86.

25. Clarendon's Instructions to Baikie, May 1, 1857, F.O. 2/23, f. 191.

26. Russell to Hutchinson, July 23, 1859, F.O. Confidential Print— Slave Trade, F.O. 541/14, pp. 86-87.

27. Foreign Office to Admiralty, March 14, 1860, F.O. 2/34, f. 146.

28. Minute by Palmerston on report by Capt. John Washington to Foreign Office, March 14, 1860, F.O. 2/34 ff. 194-96.

29. Foreign Office to Treasury, May 9, 1860, F.O. 2/34, ff. 226-27.

30. Philip D. Curtin, *The Image of Africa: British Ideas and Action, 1780-1850* (Madison, Wis., 1964), 457.

31. John E. Flint, *Sir George Goldie and the Making of Nigeria* (London, 1960), 21-22.

32. I have made a study of British expansion into northern Nigeria in the period 1875-1903 using Foreign Office and Colonial Office papers, the Salisbury and Granville papers, as well as the standard secondary sources. It is clear that there was a continuity of motives as the British moved from the Lower to the Upper Niger but also, as the slave trade diminished, that legitimate trade naturally assumed a greater prominence in the minds of the imperialists. That this consideration outweighed the French threat, territorial ambitions, investment opportunities, or any other possible strategic interests is equally clear, except where any of these might impinge on Britain's fundamental commitment to keep the Niger open for British trade.

12

THE NILE COMPLEX:
THE SUDAN AND UGANDA

THE EGYPTIAN FOOTHOLD

Since the middle of the eighteenth century when the British first began to rule in India, they had sought to develop, maintain, and safeguard the short routes to the East.[1] Different routes were favored at different times, depending on the state of international politics and technological development. Interest in the Alexandria-Suez-Red Sea route was first awakened in the 1770s after Ali Bey's rise to supremacy in Egypt and his momentary independence from Turkey had reopened the Red Sea trade. For a few years it flourished, both as a trade and dispatch route, but by 1780 the hostility of both the Porte and the Court of Directors reduced its traffic once again to a trickle. French designs on Egypt in the 1780s, although abortive, revived official British interest, and a consul was appointed in 1786 to promote communications by way of the Red Sea route and to keep an eye on the French. This effort in turn aborted when the Porte reimposed its authority over the Egyptian beys in the same year, and the consulate was finally abandoned in 1793. By 1795 the French Directory was laying plans to conquer Egypt as a *point d'appui* for an attack on India, but Bonaparte's expedition foundered in Abukir Bay, and the brief British occupations of Alexandria in 1801 and 1807 ended British concern with Egypt until Mohammed Ali's ambitions and the advent of steam navigation once again revived it.

Russia's persistent nineteenth-century efforts to exert influence over the Middle East were another reason for British concern and the cause of Britain's only war with a major power in the hundred years between Waterloo and Sarajevo. But more immediately worrisome were the unsettled and even hostile political conditions of the Middle East itself, and in the 1830s these led the British government to seek out alternative routes to India. Mohammed Ali's pref-

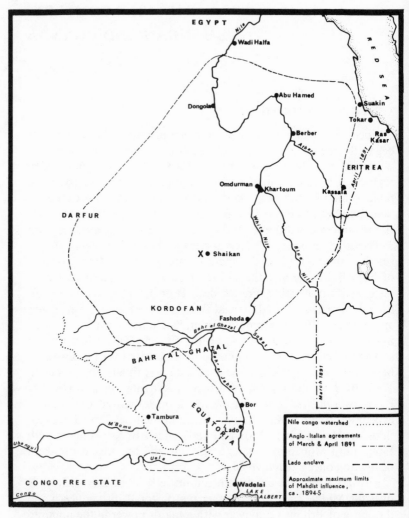

THE SUDAN, early 1890s

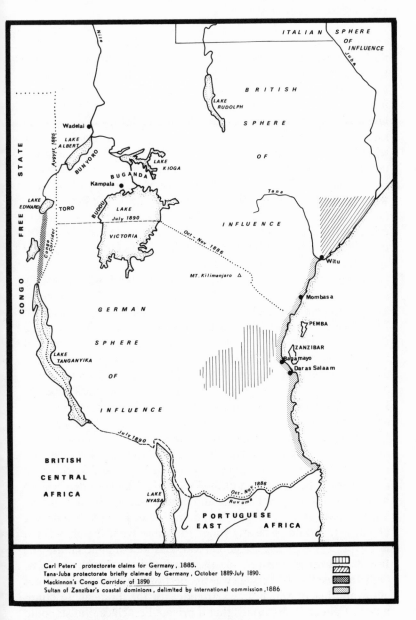

ITALIAN SPHERE OF INFLUENCE

Juba

BRITISH

LAKE RUDOLPH

SPHERE

Nile

OF

Wadelai

LAKE ALBERT

BUNYORO

LAKE KIOGA

BUGANDA

Kampala

Tana

INFLUENCE

LAKE EDWARD

TORO

BUDDU

LAKE VICTORIA

July 1890

Oct - Nov 1886

Witu

CONGO FREE STATE

August 1885

Congo Corridor

VICTORIA

MT. Kilimanjaro △

Mombasa

GERMAN

PEMBA

SPHERE

ZANZIBAR

LAKE TANGANYIKA

OF

Bagamayo

Dar es Salaam

INFLUENCE

July 1890

BRITISH

CENTRAL

AFRICA

LAKE NYASA

Oct - Nov 1886

Ruvuma

PORTUGUESE EAST AFRICA

Carl Peters' protectorate claims for Germany, 1885.
Tana-Juba protectorate briefly claimed by Germany, October 1889-July 1890.
Mackinnon's Congo Corridor of 1890
Sultan of Zanzibar's coastal dominions, delimited by international commission, 1886

EAST AFRICA in the late 1880s

erence for France and his territorial ambitions to the east and northeast resulted in the 1830s in British experiments with the Syria-Euphrates-Persian Gulf route, which, it was hoped, would be more under the Sultan's protection. For various reasons, however, it proved less satisfactory than the Red Sea route, and by 1838 that line was once again in regular use. While technology improved and made the placid seas of the Middle East more attractive for the reliable but not yet powerful steam vessels, political conditions did not improve, and the enduring political instability of the region led to the inaugural British annexation in the Middle East when Aden was occupied in 1839 to counteract Arab piracy in the Red Sea and Gulf of Aden. By 1840 a regular mail and passenger service was in operation using the Red Sea route, and the route grew in importance during the next decade despite the difficulties of reaching agreements with the Egyptian government.

During the reign of Abbas (1849-1854), who was especially hostile to French influence, a British company received a concession to connect Alexandria and Suez by a railroad through Cairo. By 1854 the Alexandria-Cairo line was almost complete and the Cairo-Suez section about to start construction when there occurred an event that greatly complicated the short route problem for Britain. In that year the viceroyalty was assumed by Mohammed Said, an old friend of the French engineer-diplomat Ferdinand de Lesseps, to whom he granted a concession to build a ship canal across the Isthmus of Suez. For years the British government was firmly opposed to the canal, and Palmerston explained why in a letter to his Foreign Secretary, the Earl of Clarendon. Construction of the canal would place a barrier between Egypt and Turkey and effectively make Egypt part of the French dominions. There was no harm in that as long as England and France were on friendly terms, but the disadvantage to Britain should France become hostile was obvious. It should be clearly stated to France what Britain wanted in Egypt: a free passage, a good road, and well-supplied inns. The British railway would provide the road and the Pasha the inns. Only the freedom of passage was in question, and Britain could not allow another power, however friendly for the moment, to dominate it. Palmerston reasoned that if private French capitalists could not find the money for their own railroads, they could not expect to find it for a distant canal. Accordingly the French government was probably behind the scheme, and its purpose was not commercial but political, and Britain had every right to oppose it.[2] British opposition proved futile, the canal was opened in 1869, and the British were obliged to accommodate themselves to the fact.

Meanwhile Ismail had succeeded to the Egyptian throne and embarked on an ambitious program of modernization. By 1876 he had bankrupted the government and was forced to call upon his European creditors to establish mixed courts (in February 1876) for adjudicating foreign claims and to create the Office of Public Debt (in May 1876) for refinancing and reorganizing the debt. Because these measures proved ineffective, the Khedive was obliged to appoint a commission of inquiry in 1878, which led to the establishment of the "European ministry" in November of that year. If Europeans were not in effective control of the Egyptian government by 1876, they clearly were after November 1878, with an Englishman at the Ministry of Finance, which controlled the revenues, and a Frenchman at the Ministry of Public Works, which controlled most of the expenditures. It was a British paramountcy because the French tacitly recognized Britain as the senior partner in the arrangement.

By the mid-1870s then, it would appear that the British had moved into Egypt to protect the bondholders, and although this is the conventional view, it is not the case. Other countries had repudiated British loans in the nineteenth century and the government had consistently refused to intervene on behalf of the creditors.[3] It was the new short route to the East that concerned the British in Egypt. And to the official British mind, the canal signified not military strategy—it was used infrequently for that purpose—but trade. By the mid-1870s British shipping accounted for three-fourths of the traffic through the canal, shipping filled not with British troops but with the produce of Europe and Asia. By 1879 the canal was carrying 13.2 percent of the total value of British exports, and Joseph Chamberlain was claiming that one-seventh of Britain's total foreign trade passed through it.[4] The expanding volume of trade with all of Asia, not India alone, made the canal vital to the British economy. Once the canal was built, Britain could not leave Egypt alone.

What threatened the security of the canal? One view holds that it was the rise of the Egyptian nationalist movement.[5] While this came to be true in 1882, it ignores the fact that the British were already paramount in Egypt by at least 1878 and that few Europeans were aware of the existence of organized nationalist sentiment until the winter or spring of 1879, after the mutinous demonstration of army officers in February. The threat came from elsewhere—from the control exercised over the canal by an uncooperative canal company dominated by Ferdinand de Lesseps and French financiers whose influence over the Egyptian government was well known, if overestimated. The instability of that government, owing to its financial decrepitude, was equally worrisome. Hence the British moved slowly into a predominant position during 1876-1878 to prevent the breakdown of the Egyptian government or its subversion by French financial interests, either of which seemed quite possible at the time and either of which could endanger the security of an important British trade route. It was imperative that stable government be restored in Egypt and especially that European financial interests not be allowed to undermine it.

Behind Herodotus's adage that Egypt is the gift of the Nile lies the fundamental anxiety that has dominated the affairs of Egypt since humans have lived in the Nile Valley.[6] As long as the occupation of Egypt appeared to be temporary, the British had little interest in controlling the upper reaches of the river, but once Salisbury had abandoned hope of evacuation (which he did about 1887), and it appeared that Britain would be indefinitely responsible for the security and stability of Egypt, anything that happened along the Upper Nile to threaten that security unquestionably would be resisted.[7] As long as the Mahdist State and Buganda remained viable, Britain had no territorial ambitions there, for neither had the technical capability of impeding the flow of the river. But when those states appeared to show signs of disintegrating from within, Salisbury took steps to fence them off from European intervention by a series of international agreements that had the effect of creating a kind of diplomatic British paramountcy along the Upper Nile long before the reconquest of the Sudan or the proclamation of the Uganda protectorate had taken place.

THE ERA OF UNOFFICIALS

The Egyptian conquest of the Sudan, begun by Mohammed Ali in 1820, was completed in the reign of Ismail. During the 1870s the region was knocked into a semblance of order and the slave trade

somewhat curtailed by Egyptian troops under European commanders. Sir Samuel Baker pushed the frontiers southward as far as
Bunyoro during his term as Governor-General (1870-1873), and his
successor, Charles George Gordon, consolidated the Egyptian
administration and dealt the slave trade some telling blows in the
late 1870s. Under Gordon, Emin Pasha (the German adventurer,
Edward Schnitzer) ruled Equatoria province, while the Bahr-el-
Ghazal was governed by an Italian named Gessi. Baker and
Gordon also occupied the Red Sea coast and extended Egyptian
control as far as Cape Guardafui, isolating Ethiopia in the interior
and threatening to encroach on the claims of the Sultan of Zanzibar.

In this period official British activity in East Africa was limited
to exerting pressure on the Sultan to prohibit the slave trade. To
this end there had been a British squadron on the east coast since
the 1820s and a consul or consul-general in Zanzibar since 1841. Sir
John Kirk, Consul-General from 1866 to 1887, exerted great personal influence over Sultan Barghash and in 1873 persuaded him
(under considerable pressure) to prohibit the export of slaves from
his dominions. At that time the British government had no interest
at all in the interior of East Africa; it was satisfied to dominate
Zanzibarian trade, to prevail in the Sultan's councils, and to leave
the mainland alone. What British interests there were on the Upper
Nile were entirely unofficial. British humanitarians, missionaries,
and traders believed that the suppression of the slave trade would
open up opportunities for legitimate trade and Christian conver-
sion, but these folk were offered no encouragement by Her
Majesty's Government, and even the British governors and *sirdars*
(military commanders) who served the Khedive were given no
official recognition. The occupation of Egypt altered nothing with
regard to the Sudan because it was seen as temporary.

Nor was this changed by the rise of Mahdism in the Sudan. In
1879 Gordon resigned in despair over ending the slave trade, and
Gessi followed the next year. Thereafter under Egyptian governors-
general, the Sudan sank back into injustice, corruption, and cruelty, the slave trade revived, and the ground was prepared for the rise
of a local religious patriot. The Mahdi quickly shook off the loose
control exercised by the Egyptian administration, and when in
November 1883 the Egyptian expeditionary force and its command-

er, General William Hicks, were wiped out at Shaikan, the British government decided to evacuate the remaining Egyptians. Gordon, sent to conduct the evacuation, was caught and massacred in Khartoum. The relief expedition under Wolseley arrived too late and ignominiously completed the withdrawal in June 1885. Of the former Egyptian governors, only Emin Pasha stayed on, precariously, in Equatoria province.

For the next two years the British government was content to ignore the Sudan. Evelyn Baring, who now ruled in Egypt, shared the humanitarians' view that Egyptian rule in the Sudan was malign, and he did not seek to be the agent for restoring it. Even if control of the Sudan should prove to be vital to the security of Egypt—and Baring was by no means convinced of that in 1885—the finances of Egypt were not yet equal to the task. Salisbury agreed, on the whole. If Egyptian or Anglo-Egyptian authority were to be restored to the Sudan, he would have liked to relegate the job to Turkish troops, but even that alternative was out of the question for the moment. In June 1885 he explained the withdrawal to his ambassador in Constantinople: "we were responsible for the condition of Egypt at the present moment, and . . . such a measure as the introduction of Turkish troops [into the Sudan] could not be contemplated until we had dealt in the first place with the financial difficulty."[8]

Even the possibility that the Nile waters might be diverted left Salisbury unperturbed. By the late 1880s the expanding delta irrigation system promised to absorb the entire supply of Nile water in low seasons, and any interruption of that supply could threaten the survival of Egypt. It seemed that just at the moment when Western engineering had greatly helped Egypt, control had been lost over the region from which the waters flowed. No less an authority than Sir Samuel Baker had warned in 1884 that barrages could easily be built in the beds of the Blue Nile and Atbara during the dry season.[9] Salisbury, however, discounted the ability of the Mahdists to divert the waters, and as long as their state remained intact and no European power intervened, he preferred to leave matters as they were.

The only activity the British permitted themselves in the Sudan during this period was the maintenance of a small garrison at Suakin on the Red Sea coast from 1887 onward. Under the command of Colonel Kitchener, it preserved peace on the southern Egyptian border, tried to reopen trade with the eastern Sudanese and to wean them away from the Mahdi and the slave trade, and kept an eye on the Italians down the coast. Neither Baring nor Salisbury had any thought of using it at this time to reconquer the Sudan. It is significant for this study, however, because it occasioned some correspondence among Salisbury, Baring, and Kitchener that reveals their intentions for the Sudan in the years ahead.

If Salisbury thought he was rid of the Sudan, he was mistaken, for events in East Africa now conspired to involve Britain in the Nile headwaters and the "back door" to the Sudan.

THE FIRST GERMAN CHALLENGE AND THE
FAILURE OF THE TURKISH DEFENSE, 1884-1888

Uganda was first thrown open to the outside world by Arab traders from Zanzibar who worked their way around the west side of Lake Victoria in the 1840s. Muslim traders from Khartoum began operating in Bunyoro and Buganda in the 1860s, and in the next decade Egyptian troops under Baker and Gordon penetrated Bunyoro in an unsuccessful effort to expand the Egyptian empire into the lakes region. Stanley arrived at Mutesa's court in 1874. In the eyes of Buganda's ruling class, the Europeans who followed him seemed even more powerful than the Muslim traders who brought the guns because the Europeans manufactured them, and it was partly for this reason that Stanley was able to persuade Mutesa to invite European missionaries to come to his land.

In response to Stanley's call, the first contingent of the Church Missionary Society arrived in 1877 from the east coast and a second group from the north in 1879, the same year in which the Roman Catholic White Fathers' mission also arrived. For the first few years they were given a cordial welcome and were able to claim numerous conversions, but the rivalry of the Protestants and Catholics puzzled the Baganda and weakened the potential of Christian influence. Hence rather than supplanting Islam, the introduction of Christianity led to a four-way religious struggle among the adherents of the traditional religion, Islam, and the two Christian sects, which disrupted both the monarchy and Baganda society and ultimately led to European intervention.

Until the end of 1884 the British government had persistently avoided any involvement in East African affairs, but German initiatives and a change of government in Britain were to change all that. In March of that year Carl Peters, one of the more restless spirits in the German colonial movement, founded the *Gesellschaft für Deutsche Kolonisation*, essentially a commercial company formed to establish a colony under government charter. Rebuffed at first by his Foreign Office, he nevertheless organized two private expeditions to the East African coast in November and December 1884. Peters himself obtained a number of protectorate treaties on the mainland opposite Zanzibar, while the Denhardt brothers did the same farther north at Witu.

The British reaction was surprisingly vigorous. The more forward spirits in Gladstone's cabinet—Dilke, Chamberlain, Granville, and Kimberley—prevailed for the moment, and Consul John Kirk was instructed to urge Barghash to send a military expedition, accompanied by Kirk, to Kilimanjaro to gain the chiefs' recognition of the Sultan's authority. If they refused, Kirk was to try to negotiate protectorate treaties with them himself on behalf of Britain. But it was all in vain. Kirk was outmaneuvered by Peters and the Denhardts who returned to Berlin in February 1885, treaties in hand, during the final days of the Berlin Conference.

While the British cabinet was still trying to use its client sultan to fend off the Germans, the conferees at Berlin had changed the rules about claiming spheres of influence in tropical Africa. Bismarck now sought to use the doctrine of effective occupation to destroy Britain's influence in East Africa by granting Peters a *Schutzbrief* for his protectorate treaties. The *Schutzbrief* was published on March 3, the day after the Berlin Conference adjourned, and in effect chartered the *Gesellschaft für Deutsche Kolonisation* to administer a German protectorate over the treaty areas.

Not content with this coup, Bismarck sought to enlarge on it by substituting German for British clientage over the Sultan of Zanzibar. When a German squadron sent out in May arrived off Zanzibar in August, Barghash was compelled to abandon his claims to the interior behind Dar es Salaam and, more damaging to British interests, behind Witu. From Witu the lakes region and the Nile headwaters seemed within reach of German expeditions. Kirk was powerless to intervene; indeed, he had been instructed by Granville in May to cooperate with the Germans, and the Sultan's signature was affixed to a protectorate treaty in December.

It appeared that Britain had failed to meet the German challenge, but private interests now intervened. British commercial activity in the East African interior had been minimal up to this time. What little there was was in the hands of Sir William Mackinnon, who had been operating a highly successful steamship line in the Indian Ocean for some twenty years when he seems to have undergone a change in character and become the promoter of a series of ill-starred commercial-philanthropic ventures in East Africa. His interest in the African mainland had been aroused by Leopold's International Association, but when its British branch collapsed of inanition in 1876, Mackinnon embarked on a scheme of his own. During 1877 and 1878 he negotiated with Barghash a concession in the Sultan's coastal dominions that eventually came to nothing because the potential for profit seemed marginal and the Sultan's second thoughts and last-minute conditions rendered the project impractical. Then after once again toying with some of Leopold's projects in the Congo and East Africa, Mackinnon lost interest in the mainland and devoted himself almost entirely to his shipping interests until 1885. Nevertheless it was Mackinnon who was destined to be the vanguard of British penetration in Uganda, and it was Peters's *Schutzbrief* that rekindled his interest.

With the aid of James Hutton and the Manchester Chamber of Commerce and Lord Aberdare, Mackinnon revived the plan of a chartered company to preserve at least part of East Africa for British trade. The government's support for the company—to be called the British East African Association—was solicited in April, but Granville, not wanting to offend Germany, revealed the whole plan to Bismarck. The upshot was that an international commission (including France but excluding any Zanzibari representatives) was appointed to delimit the Sultan's domains on the mainland. The commission was appointed in June, just as Salisbury took office, started its work in October, and after several frustrating months of trying to reach unanimous decisions was disbanded in June 1886 just before Salisbury returned to office once again. Salisbury's purpose up to this moment was still that of his predecessor: to reinforce what was left of Zanzibar's independence rather than to give official aid to a private company. This was the best way, he felt, to safeguard Britain's primary interests in East Africa, which at that time were the maintenance of free trade and the suppression of the coastal slave trade.[10]

In 1886 Salisbury placed little value on the upper reaches of the Nile, as is shown by the terms of the Anglo-German Agreement of that year, by his attitude toward the horror stories emanating from Uganda, and by his aims in supporting the Emin Pasha Relief Expedition. The Anglo-German Agreement was designed to settle issues on the coast, not in the hinterland. It divided the British and German spheres of influence by a line running from the mouth of the Umba River to the point where 1 ° south latitude intersects Lake Victoria. This gave Mackinnon some encouragement because it seemed to give the British direct access to Uganda, but the fact was that in 1886 Salisbury cared nothing for Uganda. The country was not even mentioned in the agreement, and Witu had been conceded to Germany. Salisbury had given Mackinnon a crumb and had displayed indifference to the headwaters of the Nile.

At this point the philanthropic factor made its appearance. In 1885 and 1886 humanitarian sentiment had been deeply stirred by reports from Buganda where the Kabaka, Mwanga, had begun a bloody reign by executing three Christian converts, assassinating Bishop James Hannington, and burning alive more than thirty native Christians while plundering the property of the European missionaries. Other disturbing reports came from Equatoria where Emin Pasha, the last of Gordon's lieutenants, and his troops had been holding out successfully against the Mahdists. To excitable humanitarians it appeared that Emin needed to be rescued from the "murderous hordes" of the Mahdi, whereas in fact he was more interested in maintaining his last remaining supply route through Uganda, which events in that country now threatened to cut off. Certain elements in the Foreign Service were eager to capitalize on Emin's plight by mounting an expedition to punish Mwanga and to create on Lake Albert a base from which Emin could be supplied and "from which any further operations . . . for the retention of the Upper Nile could be undertaken effectively and without anxiety."[11] But Holmwood, the consul in Zanzibar who wrote this, and Percy Anderson, at the African desk, were ahead of Salisbury and Baring who wanted Emin to evacuate Equatoria and absolve Egypt (and Britain) from any further responsibility there.

Meanwhile it was private enterprise that responded. Having received no official help or encouragement to this point, Mackinnon's interest in his East African Association had flagged somewhat in 1886, but the reports of Emin's plight revived it. The Anglo-German Treaty seemed to clear a path for him to exploit a

British sphere of influence, and an expedition to "rescue" Emin seemed a good way to introduce the British presence into the interior. Salisbury still hung back, willing to let Mackinnon take the initiative and bear the expense. Even the threat of a German expedition to relieve Emin and his troops left Salisbury unmoved. For the moment, Emin's "rescue" was left to private groups, merchants and humanitarians, who united behind a venture that they hoped would substitute legitimate commerce for the slave trade and put an end to the killing in Buganda. Mackinnon himself subscribed £10,000. Stanley was selected to lead the expedition and was instructed to make whatever agreements were necessary with the local chiefs to give the association a commercial entrée into the interior.

Salisbury, however, was not to be hustled into the Sudan by faits accomplis or by the entreaties of some of his colleagues in the Foreign Office. Both Anderson and Julian Pauncefote, the Permanent Under Secretary, were pressing him to support Mackinnon's association, and in October 1886 a telegram was received from Holmwood stating that Emin Pasha had offered in July to surrender his province if Britain would have it. Anderson at once proposed that an armed expedition, bypassing Uganda, should try to establish contact with Emin, but Salisbury quashed the project out of hand, retorting that since Emin was a German subject, it was up to the German government to protect him.

By December, however, Salisbury had changed his mind and given his approval to the Emin Pasha Relief Expedition. The Egyptian government, under Baring's guidance, was so eager to terminate its last remaining responsibilities in the troublesome Sudan that it was willing to contribute £10,000 to an expedition to evacuate Emin and his troops.[12] In Salisbury's view, no harm would be done if the Mahdists moved into Equatoria when Emin moved out, and the problem of expense had been solved by the Egyptian offer. Moreover in late 1886 and early 1887 there appeared to be no European rivals on the scene, and in the summer of 1887 Bismarck became unexpectedly cooperative. When Stanley embarked on the Relief Expedition early in 1887, the German East Africa Company had understandably expressed its apprehension lest the irrepressible explorer engage in treaty making in the hinterland of the company's sphere of influence. The German ambassador asked and received Salisbury's concurrence with the company's assumption that Germany would have a free hand south of Lake Victoria and England north of it although no demarcation line had been drawn west of the lake. In July Salisbury was gratified to learn that this delimitation was "clear and most satisfactory" to Bismarck.[13] As of the summer of 1887 then, it appeared to Salisbury that whatever tentative British interests lay along the headwaters of the Nile, they were amply protected by the Anglo-German accord and that the Emin Pasha business could be handled by Mackinnon with Egyptian support and without expense to Britain.

At that moment, however, Salisbury's view of the Nile waters began to change. By July it was apparent that the Drummond-Wolff Convention, designed to shore up Turkey as a defense for the canal, had collapsed because of French and Russian opposition. This was dismaying proof that Turkey was even weaker than Salisbury had supposed.[14] Even the Second Mediterranean Agreement of December 1887, by which Britain, Austria, and Italy undertook to guarantee the integrity of Turkey against Russia, failed to stay his growing pessimism and further altered his view of the Egyptian occupation. His note of December 12 to the Austrian and Italian ambassadors reveals what he was thinking at this time: in the event that Turkey was unable to stand up to Russia, he wrote, the Mediterranean powers should be free, jointly or severally, to occupy whatever Ottoman territory was necessary to secure the objects of the agreement.[15] Clearly by the end of 1887 Salisbury was no longer counting very heavily on Turkey, and by August 1888 he had definitely and publicly committed himself to an indefinite postponement of the evacuation of Egypt and was shifting the focus of his Middle East strategy to that country.[16]

Because the security of the canal was now seen to depend on Egypt and the survival of Egypt on the Nile, from late 1887 onward it became a fixed imperative of the British government that no power capable of interfering with the flow of the Nile should be allowed to gain a strategic position within the Nile watershed. This decision was reinforced when France and Turkey torpedoed the Suez Canal Convention in November 1888 when Salisbury wrote Baring that Britain would have to stay in Egypt and even control the Red Sea coast of the Sudan.[17] It was further reinforced when 1888 turned out to be a very dry year in northeastern Africa. The abnormal water shortage on the Nile occasioned a great deal of discussion about the possibilities of storing water at various places along the river as far south as the outlets of lakes Albert and Victoria and prompted Sir Samuel Baker to air once again his anxieties about the ease with which the Upper Nile and its tributaries could be obstructed.

Official or direct governmental intervention at this time was still out of the question, however, in part because of Baring's opposition and in part because of penury and Liberal-Unionist opposition at home. Accordingly Salisbury continued to rely on Mackinnon and the Anglo-German accord, and this still seemed feasible in 1887 and 1888 because affairs along the Upper Nile were relatively dormant. In March 1887 Mackinnon's renewed appeal for "more than ordinary support" had been firmly rejected by Salisbury who was willing to use the East African Association as long as it cost the British taxpayer nothing. But he did acquiesce in May when pressed by Anderson and Pauncefote to renew Mackinnon's mail contract between Aden and Zanzibar. Armed with this faint encouragement, Mackinnon obtained from Barghash a fifty-year concession over the Sultan's mainland possessions between the Umba River and Witu, which carried plenary judicial and political rights, including the right to collect customs duties. Salisbury approved the lease immediately, and after several months of diligent treaty making, the association could claim sovereignty over the interior to a depth of two hundred miles. In April 1888 a company was formed and £250,000 soon subscribed, and in the same month Emin Pasha was offered the management of the company's operations in Equatoria. Mackinnon and his associates seemed to be gathering momentum on their own without any significant government support, and until mid-1888 at least, Salisbury was entirely sanguine that his unofficial dog-in-the-manger policy was working well.

THE SECOND GERMAN CHALLENGE AND THE
DIPLOMATIC SETTLEMENT, 1888-1891

During the next two years the German challenge revived, led not by the German government but by Carl Peters and the *Gesellschaft für Deutsche Kolonisation* whose intention it was to launch a pincer movement from German East Africa in the south and from Witu in the north with the objective of occupying the interior behind the British coastal sphere. The plan, thinly disguised as an Emin Pasha

Relief Expedition, was announced in June 1888 and took Salisbury by surprise. In September the British Foreign Office, which had parried Mackinnon's entreaties for three years, hastily granted a charter to the Imperial British East Africa Company (I.B.E.A.) with the expectation that Mackinnon would use it to forestall the Germans in the interior. The first step in that direction was taken by the Company in February 1889 when Frederick Jackson left the coast for Wadelai with instructions to concert efforts with Stanley and Emin.

Meanwhile in the summer of 1888, Salisbury had asked Bismarck to explain German intentions with regard to Peters's expedition and had received Bismarck's assurance that it had "no official support" and that "Nyande [Uganda], Wadelai and other places to the east and north of Lake Victoria Nyanza, are outside the region of German colonization."[18] Owing to Peters's wild prophecies that Africa was to be Germany's India, he was out of Bismarck's favor, and in complaining about Peters's visionary exploits to the German explorer Wolff in December, the Chancellor stated that "the English sphere of interest reaches as far as the sources of the Nile, and I run too high a risk [in supporting Peters]."[19] At the time Britain and Germany were cooperating to suppress the slave trade in East Africa and to put down a rebellion against German rule, and Peters's expedition was an embarrassing complication. The German consulate in Zanzibar tried to stop him from landing, and when he avoided the blockade and slipped ashore north of Witu in June 1889, Hatzfeldt told Salisbury that Bismarck had repudiated the expedition.[20]

Bismarck, however, was not entirely in control of events in East Africa, and in the fall of 1889 British interests there appeared to be in danger. Peters was not to be daunted merely by the Chancellor's disapproval. Proceeding up the Tana River, he made treaties with the interior chiefs designed to establish "effective occupation." Salisbury could not afford to permit this because, despite Bismarck's disavowals, the threat remained that Berlin might again smile upon the faits accomplis of insubordinate adventurers like Peters as it had in the past. Then in October, because of British activity between lakes Nyasa and Tanganyika, which Bismarck regarded as German hinterland, the cooperative Chancellor became irritated and suddenly proclaimed a protectorate over the coast north of Witu to the Juba River. Salisbury's response was to recognize the new protectorate on the coast, while reserving British claims in the interior on the grounds of the I.B.E.A. treaties. And in December Stanley, with Emin in tow, arrived on the coast in a blaze of publicity that greatly stimulated both British and German colonial enthusiasm. They had left Equatoria in turmoil. Stanley's intervention and Emin's apparent collaboration had thoroughly demoralized and divided Emin's troops and had cost him their loyalty. When Emin ultimately withdrew with Stanley, the divided garrison, which refused to follow him, withdrew to the southern end of Lake Albert, ending the last vestige of European-style administration in the Southern Sudan. Here was an open invitation to German intervention should Bismarck change his hands-off attitude toward the Upper Nile.

By the end of 1889 both Bismarck and Salisbury were becoming uneasy about the turn of events. The prospect of a Franco-Russian alliance from 1888 onward had made Bismarck dependent on British support in the Mediterranean, and he could not bring pressure to bear on Britain in East Africa as he did in 1885-1886. It was also becoming difficult for him to exert leverage on Britain in Egypt owing to Baring's success in restoring solvency. And now, to make matters worse, Peters had jumped the traces in East Africa and was at large in the interior fouling the air of international amity. Salisbury, watching Peters and Stanley marching about making treaties and aggravating the friction between the German and British companies, feared that the situation was getting out of hand and that trouble might arise between the two countries. Both London and Berlin concluded that outstanding issues should be settled before a needless confrontation took place in East Africa. Bismarck suggested negotiations in the fall of 1889, and in December Salisbury offered to submit the matter to arbitration, specifically reserving the Nyasa region and the country west of Lake Victoria from consideration. The fact that he did not include the Upper Nile north of Buganda in his reserved list indicated that he was still sanguine that Bismarck would honor his assurances of the previous year.

Humanitarian sentiment was also pressing hard on Salisbury. By 1889 the reports of Mwanga's persecutions and the religious civil war in Buganda had built up a sense of outrage in British public opinion, which was greatly enflamed by Stanley's return and his letters to the *Times*. For a few weeks public attention was riveted on Buganda by the Church Missionary Society, the Aborigines Protection Society, and the Anti-Slavery Society, and Salisbury came under heavy criticism in the press for his reluctance to intervene. Furthermore the Prime Minister was in a vulnerable position at this time of Irish obstructionism because his slender Conservative majority could easily be toppled by a few votes controlled by vested interests, commercial or religious. Negotiations would have opened sooner but for Salisbury's winter illness and Bismarck's dismissal. This delay allowed events to build to a crisis in the spring.

The fall of Bismarck in March 1890 deprived German colonial enthusiasm of a moderating influence and revived the possibility of an official German push to the Nile. It was hard enough for Salisbury to have to depend on German support in Egypt. If Germany controlled Uganda, British dependence would become even more onerous. Accordingly when the news reached London on April 1 that Emin was to lead a German expedition to Uganda, Salisbury felt that his long-standing agreement with Bismarck was about to be overthrown, and he inquired what Mackinnon's company was doing about the matter. The Company in fact was greatly exercised over the activities of Peters and Emin and had already commissioned a large expedition under the command of its new agent, Captain Frederick Lugard, to proceed to Uganda in support of Jackson and formally establish the Company's authority. Mackinnon as well was negotiating a private treaty with Leopold, which would settle the western boundaries of the Company's sphere, provide a corridor for a British railway from Lake Tanganyika to Lake Edward in Congolese territory, and accord the Free State sovereignty over the left bank of the Nile as far as Lado. It appeared that Mackinnon was taking his charter seriously, but a few days later it was learned that Peters had already reached Uganda in February while Jackson had reached neither Uganda nor Wadelai, and on April 26 Emin's expedition left Bagamoyo for Equatoria with secret instructions to extend the German sphere of influence wherever possible on the way.

By April 1890 Salisbury had finally concluded that the Mackinnon group could not be relied on. The Prime Minister cared little what Mackinnon did in the rest of East Africa, but the Upper Nile was too important to depend on the unofficial Mackinnon treaty for its security, a treaty that Germany in any case was not likely to recognize. Salisbury opened formal negotiations in Berlin between Anderson and Krauel of the German Colonial Office to take the matter out of private hands, making it clear from the start that Uganda was not negotiable. Bismarck had always conceded that point, and by May 9 the new German government had done likewise. But so far nothing had been settled about German access to the Nile north of Uganda, which could reasonably be construed as the hinterland of the Tana-Juba protectorate, except that Salisbury had warned Hatzfeldt on April 29 that German moves in that direction would be very displeasing to Britain.

At this juncture, in the first two weeks of May, the negotiations were complicated by the I.B.E.A.'s agitation for an immediate proclamation of a protectorate southwest of Lake Victoria where Stanley had purportedly made some treaties. The Company's demands reached the public press and aroused a measure of anti-German sentiment. This in turn provoked Marschall, the new German Foreign Minister, to threaten to extend the Tana-Juba hinterland all the way to the Upper Nile. Salisbury had never taken the Mackinnon treaty seriously. He had no objection to it and eventually approved it in order to forestall Mackinnon's opposition to the Anglo-German negotiations, which had now reached a critical stage, but if the I.B.E.A. agitation jeopardized the negotiations, Salisbury was prepared to override any of Mackinnon's private arrangements. He now moved dramatically to resolve the East African crisis before enthusiasts in both countries precipitated trouble.

On May 13 Salisbury made his surprise move by dangling Heligoland before the German negotiators. The island would be ceded to Germany, he suggested, and Britain would abandon its claim to the Congo corridor and would try to persuade the Sultan to sell his coastal leases outright to Germany. In return Uganda was to be recognized as in the British sphere (this had already been conceded four days earlier), and Germany must abandon the Tana-Juba protectorate and agree to a British protectorate over Zanzibar. Hard terms these, but so eager was the Emperor to obtain Heligoland that agreement on all matters was speedily concluded in June, and the treaty was signed on July 1.

The final wording of the Heligoland treaty defined precisely the boundaries of the British sphere of influence in the Nile basin. The southern boundary was 1° south latitude, a canted extension of the line of 1886. In the east it was coterminous with the Italian sphere, and in the west with the Congo State, and north of that, the western watershed of the Nile basin. Only the northern boundary, in the depths of the Sudan, remained undefined, but Salisbury was confident that he had achieved paramountcy for Britain throughout the Nile Valley. He wrote Malet on June 14:

The effect of the arrangement will be that, except as far as the Congo State is concerned, there will be no European competitor to British influence between the 1st degree of south latitude and the borders of Egypt along the whole line of the country which lies to the south and west of the Italian Protectorate in Abyssinia and Gallaland.[21]

Peters's exploits in the interior, where he had persuaded Mwanga to sign a protectorate treaty in February, had come to naught. Over the heads of Peters and Jackson, whose antics in Uganda have some of the aspects of an *opéra bouffe*, a diplomatic solution to the Upper Nile had been found in Europe. Britain had squared its most formidable European rival and had staked out as a British sphere all that later became Kenya, Uganda, and the Anglo-Egyptian Sudan.

The French were infuriated by their exclusion from the East African settlement and insisted on compensation. Salisbury was eager to provide it so as to ease tensions with France over Egypt. Since he could not compensate France in Tunis without offending Italy and thus endangering his anti-Russian bloc, he offered West Africa and Madagascar. By the Anglo-French Agreement of August 1890, Salisbury agreed to a French protectorate over Madagascar and to the extension of French influence in West Africa from Timbuctoo eastward to Lake Chad and southward to the borders of Nigeria. France in return recognized the British protectorate over Zanzibar, but no accord was reached on the Nile watershed or on Egypt, still a sore point with France. This was to cause Salisbury problems in the future, but for the moment the French government, in the person of its Anglophile Foreign Minister, Alexandre Ribot, seemed to acquiesce and displayed no desire to contest Britain's dominant voice in the Nile Valley.

In Buganda meanwhile Mwanga had refused to sign a treaty with Jackson because he had already signed a more favorable one with

Peters on behalf of the German company. Jackson could do nothing but return to the coast empty-handed, although he did leave behind a small garrison under the command of Ernest Gedge and took back with him two Baganda envoys whose task it was to discover whether their country fell within the German or British sphere of influence. The Christian chiefs of the country had come to realize that Buganda would soon find itself within the orbit of Europe, and while they disagreed about which Europeans should exercise influence, they were not unaware of the realities of power.[22] Consequently when Lugard arrived in December with sixty-six Sudanese and Somali soldiers and a Maxim gun and when the Anglo-German partition of East Africa became known, the Catholic party, which had formerly favored a German protectorate, gave up its opposition and advised Mwanga to sign with Lugard. Abandoned by his main supporters, Mwanga angrily signed a treaty on December 26, which in return for rather vague promises of protection gave the I.B.E.A. suzerainty over Buganda and required Mwanga to accept a Resident who would have jurisdiction over all Europeans, be president of a committee controlling taxation and finance, and have authority to regulate Mwanga's relations with foreign powers. In addition it called for the cessation of the slave trade and strict controls over the arms trade in Buganda.[23] By this treaty the Buganda establishment in effect ratified the Anglo-German diplomatic settlement of the previous July.

During the final months of resolution of the Ugandan crisis, the status quo in the Sudan showed signs of becoming unhinged. Since 1885 Salisbury had been toying with the idea of an eventual reconquest of the north and had already anticipated the master strategy to be used. In a letter of August 4 of that year, he wrote:

As to the Sudan...I do not anticipate, unless the Mahdi's successor attacks us, any more expeditions. But I think the railway ought at once to be carried forward to Fatmeh (is that the name?) by which the first zone of cataracts will be turned. It will then be a matter of perfect ease to reoccupy Dongola, without any large expenditure, whenever the Egyptian Government shall feel itself in a condition to do so. Later on another railway will be wanted to turn the reach of cataracts which intervene between Dongola and Berber, and I suppose that if Egypt becomes master of Berber, it also becomes master of Khartoum, and the railway from Berber to the coast can hardly fail to follow in due time. But these anticipations are for the future, to be kept in mind as an object towards which we should work: but they are wholly out of the reach of our present penury. I have mentioned them rather to illustrate what I mean when I express a hope there may be no more expeditions. Egypt should expand southwards, but it should take its railway with it. No attempt should be made to incorporate or subjugate any part of the Nile Valley to which there is not complete military communication by rail or *flat* water with the base in Egypt. It follows that any advance must be very gradual.[24]

Salisbury's objections to the reconquest were conditional. Since a tight-fisted Parliament deprived him of resources for such an effort, the expense would have to be borne by Egypt; hence it was necessary that Egypt experience several years of balanced budgets. He was also understandably skeptical of sending other eminent men into the desert unless it was known exactly how to get them out again.[25] But the most important factor was that the Mahdists were "keeping the bed warm"—indeed to Salisbury they seemed expressly created for that purpose—until Egypt was prepared to reoccupy.[26] From mid-1887 onward, his attitude toward the Mahdists was not anxiety that they would interdict the Nile waters but that they would collapse before Baring could finance the restoration of Egyptian authority. Thus the drought of 1888, which forcefully demonstrated Egypt's dependence on the Nile, caused Salisbury no particular alarm because the Mahdist state still appeared to be in full vigor. He could bandy ideas with people like Harry Johnston who came away from his celebrated weekend at Hatfield enthusing about "our sphere of influence in the Egyptian Sudan [where] Emin Pasha will rule in England's name" but there were no definite or concrete plans to this end in the summer of 1888.[27]

Not until August 1889 did Salisbury's attitude begin to change. In that month a Mahdist force invaded Egypt and was demolished by the Egyptian army at Tushki. This seemed to reveal that the Mahdist state was weakening, and although that conclusion proved to be premature, it showed that any European power that lusted after Sudanese territory could probably gratify itself with impunity. This was what Salisbury feared from 1889 onward and was one of the reasons for the Anglo-German Treaty of 1890. But even more than Germany it was Italy that he regarded as the real enemy in the Sudan, because by mid-1889 Italy was showing a disquieting tendency to expand into the eastern Nile watershed.

As long as Italian expansionism was limited to the Red Sea slope, Salisbury was unconcerned. He was prepared to sacrifice that region, where Egypt's old claims were as valid as in the Sudan, while remaining adamant on Italian encroachments in the Nile watershed proper. In cautioning Baring not to waste money on a garrison in Tokar (near the Red Sea coast north of Eritrea), he wrote that it would do nothing to protect the Nile, such as a garrison at Kassala might do, and that it was "only by a process of forced reasoning that the Eastern Sudan, draining into the Red Sea, [could be] represented as essential to the safety of Egypt."[28]

In May 1889, however, Menelek of Ethiopia signed what was purported to be a protectorate treaty with Italy, and a few months later it was learned that Italian troops were advancing toward Kassala.[29] When in March 1890 the Italian government proposed delimitation talks, Salisbury warned the Italian Ambassador Tornielli, that as Egypt's guardian, Britain would not surrender any portion of the Sudan over which Egypt claimed sovereignty and that when it suited them, the British intended "to recover the lost Egyptian provinces."[30] Accordingly as early as March 1890, Premier Francesco Crispi understood Salisbury's position, and although he persisted in trying to soften it, he never succeeded. Baring was sent to the negotiations in Naples in August with instructions that he must insist on retaining "command of all the affluents of the Nile, so far as Egypt formerly possessed them." When Crispi refused to recognize the Sudan as Egyptian, Salisbury broke off negotiations on October 10.[31]

Crispi's impulse was to force the issue with Britain by occupying Kassala, but within the Italian government there was strong dissent. Tornielli, who appreciated Salisbury's resolution better than Crispi, feared that this would destroy the Anglo-Italian entente and warned that Italy should do nothing to "create the least suspicion of challenging British supremacy in the Nile Valley."[32] Salisbury's anxiety was somewhat assuaged by his doubt that Italy had the resources to pursue a Sudanese policy for long. His tactic was to temporize on a settlement of Anglo-Italian issues in East Africa until the expansionist Crispi fell from office and a more malleable government came in.[33]

In the winter of 1891 it appeared that a Franco-Russian entente was in the making (it actually materialized in August), and when the Marquis di Rudini succeeded Crispi in February, he was willing to make concessions in East Africa to obtain British protection against a French attack. Thus it was that agreement was speedily reached, and two protocols were signed on March 24 and April 15. The first set the boundary from the Blue Nile southward along 35° east longitude; the second from the Blue Nile north and east to Ras Kasar on the Red Sea, leaving Kassala in the British sphere. Britain thus recognized Italy's protectorate in Ethiopia, which theoretically gave Italy access to the uppermost reaches of the Atbara and Blue Nile, but the agreements bound Italy not to obstruct their flow in any way. The Italians could occupy Kassala temporarily, if they chose, until the Egyptians were prepared to replace them. While the agreements gave Italy a tentative toehold within the Nile watershed, they effectively nullified any political ambitions Italy might have entertained.

The agreements of 1890 and 1891 with Germany, France, and Italy rendered the diplomatic protection of the Nile so complete that it no longer seemed necessary to hasten the reconquest of the Sudan or to be in any hurry to come to the aid of Mackinnon's company in Uganda. And as of 1890 Salisbury did not regard the Congo State as a threat.

THE INTERNAL CHALLENGE:
UGANDA, 1890-1899

Between 1890 and the final resolution in 1899, however, the British faced three serious challenges to their diplomatic supremacy on the Upper Nile. The first of these lay in the task of breaking Uganda to the British harness.

Because of Salisbury's failure to persuade his Chancellor of the Exchequer, George Goschen, that the government should subsidize a Mombasa-Lake Victoria railroad in order to consolidate British control over the Nile headwaters, Lugard was left isolated in Uganda with his very small force. His position there was precarious and depended in large part on his role as arbiter between the rival Catholic and Protestant parties and on their fear, in turn, of the Muslim party, although he was somewhat strengthened on January 31, 1891, when Captain W. H. Williams arrived with seventy-five Sudanese troops.

Between June and December while Lugard was touring the western provinces in search of the remnants of Emin Pasha's Sudanese army, he and his Baganda allies easily defeated on two occasions the main body of the army of Bunyoro, Buganda's traditional rival. Striking off to the west, he found Emin's troops under Selim Bey on the southwest shore of Lake Albert and persuaded them to enlist in the Company service and return with him to Uganda. A string of forts in Toro was garrisoned by them on the return trip while the remainder marched to Kampala with Lugard, augmenting the Company's little army by a hundred men.

Lugard arrived in Kampala on December 31 to find a disturbed state of affairs. Captain Williams had been barely able to hold the balance, and there had been skirmishing between the two large, well-armed parties of Christians. Serious fighting broke out on January 24, 1892, precipitated in part by Lugard himself when he distributed arms to the Protestants the previous night. Superior arms and Lugard's Maxim gun won the day for the Protestants, and the Catholic party, with Mwanga, was driven from the capital.[34] Although Lugard took the Catholic missionaries under his protection, Monsignor Hirth continued to intrigue with Mwanga until the two ultimately took refuge in German territory at the southern end of the lake. From this time forward the Protestant chiefs with British support remained dominant in the government of Buganda, while the Catholic and Muslim chiefs were relegated to a subordinate role. In actuality since the outbreak of the three-way contest for power in 1888, there had been a breakdown of central authority: the former royal autocracy had been dissolved and the chiefly establishment that had replaced it had split into factions. Only the arrival of Lugard and his subsequent support of the Protestant party had enabled one faction to restore authority. It seems fair to say that the British force that arrived in Buganda with Lugard, which imposed a protectorate treaty on Mwanga and a measure of restraint on the contending parties, which helped to rout Buganda's traditional rivals, and which garrisoned the western provinces rarely before under Bagandan control became the decisive force in Ugandan politics from December 1890 onward.

In March 1892 Mwanga was persuaded to return to Kampala and resume his throne and the next month to sign, with his chiefs, a new protectorate treaty that confirmed the I.B.E.A.'s suzerainty and redistributed the provinces in a manner more favorable to the Protestant party. The Catholic chiefs received the fertile province of Buddu, the Muslims three small provinces near Kampala, and the Protestants controlled the rest. By this treaty Mwanga acknowledged that he needed Company support to rule over his divided land; indeed since the Company now exercised the decisive influence in the three-way balance of power, Mwanga had become sovereign in name only.

The scene now shifts to Britain where the I.B.E.A., finding the operation too costly, decided in May to withdraw from Uganda at the end of the year. Salisbury remained unruffled by this turn of events. He now saw the Company mainly as a means of building the railroad into Uganda, which would help consolidate Britain's sphere of influence there and also make possible the eventual occupation of the southern Sudan. But the failure of the Company would not alter Britain's claim to the region or the international agreements that guaranteed that claim. So long as no other European power challenged the claim, Salisbury was content to leave Uganda unadministered, and the Liberal government, which replaced him in August, was inclined to agree.

Frederick Lugard, however, had different ideas. By the fall of 1892 he had developed a vested interest in Uganda and had become a power unto himself. He arrived in England in October and throughout the fall campaigned hard for retention, completely winning over the British public and the press. In November the cabinet bowed to increasing public pressure and to Rosebery's threats to resign and agreed to let the Foreign Minister choose a commissioner who would go to Uganda and report on the situation. Shortly thereafter Rosebery wrung from his reluctant colleagues an undertaking to finance the Company's costs for an additional three months, from January 1 to March 31, 1893.

The man Rosebery chose was Gerald Portal, Consul in Zanzibar and known to be a strong retentionist. He arrived in Kampala in mid-March ostensibly to report but with secret orders from Rosebery not to evacuate. When the Company formally withdrew on April 1 after its subsidy ran out, Portal lived up to Rosebery's expectations and ran up the Union Jack. On May 29 he obtained Mwanga's signature on a new treaty of protection, which replaced the Company by the British government and provided for British approval of all of Buganda's foreign relations and British control of the assessment, collection, and disbursement of Buganda's revenues. Mwanga had no more freedom to maneuver than if his country had been overrun by British troops. Portal left for England immediately, leaving Captain Macdonald in charge of a provisional British administration, which, as it turned out, was never withdrawn.

In November Portal arrived in England with a report that was far too mild for Rosebery. After it was altered to the Foreign Secretary's satisfaction, it was circulated to the cabinet in December, strongly advocating annexation on the grounds that evacuation "means, practically, the renunciation of the whole of that vast territory reserved by the Anglo-German Convention [of 1890] for the sphere of British influence." Protection of the Nile waters was the central argument of the report.[35]

Allowing Rosebery to appoint Portal was one thing, however; approving his report was quite another, and the cabinet refused outright either to initial the report or to ratify Portal's protectorate treaty. Nor was Rosebery any more successful than Salisbury in wringing funds for the Uganda railroad out of a parsimonious Exchequer. Not until he replaced Gladstone as Prime Minister in March 1894 was the report approved. It was published on April 10, and the Uganda Protectorate was formally proclaimed two days later and approved by Parliament in June by a vote of 218 to 52. A year later, just before he left office, Rosebery was able to submit the Uganda railway bill to Parliament and arrange for the government to assume the debts and responsibilities of the I.B.E.A.

The extension of the I.B.E.A. protectorate of 1890 and its official successor of 1894 to the outlying provinces was only a matter of time and convenience. Only Bunyoro put up a stiff resistance, but that was largely overcome by 1894, and by 1896 most of the other states had submitted to British overrule. Since the beginning of 1891, the military expeditions sent against these provinces had demonstrated that the Baganda, in concert with I.B.E.A. troops, could dominate any region or situation in Uganda anytime they chose to do so.

Mwanga himself caused a brief flurry of trouble in the summer of 1897. Chafing under his subservience to the British, Mwanga fled the capital and raised a rebellion in Buddu, the southwestern county that had not yet come under direct British control. No one in Buganda, however, rose to his support. Throughout the crisis the Christian and Muslim chiefs remained loyal to their British connection, as did the other counties. The British and their Ganda allies easily defeated the rebels in two battles within the borders of Buddu itself, and after Mwanga's flight to German East Africa, his infant son, Daudi Chwa, was proclaimed Kabaka. The revolt smoldered on until the summer of 1899, but it was never a serious challenge to British paramountcy.[36]

Salisbury had established the British sphere of influence in the Nile Valley by diplomatic measures, but he had been unable to muster parliamentary support for a government protectorate or a Uganda railway. He left office with his strategy half complete. It was Rosebery who completed it, and he was successful because foreign threats to Britain's control of the Nile began to materialize on two fronts during his term of office. Leopold was pushing against the left bank of the river well up into the Sudan from 1892 onward, and in 1893 the French mounted the first of several expeditions aimed at the Bahr el-Ghazal.

THE BELGIAN CHALLENGE: THE SUDAN, 1892-1894

Although Leopold was the most persistent of Britain's rivals in the Southern Sudan, Salisbury never took him very seriously. In contrast to the French who sought to displace British influence on the Upper Nile, Leopold merely wished to share it. By the Mackinnon treaty he thought he had obtained part of that share—sovereign rights to the left bank of the Nile as far as Lado—but he never sought to cut the British connection between Uganda and Egypt, which the French tried to do by connecting Ubangui with French Somaliland.

It was perhaps partly for this reason that Salisbury, in approving the Mackinnon treaty, could contemplate the presence of another European power—if Leopold could be called such—on the Upper Nile. But more likely Salisbury never intended to let the treaty become operative. He always regarded it as unofficial and valued it largely as a means of keeping Mackinnon quiet during the Heligoland negotiations. Since the treaty was never formally completed, it had no force in Salisbury's eyes once the Anglo-German Treaty of 1890 set aside the whole Nile basin as a British sphere "not open to the occupation of a Foreign State." Consequently when the Van Kerckhoven expedition was launched by Leopold in the spring of 1892, Salisbury viewed it as strictly illegal and gave Leopold a curt warning to withdraw it. The King played for time by pointing out that he might make a better neighbor than the French who intended, he claimed, to establish themselves on the Nile to Britain's detriment. Nothing was visible on that horizon, however, in mid-1892, and Salisbury left office confident that his diplomatic defenses of the Nile were still intact.

The replacement of Salisbury by Rosebery, however, bolstered Leopold's determination to make good the Mackinnon agreement. Van Kerckhoven reached the Nile watershed in August 1892 and by October had occupied Wadelai where he took into Congolese service the remnants of Emin Pasha's forces who had not migrated south to Lake Albert. Rosebery's brusque demand of October that the expedition be withdrawn was rebuffed by Leopold who threatened to publish documents relating to the Mackinnon treaty, including his correspondence with Salisbury. Since Salisbury, as both Prime Minister and Foreign Secretary, had approved that treaty, the British had a weak case, and Rosebery was powerless to press further.

The Congolese expedition, however, proved to be a will-o-the-wisp. In July 1893 it occupied two small ports on the Nile but was forced to abandon them and retreat to the Congo when the local people rose in rebellion. And in January 1894 the Mahdists administered the coup de grace to Leopold's ambitions in the Southern Sudan by annihilating the remnants of Emin Pasha's army and invading Congolese territory beyond the Nile watershed.

These reversals were unknown in London, however, and so skillfully did Leopold manipulate the Belgian press and the news from the Congo during 1893 and 1894 that the Foreign Office fully believed that the Congolese were in occupation of Wadelai and other points on the left bank and had made protectorate treaties there. Rosebery was extremely upset, but since his colleagues—Gladstone and Harcourt primarily—prevented him from negotiating with Leopold, he resorted to secret instructions to his new Commissioner in Uganda, Colonel H. E. Colvile, to secure the Nile

north of Buganda from the Congolese advance by means of protectorate treaties with the local tribes. The mission sent by Colvile
under E. R. Owen found Wadelai unoccupied and no trace of the
Belgians, but this was not learned in London until May 1894, when
it was too late to be of use.

When Gladstone retired in March 1894, Rosebery was finally
free to pursue an agreement with Leopold. Still believing that the
Congolese were in occupation of parts of the Southern Sudan,
Rosebery made Leopold a handsome offer of a lease on the left
bank of the Nile all the way to Fashoda for the duration of his reign
and a lease on the Bahr el-Ghazal to the King and his successors. In
return Leopold was to recognize the Anglo-German Treaty of 1890,
abandon all claims to the Nile basin, including the "sovereign
rights" mentioned in the Mackinnon treaty, and to provide Britain
with a corridor through Congolese territory between lakes Edward
and Tanganyika. Signed on May 12, the Anglo-Congolese Treaty
promised to exclude the French from the Upper Nile permanently
at the cost of sharing access to it with the least dangerous of Britain's European rivals.

When they learned that Leopold had completely hoodwinked
them, the British could scarcely believe it. Nevertheless Rosebery
continued to regard the agreement as the solution to the Nile problem, and it was only in the face of vigorous French and German
opposition that he gave it up. The Germans insisted on a common
frontier with the Congo State, as Salisbury had predicted they
would, while the French, now in process of mounting their first
expedition toward the Nile, were outraged at the prospect of being
shut out of the Bahr el-Ghazal. So much pressure was brought to
bear on London and Brussels that the treaty was abandoned in
August.

Rosebery's diplomatic defense of the Sudanese Nile and Leopold's golden opportunity seemed to have collapsed together. After
Salisbury returned to office in 1895, two interviews with Leopold
convinced him that the King was an "egocentric old man whose
delusions of grandeur need not be taken seriously."[37] Not that Leopold gave up. In 1896-1897 a large Congolese expedition under the
Baron Dhanis headed for the Nile, but it dissolved in mutiny just as
it reached the Nile watershed at Ndirfi in February 1897. Even as
late as 1903 Leopold tried to occupy the leases granted him by the

1894 agreement, and when the British government pointed out that the treaty was long since null and void, Leopold formally annexed the region in October 1905, but he was obliged to withdraw these claims under threat of force in May 1906 and satisfy himself with the Lado Enclave for the duration of his reign. From 1894 onward, the French rather than the Belgians were regarded as the greater threat.

THE FRENCH CHALLENGE:
THE SUDAN, 1893-1899

For at least two years prior to the Anglo-Congolese Agreement Leopold had been warning the British Foreign Office about French designs on the Sudan and had actually been encouraging those designs as a means of exerting leverage on the British. An air of truth was given to the King's warnings when the French engineer, Victor Prompt, claimed in a speech in January 1893 that a barrage at the mouth of the Sobat (a Nile tributary just south of Fashoda), with similar dams at the outlets of lakes Albert and Victoria, could control half of Egypt's summer water supply and could be used to dessicate or inundate Egypt. These French ambitions could be frustrated, Leopold suggested, if Britain would only recognize his claims in the Bahr el-Ghazal. The British government, however, was not alarmed in 1893, although Rosebery took note of these straws in the wind. At this time Uganda loomed larger in his mind as the key to the Nile basin, but he did become alert to the possibility that Salisbury's "diplomatic protection" of the Sudan might have to be consolidated.

Nor were the French responsive to Leopold's blandishments until the cabinet reshuffle of January 1893 brought the ambitious Théophile Delcassé to the Colonial Ministry. Whatever their political stripe, most French politicians of this period, Delcassé included, were frustrated by their failure to force the British out of Egypt. Inspired perhaps by one of Leopold's secret agents, the Secretary-General of the *Comité de l'Afrique Française*, Harry Alis, Delcassé soon formed the idea of sending a mission to the Nile not primarily to acquire territory but to bring pressure to bear on Britain to "reopen the Egyptian question" and to provide France with compensation elsewhere in return for recognition of Britain's sphere in the Sudan. From 1893 onward this became the fixed objective—and ultimately the obsession—of the French Colonial Office, which for the next five years steadily ignored the warnings of the Ministry of Foreign Affairs to moderate its aspirations. In May Delcassé appointed P. L. Monteil head of a Nile expedition, and in the summer of 1893 its advance elements left France.

It had been unwise for Delcassé to rebuff Leopold's offers of collaboration and to attempt a unilateral French effort maneuvering Leopold out of position. Incensed by Delcassé's treachery, Leopold ordered his Congolese forces to block the French advance by occupying posts on the Uele and M'Bomu rivers, although he had given France an *"ouverture sur le Nil"* in 1887 when he had ceded all his territories on the right bank of the Ubangui. Turning now to the British, Leopold seemed assured of success when the Anglo-Congolese Treaty promised at one stroke to exclude the French permanently and to give Leopold what he sought in the Nile basin. As of mid-1894, then, France did not appear to offer any threat to the British sphere of influence in the Sudan. Even the French were only mildly interested in the Nile at this time. Although subscribing to Delcassé's long-range policy, Eugène Etienne, the influential Under Secretary for Colonies, thought it more important in November 1893 to send Monteil to Berlin on a mission to adjust the West African frontiers than to send him up the Ubangui. And in December a change of governments in Paris delayed the Monteil expedition for several months more until the new government could decide to revive it.

What reawakened French determination to exert control over the Nile was the Anglo-Congolese Agreement. Etienne explained to the Chamber on June 7, in reference to that treaty, "What you have before you is the question of Egypt," a revelation calculated to set a number of Deputies on their ears.[38] Several days later Hanotaux announced that as far as he was concerned, the treaty was null and void and that the long-delayed Monteil expedition would soon depart. On June 20 the Deputies duly voted a credit of 1.8 million francs "for the defense of French interests in Africa."[39]

Despite Etienne's histrionics, however, the immediate purpose of the expedition was not to force the Sudan issue with Britain but to force the Upper Ubangui issue with Leopold. Monteil's instructions consequently were to push no farther than a point just short of the Nile-Congo watershed, which he was explicitly forbidden to cross. The combined effect of this initiative and the collapse of the Anglo-Congolese Treaty enabled Hanotaux to extract from Leopold the Franco-Congolese Convention of August 1894. By securing French rights to the right bank of the M'Bomu, from which the Congolese garrisons now retired, the immediate purpose of the Monteil mission had been achieved and Monteil was recalled by Delcassé at the end of the month.

By limiting the Congolese occupation of the Upper Ubangui region to 5 °30″ north latitude, the Franco-Congolese Convention appeared to have given the French access to the Bahr el-Ghazal and reopened their *"ouverture sur le Nil."* But the Heligoland Treaty was still intact, and despite its more ardent spirits, the French government did not hasten to move in. In 1894 Hanotaux was still holding to his publicly announced principle of the integrity of the Ottoman Empire and was trying to forestall any rash adventures that would present the British with a good legal case against French intervention on the Upper Nile. There is also reason to believe that he was restrained by Dufferin's threat of June that Britain would treat any French incursion into the Nile Valley as an act of war. On August 10 he told Phipps of the Paris embassy that France did not dream of entering the Bahr el-Ghazal and the next day even suggested that France might be willing to acknowledge the Heligoland Treaty as part of a general settlement on Africa.[40] This concessionary attitude inspired the Foreign Office to offer a piece of Borgu in return for French recognition of the treaty, and on this basis negotiations were undertaken to resolve all outstanding African issues.

It soon became clear, however, that Hanotaux and Delcassé were not in agreement and that an exchange for the Sudan was unacceptable to the hawks in the Colonial Ministry. Instead they proposed a "self-denying" agreement that France would stop at the Nile-Congo watershed if Britain would agree not to advance beyond posts already occupied (in Uganda). Although this would have required the British to abandon their long-standing plans for the eventual reconquest of the Sudan, it still constituted a large concession from the standpoint of traditional French foreign policy, and it would have accorded Britain essentially what it wanted in the Nile Valley: the exclusion of other European powers. Its outright rejection by Kimberley and Anderson was probably a blunder, for its acceptance might have prevented Fashoda. Sanderson concludes that the obduracy of Kimberley and Anderson reflected a new attitude about empire from 1894 onward when convinced imperialists gained control of policy making in both London and Paris and rational evaluations gave way to chauvinism.[41] Whatever the cause, the negotiations had essentially failed by early November, and on November 17 the French cabinet decided to mount a new expedition to the Nile.

The Liotard mission, which replaced the defunct Monteil mission, turned out to be a *coup de théâtre* in comparison with the substantial military expeditions mounted by France in West Africa at the same time. After the breakdown of negotiations, Rosebery resumed his diplomatic defense of the Nile in the form of a parliamentary declaration by Sir Edward Grey in March 1895 (very likely inspired by Rosebery) that the combined British and Egyptian claims to the "whole of the Nile waterway" were incontestable and that any French penetration would be viewed by England as an "unfriendly act." Grey's declaration brought cries of outrage from Paris, but it temporarily caused the French government to hold its hand. Delcassé's successor, Chautemps, quietly neglected to reinforce Liotard, thus giving the British a respite. As of the summer of 1895, the French had still not offered a serious or imminent challenge to the Anglo-German partition.

The weak ministry that replaced Hanotaux in October, however, was easily led by the permanent officials at the Quay d'Orsay and the Pavillon de Flore. In November the new Foreign Minister, Berthelot, and the Colonial Minister, Guieysse, were persuaded to authorize a secret Nile expedition to be commanded by Captain J. P. Marchand. But Marchand did not leave Paris until June 1896, and even then British intelligence estimated (incorrectly, as it turned out) that the forces at his command were so sparse and scattered that any serious incursion into the Nile basin would be unlikely. Accordingly Salisbury's decision of March 1896 to begin the reconquest of the Sudan was not the result of any immediate French threat to the Nile. It came from the long-standing decision to restore Egyptian (now Anglo-Egyptian) sovereignty and from the need to make a gesture of support to the Italians who had suffered a disastrous defeat at Adowa a fortnight before and were now under siege in Kassala by the Mahdists.[42]

The Uganda salient was also strengthened that same month when the Treasury complied with Salisbury's request to release £3 million for construction of the Uganda Railway, the funds for which were voted by the Parliament in June. Also in June the Uganda Protectorate was extended over Bunyoro, advancing British administration to the threshold of the Sudan.

The reconquest of Dongola province was accomplished by Kitchener with little resistance from the Mahdists between July and September 1896. Because Dongola was the birthplace of the Mahdi, its loss was a severe blow, psychologically as well as strategically, to the Mahdist cause. The reconquest was so easily done that Kitchener began immediately to press for an advance to Berber, but Salisbury was loath to approve it for fear of arousing a French reaction in the South. His chief concern in 1896 was to wait until the completion of the Uganda Railway, which would enable him to make good on the ground the sphere of influence created by the Anglo-German partition of 1890. Cromer was easily persuaded, however, and when Kitchener was home on leave in November, he converted Salisbury as well. Funds were made available sufficient to provide some additional gunboats and to connect Wadi Halfa with Abu Hamed by rail. Berber was occupied in August 1897, and there, for the moment, Kitchener was stalled by a large Mahdist army.

Other than some outbursts in the French press about English arrogance and perfidy, the French reaction to Kitchener's expedition was surprisingly bland. Indeed the Anglo-French discussion of African issues, which had continued sporadically since 1894, went on as before, Berthelot even suggesting that France might acquiesce in a British Sudan if London could propose "some arrangement respecting Egypt that might be satisfying to France."[43] Apparently the French did not intend to raise any serious objections to the reconquest.

In August, however, reports were received that the spearhead of the Marchand expedition under Liotard had occupied Tambura on the eastern slope of the Nile-Congo watershed, and by February 1897 British intelligence was fairly certain that Marchand was bound for the Nile. Salisbury now became somewhat uneasy about French maneuvers, and he warned Hanotaux that no "other European Power than Great Britain has any claim to occupy any part of the valley of the Nile."[44] He also dispatched a secret mission down the Nile from Uganda "to make friends with the tribes before the French get there from the west."[45] The leader of the expedition, J. R. L. Macdonald, received his instructions in June but was delayed by a mutiny of Emin's old troops who had garrisoned the forts in western Uganda. Not until April 1898 could he resume his mission, but he never got as far as Lado, from want of provisions, and was forced to return to Uganda. The British Commissioner in Uganda now stepped into the breach and sent north his own expedition under Major Martyr in July. By November Martyr had reached Bor (north of Lado) but was prevented from moving on by the impenetrable *sudd*. Salisbury's tactic of closing off the Nile basin from Uganda had failed.

Meanwhile during 1897 and 1898 Marchand and other French troops following on his heels had occupied about a dozen points in the Bahr el-Ghazal, and Fashoda was reached in July 1898. Kitchener had sought to use the French advance to obtain approval to push on to Khartoum in the fall of 1897, but he was overruled by Salisbury and Cromer. Salisbury remained unruffled and unimpressed by the prospect that "upon some spot in the Nile valley a French explorer may have succeeded in inducing some chief to accept a treaty." Such a development would in no way alter the loud protest that France would make in any case when Britain eventually occupied the sphere allotted to her by the Heligoland Treaty.[46]

Accordingly the pace of Kitchener's advance was dictated not by Marchand's exploits but by the condition of the Egyptian army. While that army under Kitchener as *sirdar* was still stalled at Berber, Cromer was confident that a British army could advance to Khartoum any time it chose. Thus when it was learned in December that a large Mahdist force was concentrating near Omdurman, Cromer wrote to Salisbury that a British expedition to Khartoum would be unavoidable, not to counter French moves, but to secure territory already held by the Egyptian troops in the face of a Dervish buildup. British reinforcements were authorized by the cabinet in January 1898, and Kitchener's slow, deliberate advance began, ending on September 2 with the annihilation of the Mahdist army near Omdurman.

A week later the Mahdist steamer *Tawfiqia* appeared at Omdurman bearing the marks of her engagement with the "whites" at

Fashoda. Kitchener had no doubt who the "whites" were and on September 10 set out for Fashoda with four gunboats and a steamer. His encounter with Marchand on September 19 and the latter's ultimate withdrawal in November have been amply described. During the entire crisis Salisbury was unflappable. He was certain that if it came to war, France would be easily defeated, and as rumors of impending military coups and mobilizations poured in from France, he dismissed them as "gloomy forebodings" and mere "conjectures."[47] His strategy was simply to let Kitchener starve out Marchand while waiting for the French to come to their senses and for diplomacy to resolve the crisis in Europe.

The Prime Minister had written to Lansdowne in October 1897 that "the diplomatic question will be interesting and difficult, but the increase of those qualities conferred by a French adventurer's 'effective occupation' will not be serious."[48] The British sphere of influence would be maintained, as before, by diplomatic measures, and the diplomatic measures Salisbury had in mind were understandings with Russia on the Dardanelles and Port Arthur and with Germany on South Africa. The former allowed Russia to turn its attention away from Constantinople and gave it a free hand in the Far East, while the agreement with Germany of August 1898 created a limited Anglo-German entente. Accordingly neither Russia nor Germany was prepared to stand behind France at Fashoda in the fall of 1898, and the French occupation of the Nile Valley became a lost cause almost before it was achieved. Ultimately, in March 1899, an Anglo-French boundary agreement left the entire territory east of the Nile watershed to Great Britain.

PARAMOUNTCY: UGANDA

Because the Nile Valley became such a bone of international contention, the two aspects of British paramountcy, internal and diplomatic, will be considered separately.

Although it has been argued that Mwanga's rebellion of 1897-1899 very nearly regained him his autonomy, that contention is questionable when we recall that hardly anyone outside Buddu rose to his support. By 1897 nearly all the chiefs and power factions in Uganda were loyal to the British because the British umbrella supported their power. Mwanga was kicking against traces far too strong for him to break. Three years earlier the proclamation of the protectorate over Buganda formalized his agreement of May 1893 to accept British control of his finances and foreign policy. Few would cavil at the contention that this was a clear, if painful, acknowledgment of internal British paramountcy. But Mwanga's signature in turn was a recognition of the realities of the previous two and a half years: that since the arrival of Lugard's small force in December 1890, the I.B.E.A. had exercised the deciding influence in a country whose monarch had become a shuttlecock in a three-sided struggle for power. That influence was gradually reinforced in 1891 by the arrival of additional troops from the coast and by the enlistment of Emin's troops in the Company service. It was confirmed by the defeat of the Catholic party in January 1892 and by Mwanga's submission in April to the dominant Protestants backed by British arms. Internally, then, British paramountcy can be said to exist from the moment Lugard arrived or within a year thereafter, although the Catholic faction and later Mwanga tried to contest it. And while the outlying provinces were not all officially absorbed into the protectorate until about 1896, or much later in the case of the acephalous regions of the north, the core of what later became Uganda—the interlacustrine states of the center and south—can be said to have come under British paramountcy at roughly the same moment as Buganda because Buganda had long been the dominant state in Uganda, and its forces in combination with Lugard's had shown as early as 1891 that they could easily subdue the most formidable resistance the other states could offer. Once Lugard had arrived at the head of the I.B.E.A. forces, it was only a matter of time and administrative convenience before the outlying states were physically brought to heel.

Internal paramountcy, however, was only the culmination of a process that had already decided the fate of Uganda in Europe. Even before Lugard arrived, the chiefs of the two rival Christian factions had come to realize that Buganda was already, or was soon to be, within the ambit of European influence. They disagreed about which power should exercise that influence, but unbeknown to them, Salisbury and Bismarck had already settled that question over their heads, and the activities of Lugard and Portal merely confirmed locally a paramountcy that the Heligoland Treaty had already accorded to Britain. Salisbury, at least—and Salisbury did not often delude himself—thought that by virtue of that treaty he had sewed up a British sphere of influence that ran in a great arc from the Indian Ocean through the lakes region and down the Nile as far north as Khartoum.

The Germans in fact had already acknowledged that sphere—not its precise boundaries but in principle—well before 1890. In December 1888 Bismarck had admonished Peters that the British sphere of influence reached from Egypt all the way to the sources of the Nile. In the previous summer the Chancellor had assured Salisbury that the Nile Valley north of Lake Victoria, including Wadelai, which German imperialists viewed as the hinterland of their Tana-Juba Protectorate, was "outside the region of German colonisation," and this had been confirmed in writing by Hatzfeldt in June 1889.[49] As early as July 1887 in fact, Bismarck had agreed to the principle that the delimitation line of 1886 extended west of Lake Victoria as well and that everything north of the lake belonged in the British sphere. This is probably the earliest date at which we can identify British paramountcy in Uganda. It was certainly not achieved by the Anglo-German Treaty of 1886, which did not even allude to the country. Even though it was tentative and informal as of 1887, as of that year the Chancellor of Britain's only serious rival in Uganda had agreed in principle to the partition formalized by the Heligoland Treaty three years later.

British paramountcy can be said to have been achieved in Uganda probably by 1887 and definitely by 1890. It is in these years and a year or two before, when Anglo-German discussions on East Africa began, that we shall search for British motives. Salisbury is the man who made all the decisions, although Mackinnon was able to force the pace on occasion. It is with their reasons for appropriating Uganda that we shall be concerned.

Although Italy did not formally recognize the British sphere in Uganda until 1891, Leopold until 1894, and France, implicitly, in the treaty of August 1890, none of these powers challenged British paramountcy in Uganda as they did in the Sudan.

PARAMOUNTCY: THE SUDAN

The reconquest of the Sudan and the assertion of British control over its internal affairs was a function of the deterioration of the Mahdist state and of Italy's defeat and withdrawal from Ethiopia in 1896. But long before that—1890 is the year—the Mahdist state had been isolated from any external European influence, other than British, whether the Khalifa Abdallahi knew it or not, because from that year onward the British government was determined to prevent the intervention of any other European power and had formally settled with one of the two powers that really mattered. Every effort made thereafter by Britain to force other powers, especially France and Leopold, to recognize British paramountcy was essentially in the nature of tidying up.

The Italians were no problem. Merely by negotiating with Britain on Sudanese boundaries from 1890 onward, they tacitly acknowledged Britain's right to speak for the Sudan. And although Crispi gave the British a few anxious moments in late 1890 and early 1891, he was not representative of the Italian government of his time on this particular issue. Despite his insistence on pushing toward Kassala, his parliament and most of his colleagues were loath to challenge what Tornielli openly described in October 1890 as "British supremacy in the Nile Valley." The Italians were simply pushing as far as they dared for favorable boundary adjustments and had no intention of challenging Britain's hegemony in the Nile basin.

An accommodation with the Congo State, however, was not reached until 1894—indeed a final settlement not until 1906—and Leopold's occupation of points in Equatoria and the Bahr el-Ghazal was an actual military threat during its momentary success in 1892-1893. But the King of the Belgians lacked the resources to stand up to the Mahdists when in full vigor, and his Congolese forces were outgunned by them from 1893 until as late as 1897, after which they were outgunned by the British. Moreover for all his frantic activity, all but one of Leopold's initiatives following the Anglo-Congolese Agreement of 1894 were aimed at occupying leases that the King implicitly acknowledged Britain had a right to grant him.[50] Leopold's quixotic forays into the Nile basin, therefore, were in the nature of tilting with windmills and were no more than an irritation to the British.

The French were another matter. There was a real possibility that war might have broken out over the Fashoda crisis. The British had reason to go to war and were prepared to do so: the Nile Valley was the key to the security of Egypt and therefore of the eastern Mediterranean and the Suez Canal. But France had no reason to go to war, and had war erupted, the issue would have been decided in Britain's favor.

The possibility of war, however, has been allowed to obscure the fact that had it happened, it would not have served to dislodge the British from the Nile Valley, and the precariousness of Marchand's position when Kitchener arrived at Fashoda attests to that. Fashoda, therefore, was not caused by any substantial French capability to intervene effectively in the Nile Valley. It was a tour de force arising largely out of the romantic and unrealistic ambitions of the *officiers soudanais* and the permanent officials in the Pavillon de Flore in pursuit of one of France's lost causes. For a brief moment —September to November 1898—until the French came to their senses, the affair mushroomed into a case of national self-delusion. For all the overheated rhetoric in which the French indulged themselves in the late 1890s, their mission to the Nile was never more than a chimera.

Why was this the case? Because the more sober officials of the French government never seriously intended to occupy the Nile but rather to exert leverage on the British in Egypt. It is difficult for us today to appreciate the depth of feeling in France caused by the British occupation of Egypt. The French considered it a national humiliation exceeded only by Sudan. It was an outrageous end to France's rightful hegemony in a country where French scholars, scientists, advisers, and businessmen had long held sway and where the impact of French culture is by no means obliterated today. Every French attempt of the 1890s to gain access to the Upper Nile was a function of this resentment, and it accounts for the passion with which they threw themselves into these unpromising ventures.

Since the object was to press the British to evacuate Egypt, even a weak expedition or nominal occupation by French forces would serve to challenge Britain's diplomatic paramountcy on the Upper Nile. Marchand's much celebrated but pitifully small expedition, as well as the French occupation of about a dozen points in the Bahr el-Ghazal, were no more than a nominal challenge. Abandoned by allies and faced by a superior navy and the Anglo-Egyptian army under Kitchener, France lacked both the military and diplomatic punch to pull it off. If this view is correct, it is likely that the Fashoda crisis has been given more attention than it deserves in the history of the Nile basin.

One explanation for Fashoda is that the French never understood the depth of Salisbury's determination to remain supreme in the Nile Valley. After 1890 he regarded Britain's diplomatic paramountcy there as de jure and was totally committed to defend it. And given the comparative strength of the forces Britain was prepared to mobilize in that defense, neither France nor the Congo State constituted an effective threat. As stately as the progress of Kitchener's expedition may have been, Britain was in position in Egypt to move larger forces into the Sudan if challenged and to do so faster than any rival.

If the foregoing analysis has demonstrated that British paramountcy was achieved in the Sudan in 1890 and never effectively interrupted thereafter, we shall seek out the motives that operated on the British government from the failure of the Drummond-Wolff Convention in 1887, when the occupation of Egypt began to seem permanent, until the conclusion of the Heligoland Treaty in 1890. It is mainly Salisbury's motives that concern us because he, virtually alone, made the key decisions, although he depended heavily on the views of Baring and Kitchener.

MOTIVES

Sanderson points out that after 1894 Britain succumbed to an "imperialism of prestige" in the Sudan, which reached a climax in 1898-1899 and was not discredited until chastened by the South African War. The same may be said for British involvement in Uganda after 1892 when public opinion, excited by the reports from Uganda and by Lugard's campaign, forced the government into moves that culminated in the protectorate. Before 1890, however, Britain's motives were somewhat different. Then its position on the Nile was based on a rational analysis of what was necessary (and no more than what was necessary) for the security of Egypt.[51] Salisbury had become convinced that control of any part of the Upper Nile by a rival European power could jeopardize Britain's position in Egypt upon which the security of the canal depended. Nearly all students of the subject agree on this point. Salisbury's interest in Uganda had little to do with East Africa as such; indeed Fieldhouse maintains that all of British East Africa was looked upon primarily as a corridor to the Upper Nile.[52] What worried Salisbury in Uganda after 1887 was that the religious strife in Buganda would create conditions that invited the intervention of other European powers. And whatever Salisbury's other concerns in the Sudan may have been, they were subordinate to his hope that the inevitable reconquest could be postponed as long as possible by the continued vitality of the Mahdist state, which was "keeping the bed warm" for Britain. In both countries what was required was the avoidance of "bad" government so as to give no European power, including Britain, an excuse to intervene.

Nevertheless there were powerful secondary factors influencing the British government. Philanthropic pressure arising out of the Uganda situation in 1889 was partly responsible for the Anglo-German negotiations leading to the Heligoland Treaty. But Salisbury in this instance was moved less by humanitarianism than by the need to hold his cabinet together, and the plight of the Christians in Uganda did not weigh heavily on him until at least 1892. Indeed in 1886, before the Upper Nile began to loom large in his thinking, he had firmly refused to do anything at all to rescue either Emin Pasha or the persecuted Ugandan Christians.[53]

Before 1890, in fact, however fateful Salisbury's understanding with Bismarck may have been for Uganda, his role was essentially negative.[54] In these years it was the I.B.E.A. that took the initiative in East Africa, and the Company was largely a projection of Sir William Mackinnon's objectives. As a successful entrepreneur, Mackinnon was unquestionably lured to East Africa by the eight-fold rise in Zanzibar's trade, which occurred from 1872 to 1887, three-quarters of which was with Britain and India.[55] But he also shared the widespread feeling of that time that legitimate trade would prove the most effective means of obliterating the slave trade and bringing civilization to Africa. In the 1880s his philanthropic inclinations seem to have overborne his commercial aims. All who have written about him attest to a change of character that came over him in his late fifties and transformed the hard-headed man of business into a somewhat absent-minded philanthropist. From about 1876 onward he engaged in a series of schemes to bring "commerce and Christianity" to Africa, of which the I.B.E.A. was only the latest. Consul John Kirk, complaining of Mackinnon's careless management of the Company's affairs, wrote in 1891 that "there is too much philanthropy and Imperialism and too little regard to finance in that Company."[56] Mackinnon indeed had risen above mere commerce and aimed at nothing less than the "moral and economic transformation of East Africa."[57] While he did not make the ultimate decisions with regard to Uganda, he set things moving and to some extent forced Salisbury's hand. It seems fair to say therefore that philanthropy and trade, in that order, were important secondary motives for British intervention in the crucial period before 1890 in Uganda.

When it came to the Sudan, however, Salisbury's motives predominated and were more complicated. While the core of the country had been given over to the Mahdi, the British clung to the eastern Sudan along the Red Sea coast, where they had occupied themselves since 1883 in suppressing the slave trade among the neighboring tribes. These tribes gave only a tenuous allegiance to the Mahdi, and Baring decided that they might be enticed by friendship and legitimate trade to abandon both that allegiance and the slave trade. In January 1887 he sent to the Foreign Office a plan to this effect,[58] and Salisbury, who had been pressed by British merchants for over a year to do something to reopen the Sudanese trade which they believed to have enormous potential,[59] responded enthusiastically:

Lord Salisbury has reason to know that leading firms in Manchester are much interested in the reopening of the Soudan trade, and . . . it will be advantageous to take steps for the purpose as soon as the military and political considerations which have hitherto been held to render such a course inexpedient have ceased to exist.[60]

Baring, however, was unwilling to sit on his hands while the Mahdist state slowly disintegrated from within. Shortly after he sent his plan to London, he had written to Colonel Kitchener in Suakin:

. . . there can be no question for the present of re-establishing the authority of the Egyptian Gov't. in the Eastern Soudan . . . therefore . . . the objects which the Egyptian Gov't., acting with the full concurrence of Her Majesty's Gov't. seek to attain are two-fold.

In the first place they wish to ensure peace and tranquility on the immediate frontiers of their *de facto* possessions. In the second place they wish to make such arrangements as will enable trade to be resumed with the more remote tribes.[61]

By April Kitchener could report that every day more Arabs [sic] were defecting from the Mahdist regime and coming over to the British side.

Events do not move so rapidly in the Soudan as, no doubt could be wished, but I see a steady advance of pacification, and no tendency in the opposite direction. The Arabs are gradually gaining confidence in our peaceful intentions, and I have to be very careful that no step of mine should shake that confidence. I much prefer to see a steady improvement than a rapid change, which might bring about a corresponding relapse.

I feel sure that if this grant [of £10,000 per annum to subsidize some of the friendly sheikhs] were allowed England would largely reap the benefit by the revival of trade in the Soudan, and the fact of England paying the money would be very advantageous in many ways. Not only would it remove the idea that, owing to subsidies and assistance, the Sheikhs were again coming under Egyptian rule, but it would also give England a primary claim on the future of the Soudan without incurring the least responsibility. When we see the real wishes of the Soudanese people with regard to their future, I feel sure that the pacification will soon be accomplished, and the Soudan will take its place as a prosperous, easily-governed, and peaceful country.[62]

Kitchener's views were endorsed a fortnight later by Cameron, the British Consul at Suakin.[63] Their optimism proved to be premature, but Salisbury's response was positive, and in May Kitchener was given permission to activate Baring's plan by reopening trade with the northern Sudan (he had, in fact, already done so in April).[64] In October Kitchener was further authorized to open trade with the south.

By the following spring, however, the optimism of all concerned had become considerably more guarded. Hostilities continued in the neighborhood of Suakin, and the Secretary of the British and Foreign Anti-Slavery Society complained to Salisbury:

> The Committee have viewed with much disappointment the long-continued hostilities which have, unfortunately, prevailed in the neighborhood of Suakin, as they believe this not only retards the reestablishment of any peaceful and productive industry, but produces a state of anarchy which affords facilities for carrying on the Slave Trade.
>
> The Committee would therefore urge upon her Majesty's Gov't. the use of all means within their power for a reopening of legitimate commerce, and a peaceful settlement of the disputes among the tribes of the Red Sea coast.[65]

Salisbury assured him that "Her Majesty's Gov't. are doing what is in their power to promote the objects indicated in your letter."[66] At the same time Baring was instructing Cameron to take a more cautious approach to the tribes:

...the policy which it is desirable to follow at the present moment in the Eastern Soudan appears to me so clear as hardly to require any lengthy explanation. It should consist in standing purely on the defensive against any hostile movement or combination of the Arab tribes, in avoiding any course of action which might involve the ultimate necessity of offensive action, and encouraging legitimate trade by every means in our power.

I gather with great satisfaction from your despatch of the 28th ultimo that a perceptible increase in local trade has recently taken place.[67]

This policy was explicitly approved by Salisbury a fortnight later.[68] And in January 1889 Baring reiterated it: "I have pointed out over and over again during the last five years that the true interests of Egypt are not to reconquer, but to trade with the Soudan."[69]

Despite this persevering optimism, unrest among the eastern Sudanese tribes continued, and by the end of 1889 Baring was forced to recognize that his policy had failed. He admitted to Salisbury in December that "I do not believe that the Soudan is to be pacified either by opening or closing trade."[70] It is very likely that this acknowledgment was an important factor in causing Salisbury to resort to the diplomatic negotiations of 1890 with Germany and Italy.

Nor was the possibility of letting the Turks or Italians do the job seen as a feasible alternative. Neither power could be allowed to control the Nile Valley itself, and Salisbury was very uneasy about letting their influence expand even on the Red Sea coast. In May 1887 he wrote Baring that Italy had proposed to occupy Ras Kasar and to establish it as the boundary between the British and Italian spheres of influence, and he was disposed to agree provided Italy "give us satisfactory assurances as to the repression of the Slave Trade."[71] When it was suggested in December that the Porte take over Suakin to relieve the Egyptian budget, Salisbury had no objection on condition that the Sultan undertook not to hand it over to any other power without British consent. Her Majesty's Government "hold this condition as indispensable on account of the Slave Trade question."[72] Nothing was done about this at the time, and when the suggestion was revived a year later as a means of restoring order in the Sudan, Salisbury was still agreeable, under certain conditions; "Nothing must be done to make our operations against the Slave Trade less efficient. The Turks must engage not to concede or permit the occupation of Suakin by any other Power, nor to impose any new duties that would fetter trade, and they must give security against any encroachment on the guaranteed autonomy of Egypt."[73]

Very soon, however, disillusion with the whole situation in the Sudan began to set in. Salisbury had second thoughts about using the Turks and eventually decided that it was not feasible because in all probability they would be unable to hold Suakin for long against a determined Mahdist attack.[74] The apparent connivance of the Italians in the slave trade, to which he was alerted in June 1889, turned Salisbury against any further concessions to them in the British sphere of influence.[75] Here, too, were reasons for Salisbury to resort to a diplomatic settlement for the Sudan as an interim measure until the reconquest could be undertaken.

During the mid-1880s when Britain assumed a defensive posture vis-à-vis the Sudan, its chief objects were to suppress the slave trade and to pacify the eastern provinces by encouraging legitimate trade. The effort failed, but in any event it was an interim policy. Salisbury's ultimate aim from 1887 or 1888 onward was to take possession of the Nile Valley because the stability and security of Egypt depended on excluding all other European powers. By definition no government along the Upper Nile could be considered good that threatened Egyptian stability and security. Because of the peculiar implications that possession of the Nile Valley had for the survival of Egypt, the derivative motive of good government became the primary motive in the Sudan and Uganda, while commercial and philanthropic factors became its handmaidens, a reversal of their usual roles in the history of British expansion.

NOTES

1. The section on Egypt is adapted principally from the following works: Halford L. Hoskins, *British Routes to India* (New York, 1928); John Marlowe, *Cromer in Egypt* (New York, 1970); Charles W. Hallberg, *The Suez Canal: Its History and Diplomatic Importance* (New York, 1931); D. A. Farnie, *East and West of Suez: The Suez Canal in History, 1854-1956* (Oxford, 1969); Agatha Ramm, "Great Britain and France in Egypt, 1876-1882," in Prosser Gifford and W. R. Louis, eds., *France and Britain*

in Africa: Imperial Rivalry and Colonial Rule (New Haven, 1971), pp. 73-119; Peter Mansfield, *The British in Egypt*, (New York, 1972).

2. Palmerston to Clarendon, March 18, 1855, Broadlands Mss., GC/CL/1379/3.

3. Mansfield, *British in Egypt*, 8.

4. Hallberg, *Suez Canal*, 379; Farnie, *East and West of Suez*, 170-71, 292, 346; Hugh J. Schonfield, *The Suez Canal in World Affairs* (New York, 1953), 168-69.

5. This was the view of Ronald Robinson and J. Gallagher, *Africa and the Victorians* (London, 1961).

6. The narrative for the Upper Nile was drawn principally from the following works: Kenneth Ingham, *A History of East Africa*, rev. ed. (New York, 1965) and *The Making of Modern Uganda* (London, 1958); John S. Galbraith, *Mackinnon and East Africa, 1878-1895: A Study in the "New Imperialism"* (Cambridge, 1972); John E. Flint, "The Wider Background to the Partition and Colonial Occupation," and Marie de Kiewiet Hemphill, "The British Sphere, 1884-94," in Roland Oliver and G. Mathew, eds., *History of East Africa* (Oxford, 1963), 1:352-390, 391-432; P. L. McDermott, *British East Africa or IBEA: A History of the Formation and Work of the Imperial British East Africa Company*, 2d ed. (London, 1895); C. J. Lowe, *The Reluctant Imperialists*, vol. 1: *British Foreign Policy, 1878-1902* (London, 1967), and *Salisbury and the Mediterranean, 1886-1896* (London, 1965); G. N. Uzoigwe, *Britain and the Conquest of Africa. The Age of Salisbury* (Ann Arbor, 1974); Richard Gray, *A History of the Southern Sudan, 1839-1889* (London, 1961); Robert O. Collins, *The Southern Sudan, 1883-1898: A Struggle for Control* (New Haven, 1962); G. N. Sanderson, *England, Europe and the Upper Nile, 1882-1899* (Edinburgh, 1965); Peter M. Holt, *The Mahdist State in the Sudan, 1881-1898*, 2d ed. (Oxford, 1970); Iain R. Smith, *The Emin Pasha Relief Expedition, 1886-1890* (Oxford, 1972); John Rowe, *Lugard at Kampala* (Kampala, 1969).

7. Gladstone's occupation of 1882 was intended to be temporary, and although Dufferin's report of 1883 convinced the British they must stay on for a while to stabilize the Egyptian government, Liberals and Conservatives alike fully expected to evacuate the troops in the near future. It was not until the failure of Drummond-Wolff's mission in 1887, when hope faded that Turkey could act as an effective buffer against Russian pressure on the Middle East, that Salisbury came to regard the Egyptian occupation as permanent.

8. Salisbury to White, June 30, 1885, in H. W. V. Temperley and L. M. Penson, eds., *Foundations of British Foreign Policy from Pitt to Salisbury, 1792-1902* (Cambridge, 1938), 427-28.

9. See article in *Nineteenth Century* (July 1884), cited by W. L. Langer, *The Diplomacy of Imperialism, 1890-1902*, 2d ed. (New York, 1968), 106.

10. Flint, "Wider Background," 371-73; Galbraith, *Mackinnon*, 92-103.

11. Holmwood to Iddesleigh and Baring, Sept. 1886, quoted in Sanderson, *England*, 29.

12. Smith, *Emin Pasha Relief Expedition*, viii, 58.

13. McDermott, *British East Africa*, 12-13.

14. Sanderson, *England*, 41-42.

15. Salisbury to Austrian and Italian Ambassadors, Dec. 12, 1887, in Temperley and Penson, *Foundations*, 460-62..

16. Sanderson, *England*, 42. Flint, "Wider Background," 380; R. Robinson and J. Gallagher, "The Partition of Africa," in *New Cambridge Modern History* (Cambridge, 1962), 11:613.

17. Salisbury to Baring, Nov. 2, Dec. 22, 1888, F.O. 633/7/100, and 101.

18. Sanderson, *England*, 44; Memorandum by Hatzfeldt (referring to Bismarck's reply of 1888), June 25, 1889, F.O. Confidential Print—Africa, F.O. 403/111, pp. 114-15.

19. Lowe, *Reluctant Imperialists*, 131; Galbraith, *Mackinnon*, 120-21.

20. Ibid.

21. Salisbury to Malet, June 14, 1890, F.O. 403/142, p. 30.

22. Galbraith, *Mackinnon*, 195.

23. Ingham, *History of East Africa*, 152-53.

24. Salisbury to Egerton, Aug. 14, 1885, Salisbury Papers, A/44/9.

25. Salisbury to Portal, Sept. 29, 1887, in ibid., A/55/19.

26. Salisbury to Baring, Nov. 21, 1890, in ibid., A/55/60.

27. Quoted in Sanderson, *England*, 44.

28. Salisbury to Baring, March 28, 1890, Salisbury Papers, A/55/53.

29. Menelek repudiated the Treaty of Ucciali in 1891, pointing out that the Amharic text made no mention of a protectorate.

30. Lowe, *Reluctant Imperialists*, 138.

31. Flint, "Wider Background," 385; Lowe, *Salisbury and the Mediterranean*, 62-63.

32. Lowe, *Salisbury*, 64.

33. Salisbury to Baring, Nov. 21, 1890, F.O. 633/7/110.

34. The authoritative account of the Battle of Mengo is found in Rowe, *Lugard*, 18-26.

35. Sanderson, *England*, 111-12.

36. D. A. Low, "Uganda: the Establishment of the Protectorate, 1894-1919," in Vincent Harlow and E. M. Chilver, *History of East Africa* (Oxford, 1965), 2:72-73.

37. Collins, *Southern Sudan*, 71.

38. Quoted in Sanderson, *England*, 161.

39. Ibid., 170.

40. Ibid., 191.

41. Ibid., 203, 211.

42. Ibid., 239-40, 244-45; Uzoigwe, *Britain*, 221-22, 263.

43. Sanderson, *England*, 232-33.

44. Ibid., 319.

45. Ibid., 255.

46. Ibid., 262, citing Salisbury to Landsdowne, Oct. 22, 1897.

47. Uzoigwe, *Britain*, 278.

48. Lowe, *Reluctant Imperialists*, 210.

49. Ibid.

50. The sole exception was Leopold's impulsive proclamation of sovereignty over the left bank of the Nile in October 1905. He was forced to reverse himself in the face of British threats. But by then the Anglo-Egyptian Condominium had already been proclaimed.

51. Sanderson, *England*, 392.

52. David K. Fieldhouse, *Economics and Empire 1830-1914* (Ithaca, 1973), 383.

53. See minute by Salisbury on letter from Kirk to Anderson, Oct. 14, 1886, F.O. 403/78, p. 12.

54. Galbraith, *Mackinnon*, 13.

55. Ibid., 25-27, 29.

56. Kirk to Cawston, Dec. 16, 1891, quoted in ibid., 29-30.

57. Ibid., 48.

58. Baring to Iddesleigh, Jan. 9, 1887, F.O. 407/70, p. 20.

59. See, for example, the correspondence relating to a Sudanese chartered company, Feb. 27, 1886, Cab. 37/16, #68.

60. Pauncefote to Thompson, Jan. 22, 1887, F.O. 407/70, p. 22.

61. Baring to Kitchener, Jan. 15, 1887, in ibid., 23-24.

62. Kitchener to Baring, April 14, 1887, in ibid., p. 137.

63. Cameron to Baring, April 30, 1887, in ibid., p. 151.

64. Salisbury to Baring, May 27, 1887, in ibid., p. 150.

65. Allen to Salisbury, March 8, 1888, F.O. 541/28, p. 540.

66. Pauncefote to British and Foreign Anti-Slavery Society, F.O. 541/28, p. 541.

67. Baring to Cameron, March 14, 1888, F.O. 407/72, p. 104.

68. Salisbury to Baring, March 29, 1888, in ibid., p. 112.

69. Baring to Salisbury, Jan. 2, 1889, F.O. 407/87, p. 25.

70. Ibid., Dec. 11, 1889, F.O. 407/90, p. 34.

71. Salisbury to Baring, May 3, 1887, F.O. Confidential Print-Africa, F.O. 403/89, p. 158.

72. Ibid., Dec. 20, 1887, F.O. Confidential Print-Africa, F.O. 403/90, p. 113.

73. Ibid., Dec. 14, 1888, F.O. 407/75, p. 57.

74. Ibid., Dec. 25, 1888, ibid., pp. 81-2.

75. See Oswald to Currie, June 13, 1889, F.O. Confidential Print-Africa, F.O. 403/124, pp. 15-16.

CONCLUSION

The British achieved paramountcy over a number of distant lands and peoples just as free trade, aborigines protection, and governmental reform were becoming powerful influences in British society at home, and each of these movements—for they each had an organization and a following as well as widespread fashionability—exerted a powerful influence in turn on overseas expansion. In Asia the philanthropic impulse was weak. There, in Burma and Malaya in the 1820s, power was exercised by the East India Company mainly to protect free trade by means of imposing good government on chiefs and princes who did not respect the sanctity of peaceful trade. A decade or so later, in Sind and the Punjab, stable government and the revival of the Indus valley trade were the joint goals of Lord William Bentinck, under whom paramountcy was achieved. The much-discussed Russian threat did not loom large in his thinking, and in none of these places is there any evidence of a desire for territorial aggrandizement. Indeed the evidence all points the other way—to the positive distaste for additional administrative responsibilities. And in Malaya the evidence that expansion was caused by strategic concerns or anxiety over foreign rivals has been shown to be weaker than the evidence for other motives.

In Africa philanthropy played a much larger role except in the initial stages of expansion at the Cape. The attempt to impose good government on the Xhosa frontier in the 1820s and 1830s was mainly for commercial reasons. But elsewhere—along the rest of the South African coast where paramountcy was achieved by 1842, on the Gold Coast where it was achieved over a period from about 1826 to 1843, and along the Niger coast in the 1850s—aborigines protection or slave trade abolition played either the principal or a significant role in expansion. On the Gold Coast, it is true, trade was chiefly on the minds of the local factors, but the Colonial Office and its local representatives as well as Captain Maclean were chiefly motivated by the need to abolish the slave trade. On the west coast, legitimate trade was first seen as the engine to displace the traffic in slaves, but when its promise failed, it came to be realized that only the imposition of good government could achieve that end. On the South African coast in the 1840s commercial factors were always secondary, and the exercise of enlightened governmental control over the Boers was recognized as prerequisite from the start.

These footholds were the staging platforms for the greater part of late nineteenth-century British expansion. It can be shown from separate studies I have made that the earlier motives continued to apply in the hinterlands of Burma, Malaya, Southern Africa, and Nigeria. The Burmese were permanently alienated by their defeat in the first Anglo-Burmese war and remained hostile to peaceful trade with the British for most of the century. In Malaya it was neither a strategic concern for foreign rivals nor territorial aggrandizement that caused Kimberley to launch the final stages of expansion in the 1870s but to cordon off the growing peninsular trade from the rising protectionism of Britain's trading rivals in Southeast Asia and to impose governmental controls over the internal turbulence and piracy that inhibited that trade. In Central Africa it was Salisbury, not Rhodes, who made the decisions that led to paramountcy in the years between 1887 and 1889, and Salisbury was uninterested in Rhodes's financial schemes, mineral exploitation, and railroad projects except insofar as they increased the trade potential of the region. Salisbury injected the imperial factor into the Rhodesias and Nyasaland primarily to preserve free trade from the encroachments of Germany and Portugal, and even of Rhodes's group itself, and secondarily to prevent as far as possible the mistreatment of the native population. In Northern Nigeria Her Majesty's Government sought to avoid administrative expense and territorial control by turning the job over to the Royal Niger Company. Both Goldie and the government wanted to preserve the Niger trade against French protectionism and the resistance of tribal and feudal regimes—the principal factor—while the government was willing to allow Goldie to cloister the river's trade in return for minimal safeguards against mistreatment of the native population.

Only in eastern Africa were there no early nineteenth-century footholds. In Egypt, as Robinson and Gallagher have shown, it was not finance but the security of the Suez Canal that inspired paramountcy. And what did the canal imply? Not military strategy, for which it was used infrequently, but British mercantile shipping, which dominated the canal from the outset. The expanding volume of trade with all of Asia and not India alone made the canal important to the British. And since nothing could be permitted to threaten this bottleneck—neither an uncooperative French company nor an unstable Egyptian government—Britain sought to refashion that government to its own design.

The Nile Valley was the backbone of the East African empire. Zanzibar, Kenya, and Tanganyika were only later appendages. But in the Sudan and Uganda the motives that prevailed elsewhere half a century earlier continued to prevail. As the nineteenth century progressed and Britain became ever more dependent on the foreign trade that made the nation wealthy and powerful, and as its peculiar commitment to aborigines protection was revived by the resurgence of the East African slave trade, good government became an increasingly powerful motive in regions where stability of trade and human rights were not taken seriously by local potentates. In the remote reaches of the Upper Nile where chaotic government endangered the security of Egypt, and hence the canal, or damaged trade potential by gross violations of humanity, good government became the principal motive, a reversal of its usual role in British expansion.

At the moment when British paramountcy was achieved in key portions of what later became the British Empire—from approximately 1820 to 1890—the chief imperatives of expansion were neither financial nor strategic but commercial, philanthropic, and governmental. If there was any change from the reluctant sporadic and small-scale expansion of the early years to the more aggressive and deliberate efforts of the 1880s, it was quantitative, not qualitative. Even in the midst of the Scramble, the British did not lose sight of their main interests. They concentrated, as before, on the free flow of trade, on the abolition of human servitude (although this was now a secondary consideration in most places), and on what was now becoming the principal end in itself: securing everywhere the kind of government that would best serve the other ends. If this now required pegging out vast claims for the future, it was simply a function of the rising protectionism of the other industrial powers, which was dramatically altering the rules of the game and threatening Britain's long-standing commercial preponderance.

In trying to understand British motives, we must distinguish between national interests and threats to those interests. Whether the threat was peripheral—from local nationalism or proto-nationalism—or from tribal turmoil or misgovernment, or later from European rivalry, these did not alter Britain's underlying aims. It may be that there was a significant change of attitude in France, or Germany, or Italy in the late nineteenth century, which caused those nations to lust after empire as the symbol of great power status, but the only significant change of British attitudes was a slightly greater emphasis on imperialism as one of the tools of foreign policy. From Waterloo to Serajevo the British pursued remarkably consistent foreign policy goals, even if they were at times dimly perceived. At whatever part of the century we may look, when it was necessary to indulge in imperialism to achieve their goals, they did so. When it could be avoided, it was. For Britain the Scramble was no more than the culmination of a continuum. British expansion throughout the nineteenth century was characterized by an organic continuity that distinguishes it from all other Western imperialisms.

BIBLIOGRAPHIC ESSAY

Some conception of the immensity of literature on nineteenth-century imperialism can be obtained by referring to my *Modern European Imperialism: A Bibliography of Books and Articles, 1815-1972*, 2 vols. (Boston, 1974). This essay is limited mainly to the papers and published works that I found most useful.

MANUSCRIPTS

None of the manuscripts I have looked at have been untouched, but there is much still to be gleaned from them in the light of new approaches, new interpretations, and changing perspectives on the modern Western empires as they recede into the past.

The most useful of the India Office Records for the era of expansion are the categories L/P & S, Political and Secret and P, Proceedings. The former comprises the correspondence between the Court of Directors and Calcutta as well as reports drawn up by Company servants and treats the "foreign relations" of the government of India with Burma, Malaya, Sind, the Punjab, Afghanistan, and the native states. The latter contains correspondence, memoranda, and similar material accumulated in Calcutta relating to these same countries. There is as yet no satisfactory guide or index to the India Office Records that follows the new classifications of the archives. For each class of archives one must turn to the mimeographed or typescript lists and indexes available at the India Office Library, or in some cases to the recently published guides to various sections of the records available for sale by the library.

The South African documents are to be found in the Colonial Office records. For the period before 1850, the most fruitful sources are the approximately three hundred volumes of in-letters (Cape of Good Hope-Original Correspondence, C.O. 48) and the nearly fifty volumes of out-letters (Cape of Good Hope-Entry Books, C.O. 49), as well as several volumes of Natal-Original Correspondence (C.O. 179) beginning in 1846. There are no area registers for the period before 1849 and the general indexes are virtually useless, but each volume of Original Correspondence and Entry Books has a helpful table of contents.

Not surprisingly the Foreign Office records are the most useful for West Africa and the Nile region. For the former, F.O. 84, Slave Trade-General Correspondence, comprises nearly four hundred volumes for the period 1849-1861, while F.O. 2, Africa-General Correspondence, contains about forty volumes for the same period. For the Nile one can first go to the Foreign Office Confidential Prints for the most important documents, especially to F.O. 403, Africa; F.O. 407, Egypt and the Sudan; and F.O. 541, Slave Trade. For affairs sufficiently important to be brought to the attention of the whole cabinet, as was the case with Egypt and the Sudan, one can also find a further selection of documents in the Cabinet Papers beginning in 1880. There are published lists of Cabinet Papers, but the sole copy of a printed "List of Foreign Office Confidential Prints" is to be found in the Langdale Room of the Public Record Office. A brief description of the contents of various classes of Foreign Office papers for the nineteenth century will be found in the four-volume *List of Foreign Office Records*... (date varies), reprinted by Kraus, 1963-1965.

The National Register of Archives (NRA) in Chancery Lane has located and cataloged the private papers of thousands of British citizens. The most helpful for this study were the papers of the first Earl of Auckland, Sir George Thomas Napier, Lord Palmerston, the fourteenth Earl Derby, the third Earl Grey, and Lord Salisbury. Other key figures whose papers are listed by the NRA are the first Earl Amherst, Lord William Bentinck, Colonel Henry Pottinger, the first Earl Ellenborough, Lord John Russell, Benjamin Disraeli, Sir William Mackinnon, and Lord Cromer. Three important personages in West African expansion for whom no NRA report exists are George Maclean, whose papers apparently exist only in scattered fragments, John Beecroft, and Macgregor Laird, who burned all his papers just before his death.

PUBLISHED DOCUMENTS

Although documents intended for publication are often designed to obscure rather than clarify, flashes of candor occasionally illuminate their pages. *The Parliamentary Papers* and *Parliamentary Debates* are fundamental. A *General Index* to the former, in several volumes beginning with the year 1801, has been reprinted by the Irish Universities Press. The two best selections for nineteenth-century foreign policy are H. W. V. Temperley and L. M. Penson, eds., *Foundations of British Foreign Policy from Pitt to Salisbury, 1792-1902* (Cambridge, 1938), and Joel H. Wiener, ed., *Great Britain: Foreign Policy and Span of Empire, 1689-1971, A Documentary History*, 4 vols. (New York, 1972), the latter also including documents on imperial expansion.

The two best collections of Colonial Office papers, which reveal that the expansionist impulse was alive and well in the early and mid-nineteenth century, are Vincent Harlow and F. Madden, eds., *British Colonial Developments, 1774-1834* (Oxford, 1953), and J. S. Bell and W. P. Morrell, eds., *Select Documents on British Colonial Policy, 1830-1860* (Oxford, 1928).

For the bailiwick of the East India Company in the critical period of the 1820s and 1830s, the indispensable source is Sir Cyril H. Philips *The Correspondence of Lord William Bentinck: Governor-General of India, 1828-1835*, 2 vols. (Oxford, 1977), which paints a somewhat less belligerent picture then Ellenborough's (Edward Law's) *A Political Diary*, 2 vols. (London, 1881). John W. Kaye, *The Life and Correspondence of Sir Charles Metcalfe*, 2d ed. (London, 1858), contains correspondence from Ellenborough not to be found in Philips. A selection of Sind documents are in *The Affairs of Sinde, Being an Analysis of the Papers presented to Parliament and the Proprietors of East India Stock ... by an East India Proprietor* (London, 1844). Two old but still useful collections are Ramsay Muir, *The Making of British India, 1756-1858, Described in a Series of Despatches ... and Other Documents* (Manchester, 1915), and George Anderson and M. Subhedar, *The Expansion of British India, 1818-1858*, 2 vols. (London, 1918).

For the period of South African history treated in this study, the two most important collections of documents are John C. Chase, ed., *The Natal Papers ... 1493 to 1843* (Graham's Town, S.A., 1843; repr. Cape Town, 1968), and John Bird, ed., *The Annals of Natal, 1495 to 1845*, 2 vols. (Cape Town, 1885; repr. 1965). Most of the documents in both collections are concentrated in the years 1824-1845. These may be supplemented by George W. Eybers, ed., *Select Constitutional Documents Illustrating South African History, 1795-1910* (London, 1918; repr. New York, 1969), by the scattering of nineteenth-century documents in G. M. Theal, ed., *Records of South-Eastern Africa*, vol. 9 (London, 1903), by Theal's voluminous collection, *Records of the Cape Colony, 1793-1831*, 36 vols. (London, 1897-1905), and by the journals and diaries published by the Van Riebeck Society in Cape Town.

The most comprehensive selection of documents for the Gold Coast (Ghana) is found in George E. Metcalfe, *Great Britain and Ghana: Documents of Ghana History, 1807-1957* (London, 1964). A few items not contained in Metcalfe may be found in J. J. Crooks, ed., *Records Relating to the Gold Coast Settlements from 1750 to 1874* (Dublin, 1923; repr. London, 1973), and Colin W. Newbury, *British Policy towards West Africa: Select Documents, 1786-1874* (Oxford, 1965), which also contains documents on the Niger Coast. Some interesting contemporary vignettes about the Niger Coast are in Thomas L. Hodgkin, *Nigerian Perspectives: An Historical Anthology*, 2d ed. (London, 1975).

For the diplomacy that swirled around the Upper Nile, see the volume of documents that accompanies C. J. Lowe, *The Reluctant Imperialists* (London, 1967), as well as the two works mentioned above by Temperley and Penson and by Wiener.

SECONDARY WORKS

The better-known interpretations of modern imperialism have been noted in the introduction to this book, while the most recent groundswell of scholarship on the subject has been summarized by William Roger Louis and his colleagues in *Imperialism: The Robinson and Gallagher Controversy* (New York, 1976). Although I am aware of no major contribution to the debate since that time, publication in the field continues to be lively. One of the foremost protagonists in that controversy, D. C. M. Platt, has edited a collection of short studies, *Business Imperialism 1840-1930: An Enquiry Based on British Experience in Latin America* (Oxford, 1977), and published an article, "British Portfolio Investment Overseas before 1870: Some Doubts," in *Economic History Review* (February 1980), but both are in the nature of reinforcing his earlier arguments. Ronald Hyam's *Britain's Imperial Century, 1815-1914: A Study of Empire and Expansion* (New York, 1976) offers a bizarre, Freudian explanation of imperial expansion but is primarily a comprehensive and perceptive survey of nineteenth-century British imperialism, summarizing without particular stress the entirety of motives that operated in different parts of the world. Daniel R. Headrick has recently published a technological interpretation of imperial expansion, suggesting that the technological advances of the 1860s and 1870s made imperialism cost effective in the late nineteenth century: *The Tools of Empire: Technology and European Imperialism in the Nineteenth Century* (New York, 1981).

Most of the books that follow have contributed something to my analysis, although this should not be taken to imply that any of their authors have endorsed it. A few additional works, important in the field but not especially relevant for this book, are included. Works relating to the general discussion of chapters 1-4 follow immediately. Others that address the same topics regionally will be found among the ensuing area studies.

For the awareness of nineteenth-century British statesmen of the rising importance of African and Asian trade and their anxiety over growing European competition, the older studies are still useful: Leone Levi, *History of British Commerce and of the Economic Progress of the British Nation, 1763-1870* (London, 1872); Arthur L. Bowley, *A Short Account of England's Foreign Trade in the 19th Century: Its Economic and Social Results* (New York, 1905); Sir John H. Clapham, *The Economic Develop-*

ment of France and Germany (Cambridge, 1921) and *An Economic History of Modern Britain*, vols. 1 and 2 (Cambridge, 1926 and 1932). Robert W. Seton-Watson's classic, *Britain in Europe, 1789-1914: A Survey of Foreign Policy* (Cambridge, 1937), while stressing diplomacy and military strategy, also reflects the abiding concern of foreign ministers for the welfare of British trade. For the dramatic impact of industrialization on the changing pattern of nineteenth-century trade, there is David Landes' excellent study, *The Unbound Prometheus: Technological Change and Industrial Development in Western Europe from 1750 to the Present* (Cambridge, Mass., 1969). Samuel B. Saul, *Studies in British Overseas Trade, 1870-1914* (Liverpool, 1960), argues against the Hobsonian thesis of surplus capital and deals with the relationship between expanding trade and empire. Werner Schlote, *British Overseas Trade from 1700 to the 1930's* (Oxford, 1952), is a good statistical analysis of the growing complexity of that trade.

The convoluted linkage between Britain's overseas interests and imperial expansion will be found in the following works. Philip D. Curtin, *The Image of Africa: British Ideas and Action, 1780-1850* (Madison, Wis., 1964), shows how notions of racial and cultural superiority, humanitarianism, utilitarianism, and laissez-faire shaped the attitudes of British statesmen as Africa was about to pass under European control. D. A. Low, *Lion Rampant* (London, 1973), suggests a conceptual model for the progressive exercise of alien power from the precolonial into the colonial period. Two studies of the late nineteenth century that demonstrated the continuity of British expansionism are C. J. Lowe, *The Reluctant Imperialists*, vol. 1; *British Foreign Policy, 1878-1902* (London, 1967), accompanied by a volume of documents, and Richard Faber, *The Vision and the Need: Late Victorian Imperialist Aims* (London, 1966), a popularization of the fin-de-siècle attitudes that administered the empire. The continuing commitment of foreign secretaries of all parties, especially to the abolition of the slave trade, is reflected in vol. 2 of the *Cambridge History of British Foreign Policy* (New York, 1923), in Reginald Coupland, *The British Anti-Slavery Movement*, 2d ed. (New York, 1964), and in the following biographical studies: Algernon Cecil, *British Foreign Secretaries, 1807-1916: Studies in Personality and Policy* (London, 1927), Wendy Hinde, *George Canning* (London, 1973), Charles A. Petrie, *George Canning* (London, 1930), Jasper Ridley, *Lord Palmerston* (London, 1970), and Donald Southgate, *"The Most English Minister" . . . The Policies and Politics of Palmerston* (New York, 1966). Where the pursuit of British interests did not establish a linkage with imperial expansion, for reasons explained in chapter 4—a subject equally as fascinating and that provides a needed perspective to a book such as mine—has been explored at length by D. C. M.

Platt in a number of his studies. Two that relate to Latin America are *Business Imperialism*, referred to above, and his chapter entitled "Economic Imperialism and the Businessman: Britain and Latin America before 1914," in Roger Owen and Bob Sutcliffe, *Studies in the Theory of Imperialism* (London, 1972). Three other works that provide the same perspective for China and the Congo are Michael Greenberg, *British Trade and the Opening of China, 1800-42* (Cambridge, 1957), Edward Le Fevour, *Western Enterprise in Late Ch'ing China: A Selective Survey of Jardine, Matheson and Company's Operations, 1842-1895* (Cambridge, Mass., 1968), and Roger Anstey, *Britain in the Congo in the 19th Century* (New York, 1962).

D. C. M. Platt is the chief authority on the connection (or lack of it) between British foreign policy, imperial expansion, and economic factors in particular, and my notes indicate my indebtedness to him, although we disagree on several of our conclusions. Three of his most influential studies in this field, all of which appeared in a burst of scholarship in 1968, are *Finance, Trade and Politics in British Foreign Policy, 1815-1914* (Oxford); "Economic Factors in British Policy during the 'New Imperialism,'" *Past and Present* (April 1968); and "The Imperialism of Free Trade: Some Reservations," *Economic History Review* (August 1968). In this connection should also be mentioned David Fieldhouse's important survey, *Economics and Empire, 1830-1914* (Ithaca, N.Y., 1973), two contributions to W. R. Louis's summary by Platt and W. W. Rostow, as well as several other works that appear in the Notes for the Introduction. The very early influence of free trade policy on expansion is reflected in Bernard Semmel, *The Rise of Free Trade Imperialism: Classical Political Economy, the Empire of Free Trade and Imperialism, 1750-1850* (Cambridge, 1970).

The best introductory survey of the British raj is still perhaps the older work of Edward J. Thompson and G. T. Garrett, *The Rise and Fulfilment of British Rule in India* (London, 1934), conventional but not without insight into the rise of Indian nationalism. Sir Percival Griffiths, *The British Impact on India* (London, 1952), stresses the ideological impact. Two teams of Indian scholars headed by R. C. Majumda have contributed two important works from the Indian point of view: *An Advanced History of India* (London, 1946), comprehensive and exhaustively researched, and *British Paramountcy and Indian Renaissance* (Bombay, 1963). The usual topical analyses can be found in the *Cambridge History of India*, vol. 5: *British India, 1497-1858*, 3d repr. (Delhi, 1968), originally published in 1929. The importance of the trading factor in early British expansion in India is reflected in different ways by the following studies. K. M. Panikkar, *Asia and Western Dominance: A Survey of the Vasco da Gama Epoch of Asian History, 1498-1945* 2d ed. (London, 1959), stresses the maritime nature of British paramountcy. The role of the private trade is brought out in Robert M. Martin's highly critical contemporary work, *The Indian Empire*, vol. 1 (London, 1858). Sir Cyril H. Philips has contributed a study of the struggle between the Court of Directors and the Board of Control in *The East India Company, 1784-1834*, 2d ed. (Manchester, 1961). A reliable popularization of expansion under the Company will be found in Brian Gardner, *The East India Company: A History* (London, 1971). The role that British attitudes toward India played in the expansion of paternalistic control is portrayed by George D. Bearce, *British Attitudes towards India, 1784-1858* (London, 1961). Bearce should be supplemented by Henry T. Prinsep, *History of the Political and Military Transactions in India during the Administration of the Marquis of Hastings, 1813-1823*, 2 vols. (London, 1825), reflecting the disdain in which the Indian capacity for self-government was held; Ainslee T. Embree, *Charles Grant and British Rule in India* (New York, 1962), showing how idealism tempered the commercial factor; and Francis G. Hutchins, *The Illusion of Permanence: British Imperialism in India* (Princeton, 1967), showing how early British optimism about Indian potential changed to disillusion before the century was far gone.

Two useful eyewitness accounts of early British expansion in Burma are Henry Gouger, *Personal Narrative of Two Years' Imprisonment in Burma, 1824-1826* (London, 1860), and John Crawfurd, *Journal of an Embassy from the Governor-General of India to the Court of Ava in the Year 1827*, 2d ed. (London, 1834). Three still reliable older surveys are Daniel G.E. Hall, *Burma* (London, 1950), John F. Cady's scholarly *History of Modern Burma* (Ithaca, N.Y., 1958), and Dorothy Woodman, *The Making of Burma* (London, 1962). On Calcutta's concern for orderly trade with its eastern neighbor and its awareness of its rising importance there are many testimonials: Anil C. Bannerjee, *The Eastern Frontier of British India, 1784-1826* (Calcutta, 1943), Walter S. Desai, *History of the British Residency in Burma, 1826-1840* (Rangoon, 1939), Amales Tripathi, *Trade and Finance in the Bengal Residency, 1793-1833* (Calcutta, 1956), D. G. E. Hall, *Henry Burney, A Political Biography* (London, 1974), and his earlier article, "Anglo-Burmese Conflicts in the 19th Century: A Reassessment," *Asia* 6 (1966), and G. P. Ramachandra, "The Canning Mission to Burma of 1909/10," *Journal of Southeast Asian Studies* 1 (1979). In this same connection, J. S. Furnivall's *Colonial Policy and Practice: A Comparative Study of Burma and Netherlands-India* (New York, 1956) is ostensibly an area study, but its observations, including those on "good government," are generally applicable throughout south and southeast Asia. The nationalist point of view, holding that the Company's Governors-General nurtured an abiding lust for power, is well represented by Maung Htin

Aung, *A History of Burma* (New York, 1967), and *The Stricken Peacock: Anglo-Burmese Relations, 1752-1948* (The Hague, 1965). Recent revisionist studies include Oliver B. Pollak, *Empires in Collision: Anglo-Burmese Relations in the Mid-Nineteenth Century* (Westport, Conn., 1979), which maintains that trade was not the primary factor in Burma, and Laurence Kitzan, "Lord Amherst and the Declaration of War on Burma, 1824," *Journal of Asian History* 9 (1975) and "Lord Amherst and Pegu: The Annexation Issue, 1824-1826," *Journal of Southeast Asian Studies* 2 (1977), which offer a new slant on Amherst's motives. A comment on Michael Adas's article will be found in the notes to chapter 6.

A most important addition to recent scholarship on British expansion in the Indus valley is Edward Ingram's lucid account, *The Beginning of the Great Game in Asia, 1828-1839* (Oxford, 1979), although his conclusions differ from mine owing to the stress on Ellenborough's role rather than Bentinck's. A fitting sequel to Ingram is James A. Norris, *The First Afghan War, 1839-42* (New York, 1967). Equally well researched is Robert A. Huttenback, *British Relations with Sind, 1799-1843: An Anatomy of Imperialism* (Berkeley, 1962), which maintains the conventional importance of the Russian threat. Kala Thairani, *British Political Missions to Sind...1799 to 1843...* (New Delhi, 1973), adds little if anything to Huttenback. The same period seen through the eyes of the general who ultimately occupied Sind will be found in Hugh T. Lambrick's scholarly biography, *Sir Charles Napier and Sind* (Oxford, 1952). Two important monographs for the Punjab in the pre-Sikh War era are J. D. Cunningham's contemporary account, *A History of the Sikhs from the Origin of the Nation to the Battles of the Sutlej* (London, 1849), and Gulsham L. Chopra, *The Punjab as a Sovereign State, 1799-1839* (Lahore, 1929), tinged by a nationalist bias. Bentinck's motives are explored comprehensively in J. Rosselli, *Lord William Bentinck: The Making of a Liberal Imperialist, 1774-1839* (Berkeley, 1974).

Three good introductory surveys of Malaya, all largely from secondary sources, are Richard O. Winstedt, *A History of Malaya* (Singapore, 1935), Joseph Kennedy, *A History of Malaya, A.D. 1400-1959* (London, 1962), and N. J. Ryan, *A History of Malaysia and Singapore* (Kuala Lumpur, 1976), primarily a college text. There is no want of excellent studies for the critical years of the early and mid-nineteenth century. Originally published in 1925, L. A. Mills, *British Malaya, 1824-67*, 2d ed. (Kuala Lumpur, 1966), is still the standard history for that period. It might be preceded by Kennedy G. Tregonning, *The British in Malaya: The First Forty Years, 1786-1826* (Tucson, Ariz., 1965), and supplemented by Nicholas Tarling, *British Policy in the Malay Peninsula and Archipelago, 1824-1871* (Oxford, 1957), which broadens the geographic perspective. C. D. Cowan, *Nine-*

teenth Century Malaya: The Origins of British Control (London, 1961), makes a strong case for the fear of international rivalries in southeast Asia. Two recent studies by C. M. Turnbull pay particular attention to racial relations as a factor in British expansion: *The Straits Settlements, 1826-67: Indian Presidency to Crown Colony* (London, 1972) and *A History of Singapore, 1819-1975* (Kuala Lumpur, 1977), the latter also useful for Raffles's aims. For the beginnings of the concluding phase of expansion under Gladstone's ministry of 1868-1874, there are two studies by W. D. McIntyre, *The Imperial Frontier in the Tropics, 1865-75* (London, 1967) and "Britain's Intervention in Malaya: The Origin of Lord Kimberley's Instructions to Sir Andrew Clarke in 1873," in J. Bastin and R. Winks, *Malaysia: Selected Historical Readings* (Kuala Lumpur, 1966), and C. N. Parkinson, *British Intervention in Malaya, 1867-77* (Singapore, 1960). Together these reflect the continuity of British motives throughout the previous half-century. An easily readable and balanced portrait of Raffles will be found in Maurice Collis, *Raffles* (London, 1966), although it does not replace the definitive biography by C. E. Wurtzburg, *Raffles of the Eastern Isles* (London, 1954).

The standard reference for South Africa in the European period, first published in 1928, is still Eric A. Walker, *A History of Southern Africa*, 3d ed. correc. (London, 1962), supplemented by the customary topical studies of the *Cambridge History of the British Empire*, vol. 8: *South Africa, Rhodesia and the High Commission Territories*, 2d ed. (Cambridge, 1963). The most recent survey, T. R. H. Davenport, *South Africa: A Modern History* (London, 1977), is a clearly written, conventional account from the earliest times stressing the development of the white community. For the definitive period of expansion that shaped the mold, during and after the Great Trek, there are numerous good studies, old and new. Volume 2 of George M. Theal, *History of South Africa, 1795-1872* (London, 1919-1927), covering the 1820s to the mid-1840s, is still useful for narrative detail. William M. Macmillan *Bantu, Boer and Briton: The Making of the South African Native Problem*, rev. ed. (Oxford, 1963), is the most valuable basic account of race relations and frontier tensions in the 1830s and 1840s, centering on the career of the Reverend John Philip. John S. Galbraith, *Reluctant Empire: British Policy on the South African Frontier, 1834-1854* (Berkeley, 1963), regards British policy at this time as an utter failure attributable to an unworkable combination of philanthropy and greed. Two accounts of the Great Trek, the former still authoritative, the latter more readable, are Eric A. Walker, *The Great Trek* (London, 1934; 5th ed., 1965), and Johannes Meintjes, *The Voortrekkers: The Story of the Great Trek and the Making of South Africa* (London, 1973). Two excellent studies of Natal are Alan F. Hattersley, *The British Settlement of Natal: A*

Study in Imperial Migration (Cambridge, 1950), and Edgar H. Brookes and C.deB. Webb, *A History of Natal* (Pietermaritzburg, 1965), the latter containing an extensive bibliography. The transition from the Trek to the Rhodes era is covered from four quite different perspectives by C. W. De Kiewiet, *British Colonial Policy and the South African Republics, 1848-1872* (New York, 1929), C. J. Uys, *In the Era of Shepstone: Being a Study of British Expansion in South Africa, 1842-1877* (London, 1933), David Welsh, *The Roots of Segregation: Native Policy in Colonial Natal, 1845-1900* (London, 1971), and John B. Wright, *Bushman Raiders of the Drakensberg, 1840-1870* (Pietermaritzburg, 1971). For the importance of the frontier trade in the early nineteenth century, see S. Daniel Neumark, *Economic Influences on the South African Frontier, 1652-1836* (Stanford, Calif., 1957). The history of the Zulu nation until its collapse in 1879 will be found in Donald R. Morris, *The Washing of the Spears* (New York, 1965). Brian Roberts, *The Zulu Kings* (London, 1974), is a popularized account of the same period.

The two best introductions to British West Africa are John E. Flint, *Nigeria and Ghana* (Englewood Cliffs, N.J., 1966), and John D. Fage, *A History of West Africa: An Introductory Survey* (Cambridge, 1969). For the Gold Coast alone, W. W. Claridge, *A History of the Gold Coast and Ashanti*, 2 vols. (London, 1915), is still useful for its massive detail. W. E. F. Ward, *A History of Ghana*, 3d ed. (London, 1966), is a conventional, even-handed introductory survey by a knowledgeable colonial official. Its companion piece for Nigeria is Alan Burns, *History of Nigeria*, 8th ed. (London, 1972). Michael Crowder, *A Short History of Nigeria*, rev. ed. (New York, 1966), is more scholarly than its title suggests and reflects the African point of view better than Burns. There are three interesting collections of short studies covering French as well as British areas. J. F. A. Ajayi and M. Crowder, eds., *History of West Africa*, vol. 2 (New York, 1973), focuses on affairs internal to West Africa, while J. B. Webster and A. A. Boahen, *History of West Africa: The Revolutionary Years—1815 to Independence* (New York, 1970), broadens the perspective to international relations. Both are refreshing for their Afrocentric emphasis, and the latter contains a useful bibliography of articles. The surprisingly stout and sophisticated military resistance to European expansion is revealed in Michael Crowder, ed., *West African Resistance: the Military Response to Colonial Occupation* (London, 1971), although it was of marginal use for my study because it deals mainly with the late nineteenth and early twentieth centuries. One would expect the earlier period to be treated in John D. Hargreaves, *Prelude to the Partition of West Africa* (London, 1963), but here too the emphasis is on the period after 1860 and on diplomatic relations. Monographic studies of the early years on the Gold Coast include

Adu A. Boahen, "Politics in Ghana, 1800-1874," in Ajayi and Crowder, vol. 2; George E. Metcalfe, *Maclean of the Gold Coast... 1801-1847* (London, 1962), more of a reference work than an interpretive study; William T. Balmer, *A History of the Akan Peoples of the Gold Coast* (New York, 1969), which treats the British intervention in the context of the ancient feud between the Asante and the Fante; and Georg Norregard, *Danish Settlements in West Africa, 1658-1850*, English translation (Boston, 1966), which adds a somewhat different perspective for English-speaking readers. The comparable period on the Niger Coast has received more attention, especially from Nigerian historians. The changing role of the missions during the expansion of British influence is portrayed in J. F. A. Ajayi, *Christian Missions in Nigeria, 1841-1891: The Making of a New Elite* (Evanston, Ill., 1965). Broader topically but narrower geographically is S. O. Biobaku's study of the reaction of Africans to the advent of the European in *Yorubaland: The Egba and Their Neighbors, 1842-1872* (Oxford, 1957). A useful political history from the African viewpoint of one of the most vigorous rivals of the palm oil ruffians is E. J. Alagoa, *The Small Brave City-State: A History of Nembe-Brass in the Niger Delta* (Madison, Wis., 1964). The flavor of Baikie's motives and activities can be tasted in Howard J. Pedraza's little book, *Borrioboola-Gha: The Story of Lokoja, the First British Settlement in Nigeria* (New York, 1960). The early chapters of John E. Flint, *Sir George Goldie and the Making of Nigeria* (London, 1960), reflect the mixture of idealism and commerce that motivated some of Goldie's predecessors, including Baikie. The early importance of the West African trade to Europeans can be seen in Edward Reynolds, *Trade and Economic Change on the Gold Coast, 1807-1874* (London, 1974), and Kenneth O. Dike, *Trade and Politics in the Niger Delta, 1830-1885: An Introduction to the Economic and Political History of Nigeria* (Oxford, 1956), the latter showing clearly how the flag followed trade, while John E. Flint, "Economic Change in West Africa in the Nineteenth Century," in Ajayi and Crowder, vol. 2, points out that European trade was a minor factor in the total West African economy of the early nineteenth century. A. J. H. Latham, *Old Calabar, 1600-1891: The Impact of the International Economy upon a Traditional Society* (Oxford, 1973), explains the crucial role of economic change in native society as a factor in European penetration. Anthony G. Hopkins, *An Economic History of West Africa* (New York, 1973), focuses on the Scramble.

Fascination with the Suez Canal and the upper reaches of the Nile has produced a flood of writing from the late nineteenth century to the present day, any assessment of which must be arbitrarily selective. For Britain's diplomatic efforts to maintain a line of defense for the canal, C. J. Lowe's two studies provide the best summary accounts: *The Reluctant Imperialists*

and *Salisbury and the Mediterranean, 1886-1896* (London, 1965). William
L. Langer, *European Alliances and Alignments, 1871-1890* (New York,
1931), is still distinguished for its reach and scholarship. For the enormous
complexity of the struggle for the Upper Nile from various angles, see G.
N. Sanderson, *England, Europe and the Upper Nile, 1882-1899: A Study in
the Partition of Africa* (Edinburgh, 1965), the most authoritative study, as
well as the following: William L. Langer, *The Diplomacy of Imperialism,
1890-1902*, 2d ed. (New York, 1951); Ronald Robinson and J. Gallagher,
Africa and the Victorians: The Official Mind of Imperialism (London,
1961), and "The Partition of Africa" in *New Cambridge Modern History*,
vol. 11 (Cambridge, 1962); G. N. Uzoigwe, *Britain and the Conquest of
Africa: The Age of Salisbury* (Ann Arbor, 1974), revealing Salisbury as a
more aggressive imperialist than usually supposed; Iain R. Smith, *The
Emin Pasha Relief Expedition, 1886-1890* (Oxford, 1972); and the two fine
collections edited by Prosser Gifford and William Roger Louis, *Britain and
Germany in Africa* (New Haven, 1967) and *France and Britain in Africa*
(New Haven, 1971), both subtitled *Imperial Rivalry and Colonial Rule*.
The East African connection with the Nile is explored in Kenneth Ingham,
A History of East Africa, rev. ed. (New York, 1965), a good introduction,
and in an excellent collection of monographs edited by Roland Oliver and
Gervase Mathews, vol. 1 of *History of East Africa* (Oxford, 1963),
especially the chapters by John E. Flint and Marie De Kiewiet Hemphill.
John S. Galbraith, *Mackinnon and East Africa, 1878-1895: A Study in the
"New Imperialism"* (Cambridge, 1972), portrays Mackinnon, despite his
deficiencies, as the initiator of expansion in Uganda. In compiling his
*British East Africa or IBEA: A History of the Formation and Work of the
Imperial British East Africa Company* (London, 1893), P. L. McDermott
had access to the records Mackinnon burned, but the work is chiefly a
defense of the Company by its Secretary. British concern for access to Asia
since the eighteenth century is broadly examined in Halford L. Hoskins,
British Routes to India (New York, 1928). Three studies of the Suez Canal
in its global setting from different points of view are Charles W. Hallberg,
The Suez Canal: Its History and Diplomatic Importance (New York, 1931),
Hugh J. Schonfield, *The Suez Canal in World Affairs* (New York, 1953),
and D. A. Farnie, *East and West of Suez: The Suez Canal in History, 1854-
1956* (Oxford, 1969), the last being less an interpretation than a mine of
information. The nineteenth-century diplomatic preliminaries and construction of the canal up to the British occupation are discussed in John
Marlowe, *The Making of the Suez Canal* (London, 1964). John Pudney,
Suez: de Lesseps' Canal (New York, 1968), is a readable and well-docu-
mented popularization treating the entire history up to 1967. Unique
among survey histories of modern Egypt is the exhaustive study by Jacques

Berque in the *Annales* tradition, *Egypt: Imperialism and Revolution*, English translation (London, 1972), but there are several well-researched popular surveys, including John Marlowe, *The History of Modern Egypt and Anglo-Egyptian Relations, 1800-1956*, 2d ed. (Hamden, Conn., 1965); P. J. Vatikiotis, *The Modern History of Egypt* (New York, 1969); J. C. B. Richmond, *Egypt, 1798-1952* (New York, 1977); and Mohammed Rifaat, *The Awakening of Modern Egypt* (London, 1947), the last displaying a nationalist bias. Nadav Safran, *Egypt in Search of Political Community: An Analysis of the Intellectual and Political Evolution of Egypt, 1804-1952* (Cambridge, Mass., 1961), explores the evolution of political thought rather than political parties. John Marlowe, *Cromer in Egypt* (New York, 1970), is an administrative biography beginning in 1876, sympathetic but not uncritical. And one should not ignore Cromer's own account, *Modern Egypt*, which has been through many editions since 1908. Ismaïl's financial difficulties are explored in David S. Landes, *Bankers and Pashas: International Finance and Economic Imperialism in Egypt* (Cambridge, Mass., 1958). E. R. J. Owen, *Cotton and the Egyptian Economy, 1824-1914: A Study in Trade and Development* (Oxford, 1969), cracks the myth of Britain's responsibility for a one-crop economy. The Sudan is not as well served, but two excellent surveys will introduce the interested student to further reading: Mekki Shibeika, *The Independent Sudan* (New York, 1959), which covers mainly the period 1820-1900, and Peter M. Holt's briefer *Modern History of the Sudan, from the Funj Sultanate to the Present Day* (New York, 1961). The endless Anglo-Egyptian quarrel over the Sudan is treated by Mekki Shibeika, *British Policy in the Sudan, 1882-1902* (London, 1952), and Mekki Abbas, *The Sudan Question: The Dispute over the Anglo-Egyptian Condominium, 1884-1951* (New York, 1952). Robert O. Collins, *The Southern Sudan, 1883-1898: A Struggle for Control* (New Haven, 1962), shows how the Mahdist invasions weakened the South's capacity to resist British expansion. Two competent surveys of Uganda from precolonial times to independence are Kenneth Ingham, *The Making of Modern Uganda* (London, 1958), and Donald A. Low, *Buganda in Modern History* (Berkeley, 1971). For an understanding of the critical years of 1890-1892, the second volume of Lord Lugard's *The Rise of Our East African Empire* (London, 1893) is indispensable. In conjunction with it should be read *The Diaries of Lord Lugard*, vol. 2, *East Africa, December 1890 to December 1891*, edited by Margery Perham (Evanston, Ill., 1959). A briefer introduction to the same period can be found in John Rowe, *Lugard at Kampala* (Kampala, 1969).

INDEX

About the Author

JOHN P. HALSTEAD was formerly with the State University of New York at Buffalo and is now Professor of History at the American University in Cairo. He specializes in nineteenth and twentieth-century imperialism and colonial nationalism and has published *Rebirth of a Nation*, a monograph on Moroccan nationalism, and a two-volume bibliography entitled *Modern European Imperialism: A Bibliography of Books and Periodical Articles, 1815-1972.*